Before Scopes

Charles A. Israel

Before Scopes

EVANGELICALISM

EDUCATION

AND

EVOLUTION

IN TENNESSEE

1870–1925

The University of Georgia Press
Athens and London

© 2004 by the University of Georgia Press
Athens, Georgia 30602
All rights reserved
Designed by Louise OFarrell
Set in 10.5/13 Bulmer by BookComp
Printed and bound by Thomson-Shore
The paper in this book meets the guidelines for
permanence and durability of the Committee on
Production Guidelines for Book Longevity of the
Council on Library Resources.

Printed in the United States of America
08 07 06 05 04 c 5 4 3 2 1
08 07 06 05 04 p 5 4 3 2 1

Library of Congress Cataloging-in-Publication Data
Israel, Charles A. (Charles Alan), 1973–
Before scopes : evangelicalism, education, and
evolution in Tennessee, 1870–1925 / Charles A. Israel.
p. cm.
Includes bibliographical references and index.
ISBN 0-8203-2645-3 (hardcover : alk. paper) —
ISBN 0-8203-2646-1 (pbk. : alk. paper)
1. Religion and science—United States—History—
19th century.   2. Religion and science—United
States—History—20th century.   3. Church and
State—United States—History—19th century.
4. Church and State—United States—History—20th
century.   5. Scopes, John Thomas—Trials, litigation,
etc.   6. Evolution—Study and teaching—Law and
legislation—United States.   I. Title.
BL245.I87 2004
277.68'08—dc22   2004008791

*British Library Cataloging-in-Publication Data
available*

To John William

Train up a child in the way
he should go: and when he
is old he will not depart
from it.
—Proverbs 22:6

Contents

Preface

"In the beginning," states the first chapter of Genesis, "God created the heaven and the earth." And in March 1925 the Tennessee General Assembly made it dangerous to say otherwise; it was illegal "to teach any theory that denies the story of the Divine creation of man as taught in the Bible, and to teach instead that man has descended from a lower order of animals." With the antievolution law's passage and the state's prosecution of Rhea County schoolteacher John Scopes later that year, Tennessee earned itself national attention as a fundamentalist bastion, the proverbial buckle of the southern Bible Belt. The spectacular trial has long captivated historical and popular attention, inspiring numerous books, plays, and films. The notoriety has stuck: any mention of antievolution anywhere, even in 2004, apparently requires a reference to the 1925 trial. But why did Tennessee pass the law in the first place? *Before Scopes* answers this question, examining the actions of white Tennessee Baptists and Methodists in the half century before the trial.

The *Scopes* trial began in a struggling New South industrial town in southeastern Tennessee; this book began as an idea in an Indiana cornfield, was nurtured in the southern industrial center of Houston, and is finally approaching completion back in southeastern Tennessee atop the Cumberland Plateau. Along the way I have benefited from the financial assistance of universities and foundations and have been graced with the generous intellectual support of many friends and colleagues. Each has helped to make this book better; none but me, of course, can be blamed for any infelicitous statements and errors of fact or interpretation that remain.

Research for this book has been supported by a graduate fellowship and research stipend from Rice University, a Dr. Lynn E. May Study Grant from the Southern Baptist Historical Library and Archives, and a fellowship from the Spencer Foundation for Research Related to Education.

Having worked on this manuscript while attached to three different universities over a great number of years, I find myself indebted to more librarians and archivists than I can name. The interlibrary loan staffs of Rice University's Fondren Library and the Tennessee State Library and Archives deserve special praise for keeping me well supplied with reel after reel of microfilm throughout the second half of the 1990s. Librarians at Texas A & M and the University of the South have also helped as I have revised the manuscript over the past three years. Archivists at the Southern Baptist Historical Library and Archives, Union University Archives, and Vanderbilt University Special Collections all served as helpful guides to their repositories. I especially thank Vincent McGrath at the Tennessee State Library and Archives and Von Unruh of the Tennessee Annual Conference Archives of the United Methodist Church.

I have further benefited from professional colleagues who have taken time to comment on portions of this work or have otherwise aided in its germination. Primary thanks must of course go to John B. Boles. Beyond his enthusiasm and great intellectual support for this project, he has been a model scholar, mentor, and friend. Paul Harvey provided a particularly thorough critique of the entire manuscript, offering numerous suggestions that were greatly appreciated if not always closely followed.

Scott Billingsley, Mary S. Hoffschwelle, Ernie Limbo, Beth Barton Schweiger, J. Douglass Smith, John Abernathy Smith, David B. Tyack, and the members of the Houston Area Southern Historians Seminar have all given generously of their time to comment on portions of this research and to discuss religion, education, history, modernity, and barbeque—sometimes all at once. Thanks as well to everyone at the University of Georgia Press, especially Jon Davies, Ellen D. Goldlust-Gingrich, and Derek Krissoff, who have eased the publication process and made it seem almost enjoyable. I have been fortunate to find keen intellects, generous colleagues, and good friends in Texas, Tennessee, and places in between as I worked on this project. Several deserve special thanks: At Rice, Carolyn Earle Billingsley, Patti Bixel, Pat Burgess, Edward Cox, David Dillard, Ira Gruber, Randal Hall, Bethany Johnson, Susan Hanssen, Melissa Kean, Paul Levengood, Scott Marler, Alan Matusow, Gerald McKenney, Evelyn Thomas Nolen, Jason Phillips, Elizabeth Hayes Turner, and Steve Wilson; at Texas A & M, Cam Addis, Carlos Blanton, Walter Buenger, April Hatfield, and Andrew Kirkendall; at the University of the South, Paul Bergeron, John Charles Bradbury, Woody Register, and Houston Roberson. John Willis has heard about this project, first from afar and now as a colleague, and has offered valuable advice and great friendship for more than a decade.

Katherine Christy Israel has lived with this project from its beginning, offering her love and an excellent reason to leave the research and come home every day. My parents, Don and Katherine Israel, were my first and best teachers; I hope they are pleased with the path I have followed and that I too can succeed at training up the next generation. John William, to whom *Before Scopes* is dedicated, is just beginning as work on the book is ending; may his path be long, wide, and fruitful.

Before Scopes

1. *Laying Foundations*

Constructing a Christian
Civilization in the New South

An 1879 unsigned editorial in the *Memphis Baptist,* most likely written by the regional weekly newspaper's conservative editor, James R. Graves, proposed a vision of the future of southern society. The article began with an account of workmen digging the foundation for the new *Tribune* building in New York and the author's fascination with "that strong and immovable foundation" of granite and concrete. Graves then turned his observations southward, presenting both a brief of industrial development for the New South and a call for schools and churches to lay firm foundations in sound education and religion that would anchor the region's anticipated development to the religious tenets of white southern Evangelicals: "In the South we are laying foundations. The old building has been torn down. A new South is being built. What it will be a hundred years hence it may be difficult to say. Much, almost everything, depends on the nature and character of the foundations." He listed several industrial developments—the opening of new mines, the growth of new mills and industries, and other "signs of material prosperity"—praising them as keys to southern rebirth. They would provide the foundations for a new economy after the "old dispensation" of slavery had passed away.[1]

Though he was proud and supportive of the New South's industrial growth and its anticipated future prosperity, Graves saw greater promise in a different kind of substructure: "If the foundations are laid in the general education and Christianization of the people, white and colored, we may expect the future to produce a civilization unsurpassed in other lands." Graves did not suggest that education and religion were separate endeavors; rather, he argued that both were essential to the South's future. He noted with equal pleasure how "the States [had] made liberal provision for the schools," how the tax-supported and state-run "common school [was] gradually working its way into the intellectual life of the people," and how "all the denominations [had] labored earnestly to lay the foundations of their colleges and universities."[2]

Rebuilding churches and establishing schools would not be enough; Graves worried about the orthodoxy of both the churches and the school curriculum. Continuing his construction metaphor, Graves urged school builders to "avoid 'hay, wood, and stubble' " in the foundations and instead to "use the best materials, as 'gold, silver, and precious stones.' " Such an educational building project could best be grounded in a stable southern church "resting upon 'Jesus Christ himself as the chief corner-stone' " and using "the word of God" as its "square and rule," from which "no departure" could "be allowed." Having thus pronounced a plan to undergird southern industry with suitable education and religion, Graves concluded his editorial with a prediction masking an admonition: "With such foundations, and such superstructures rising to the glory of God, our Southland, in years to come, will not be the least among the thousands of Israel."[3]

Before Scopes is an investigation of white Tennessee Baptists' and Methodists' late-nineteenth- and early-twentieth-century efforts to build and maintain those "foundations" for both church and state and to justify Evangelicals' earthly and heavenly authority for doing so. Though they would be active preachers of individual morality and at times leaders in efforts to shape society through such campaigns as the legal prohibition of alcohol, Tennessee Protestants showed their most consistent efforts to mold society in their concerns for the proper education of youth.

Schooling would prove important to Tennessee Evangelicals for a variety of reasons, and a study of this evangelical emphasis on education illuminates the relationship between religion and society in the New South. Fearing that children schooled outside the church would remain beyond its reach, many church leaders initially rejected public schools and advocated religious education as essential to denominational self-preservation. Such opposition was usually short lived. Given Tennessee's great masses of uneducated children and adults, Baptists and Methodists, who recognized a responsibility to the state and to human society as a whole, accepted and even promoted public schools at the turn of the century. Education—both popular and denominational— could be the "hand-maid to religion" and would aid in the spread of religion and morality throughout the state, the South, and the nation.[4] Although many historians have perhaps rightly criticized southern Protestants for focusing so much on individual salvation that they overlook important human-to-human social relations, the Baptist and Methodist emphasis on education suggests a broader interpretation of white southern evangelical theology and practice than has generally been recognized. As the Central Baptist Association's Committee on Education proclaimed, "Inasmuch as the Church is commissioned not only to save but to develop all of human life, education falls within the scope of the church's divine work among men."[5] Education was not just another church endeavor; most leaders considered it vital to the church's earthly mission.

An understanding of and regard for religion—both in its personal forms of individual belief, devotion, and world ordering as well as in its institutional forms of religious associations, churches, and denominations—are vital components of social and cultural history. Investigating the history of the South, a region recognized by natives and outsiders alike as especially or peculiarly religious, requires sensitivity to the place of religion in the regional culture. The roots of the South's peculiar religiosity stretch back at least to the beginning of the nineteenth century, when the Great Revival in the West sprang from a series of camp meetings on the Kentucky-Tennessee frontier and spread religious fervor and an evangelical framework throughout the region.[6] In spite of the efforts of southern Christians beginning in the 1850s and continuing well into the twentieth century to claim recognition for the region as especially religious (with *religious* understood by native southerners to denote orthodox Protestant Evangelicalism), the larger nation did not seem to notice until the 1920s.

National attention to the South's religiosity came largely as a result of the high-profile defense by many southern individuals and denominations of certain "fundamentals" of the Christian faith. Though a national movement that began and had many clearly identified supporters in Pennsylvania, Minnesota, California, and other states, the fundamentalist crusade against theological liberalism and the teaching of evolution in public schools had its greatest success in the American South and particularly in Tennessee.[7] The event that crystallized national attention was the so-called Scopes Monkey Trial of 1925, an East Tennessee media circus masquerading as a circuit-court trial in which the jury found high-school teacher John T. Scopes guilty of breaking a recently enacted state law prohibiting instruction about human evolution in publicly funded schools. Major national newspapers covered the trial's larger-than-life opponents, atheistic defense attorney Clarence Darrow and crusading old Populist William Jennings Bryan. Chicago-based WGN broadcast large portions of the proceedings to a growing radio audience. By some estimates, reporters filed 135,000 words per day on the trial, announcing to a national audience the peculiarity and pervasiveness of religion in the South. Acerbic journalist H. L. Mencken relished the opportunity presented by the *Scopes* trial, grafting a negative interpretation onto the national recognition of a peculiar brand of southern religion and labeling the region a "cesspool of Baptists, a miasma of Methodists, snake charmers, phony real estate operators, and syphilitic evangelists."[8]

Taking the spectacle of the *Scopes* trial as its end point, *Before Scopes* goes back a half century, to the 1870s, to explore the trial's regional origins. Specifically, this book addresses the essential roles of religious belief, ideology, and expression—individual and denominational, formal and popular—in Tennessee's social, cultural, and political history during the fifty years that preceded the antievolution law. Southern Evangelicals perceived their region as particularly religious and especially orthodox; they were determined to maintain, if not to reinforce and enlarge, a regional focus on piety. Thus, they took great interest in preserving and transmitting their culture to the rising generations. As Graves's *Memphis Baptist* editorial notes, southern Evangelicals concerned about the nature of the "foundations" of the New South were also anxious about the content and control of their children's education. Despite professing to recognize distinctions between the responsibilities and realms of church and state, many Tennessee parents and religious leaders did not neatly divide education into sacred and secular. As Tennessee's system of public education grew and its curriculum became the province of state-level legislators and administrators, parents and local community (including church) leaders came to understand that questions of politics and governance had important religious implications for efforts to build a New South with firm spiritual foundations.

Southern religion was at once intensely personal, focused on the central evangelical themes of salvation and a personal relationship with God, and pervasively communal and institutional, affecting almost every aspect of life and society. While many of the individual and personal aspects of religion elude the historian's net, religion in its institutional forms—in denominations particularly but also on smaller community-church levels—is often easier to detect if not to understand. *Before Scopes* concentrates on the two largest white evangelical denominations in Tennessee: the regular Baptists of the Tennessee Baptist Convention (and by extension the Southern Baptist Convention) and the Methodists of the Holston, Memphis, and Tennessee Conferences of the Methodist Episcopal Church, South.[9] The book focuses on these institutions' internal and external affairs by examining the written records of their thoughts and activities as expressed in church, association, conference, and convention minutes as well as in their state denominational newspapers, the *Nashville Christian Advocate* and the *Nashville Baptist and Reflector*.[10] The institutional records are supplemented by diaries, letters, and other personal sources to explain the thoughts and actions of a significant number of religious Tennesseans throughout this crucial half century.

Black Evangelicals—perhaps to a greater extent than their white counterparts—were clearly interested in education and religion but had a very different relationship to the state and to the public schools in late-nineteenth- and early-twentieth-century Tennessee. The presence of so many uneducated freedpersons would justify great public and private expenditures for black education, and black citizens would ardently support public schools under local black control. When the end of the nineteenth century brought the disfranchisement of black citizens and a related decrease in funding for black public schools, black parents and churches found themselves with educational concerns very different from those of white Tennesseans. In most cases, black children received fewer years of formal education than white Tennesseans and thus were much less likely to encounter evolutionary theories in the public school classroom. In the relative absence of state-funded and -controlled public education, informal sources of education—families and churches especially—retained a greater amount of control over black children's schooling. Many black Tennesseans would see evolution as a threat to their religion, but few encountered the theory directly, and most lacked the political tools white evangelical citizens wielded to drive Darwin from the classroom.[11]

While using many denominational sources, *Before Scopes* does not simply examine the churches in isolation but instead focuses on broader patterns of religious expression and activity in the turn-of-the-century South. This book investigates how religious thoughts and actions both shaped and were shaped by the surrounding society. Postbellum southern churches, like their antebellum ancestors, focused on the process of evangelism—spreading the Gospel and preaching repentance to individual sinners—but also sought to expand more directly the influence of religion on the surrounding society. Such a focus on social conversion—a theme typically more at home in discussions of the Social Gospel movement—appears to contradict what Samuel Hill long ago identified as the "central theme" of southern religion. The "southern church," Hill argues, " 'makes all of individual Christianity' and regards the conversion of men as virtually the whole task of the church."[12] As such, Hill continues, white southern Evangelicals have historically emphasized the vertical relationship of the individual sinner to God over almost any recognition of horizontal human-human relationships or temporal social affairs.

Such a summary does not always ring true for white Tennessee Protestants. While efforts at conversion were of utmost importance, a great majority of the state's Methodist and Baptist leaders and apparently a significant portion of the rank and file were also interested in earthly society, even if only to better shape conditions to facilitate future conversions. In 1882 Oscar Penn Fitzgerald, who edited the *Nashville Christian Advocate* between 1878 and 1890, acknowledged the churches' dual orientation, explaining that "though divine in its origin, . . .

the Church is planted in the soil of this world" and as such must take notice of earthly conditions.[13]

Fitzgerald and other Tennessee Evangelicals founded and expanded Sunday schools to minister to the young people of the church and to lay the seeds for conversion. Such efforts did not stop there, however; these leaders also sought other means to reach a wider audience, and the system of public schools developing in the early postbellum years proved to be the perfect vehicle for their aspirations. Through concerns about education in Tennessee, mainstream Methodists and Baptists demonstrated consistent, sustained interest not just in vertical human-divine relationships but also in horizontal human-human relationships and questions of social organization. Tennessee Evangelicals wanted control of the schools to teach children the religion of their fathers and mothers. The Evangelicals also sought to use public schools to create the type of society they desired to see on the earth, in the state, in the present time. Theirs were temporal, not just eternal, interests.

Seeing concern over the content and control of education as a key expression of Evangelicalism in the New South, *Before Scopes* also expands the definition of *education* beyond a simple notion of what occurs in the schoolroom. Adopting Bernard Bailyn's invitation to see "education not only as formal pedagogy but as the entire process by which a culture transmits itself across the generations," the book expands the definition and describes education as something far broader than what occurs formally in schools. John Hardin Best has recently turned Bailyn's keen insight toward the South, setting a research agenda that describes southern schooling as much more complex than simply a later development of the New England common-school ideal. Building on Bailyn's conceptions, Best argues that the only way to understand education in the South is to accept that the formal "education of the South arose from nonformal sources, from the southern culture, traditions, and institutions more fundamental than mere schools."[14]

Before Scopes is in part an educational history along the lines outlined by Bailyn and Best. This book examines fifty important years in the development of education in Tennessee, from the enactment of the foundational public school legislation of 1873 through the opening of Vanderbilt and Southwestern Baptist Universities in 1875 to the passage of the reactionary Butler antievolution bill of 1925. *Before Scopes* briefly describes the founding of schools, the training and selection of teachers, the reform efforts of the early-twentieth-century Progressives, and the changing relationship of denominational colleges to their founding churches and state-funded counterparts. But the purpose of this volume is less to chronicle the growth of schools than to understand what happened to those "nonformal sources" and the "culture, traditions, and institutions" surrounding the newly emerging public schools. Perhaps the most important of those nonformal sources, the parents and churches, did not go away but became increasingly vocal about the schools.

While examining the growth of formal schooling in Tennessee, *Before Scopes* also explores the place of evangelical religion in shaping the changing role and understanding of the family in the New South. Antebellum education was almost the exclusive prerogative and responsibility of the individual family and particularly of the head of household, who bore responsibility for determining what kind and what extent of education, if any, children were to receive. Antebellum Tennessee courts recognized a patriarch's almost absolute power over his household. By 1913, however, the Tennessee General Assembly had passed a statewide compulsory-education law requiring children's school attendance for a minimum number of days each year and punishing parents for noncompliance.

Several religious Tennesseans in the 1860s and early 1870s opposed the creation of a system of public education as an undue infringement on parental rights and responsibilities. Many of these people feared that state schools would be entirely secular and thus would threaten to undermine religion. However, by the early 1880s, Tennessee's Methodists and Baptists, led by Fitzgerald, had accepted the public schools. Believing that parents and churches would continue to provide sufficient denominationally religious instruction to complement the public schools' nonsectarian teaching, religious leaders endorsed the schools as colaborers in the evangelical mission. But in the first decades of the twentieth century, as evidence mounted that many parents were failing to live up to the responsibilities assigned by Fitzgerald and others, many Tennessee evangelical leaders became concerned. They called for more explicitly religious instruction in the state's common schools, including required daily Bible-reading exercises. When instruction in biological evolution appeared to threaten the religious culture of the public schools, Tennessee Evangelicals reasserted parental control of education specifically to ban Darwin from the state's classrooms.

Religion and education also extended into the broader arena of southern political culture. Religious ideas of what constituted proper education influenced the actions of individual parents, legislators, bureaucrats, and activists as control of education shifted from local communities to state agencies. Nineteenth-century debates regarding education were largely isolated within individual rural areas and small communities, and public schools rarely strayed far from the community's wishes. The first public schools in Tennessee were extremely decentralized, and local school boards were quite responsive to parental desires. As education grew more formal and as public elementary schools became the common experience of Tennessee children, their parents as well as church leaders to a great degree delegated responsibility for education to the new institutions. Following the success of Progressive-era drives for centralization, standardization, and professionalization of schools, curricula, and teachers, parents and church and community leaders moved from their former position as arbiters of educational standards to lobbying the state legislature to regain a potent voice in the governance of public schools. State religious leaders recognized the new power of the teachers, schools, and educational bureaucracy to shape the minds of future generations. As Baptist educator Rufus Weaver explained, it would become necessary "to enter . . . into politics to preserve the rights of the little child." And most Tennessee Evangelicals believed that these rights included religious instruction and, later, protection from the supposedly irreligious theory of evolution.[15]

From at least the 1870s, Tennessee religious leaders had been concerned about not just the industrial but also the religious and educational "foundations" of the New South. Changing political conditions in the twentieth century forced these leaders to seek new and often more explicitly political means for securing their old goals.

Chapter 2 addresses denominational efforts to rebuild following the Civil War and white Evangelicals' relationship to public education up through the beginning of the twentieth century. During the 1860s and 1870s, many state religious leaders objected to the initial Reconstruction-era creation of public schools, believing instead that education was the exclusive province of church and home. By the 1880s, however, Tennessee's Methodist and Baptist leaders had accommodated the growth of publicly funded elementary education along the lines of a "home rule" compromise outlined by Fitzgerald in the Methodists' *Nashville Christian Advocate.* By avoiding statewide legislation on religion and public education, Fitzgerald believed that Tennessee Christians could escape the ethnic and sectarian strife that had befallen several other regions over questions of religion in the schools. Parrying potential constitutional barriers, Fitzgerald's compromise eschewed state legislation ordering religious observance or teaching in the schools in favor of decisions by local school boards that probably could not be legally challenged. Public schools would be decentralized and under the control of predominantly evangelical Protestant parents, local school commissioners, and local community leaders, parties that would presumably guarantee a place for religion in the curriculum.

A large part of Fitzgerald's home rule compromise depended on the establishment and growth of denominational colleges to complete the education begun in the public schools, to provide teachers for state schools, and to supply the religious and secular leaders of the New South with a morally and religiously sound education. Chapter 3 examines the history of religious higher education—specifically, the Methodists' Vanderbilt University in Nashville and Southwestern Baptist University (which changed its name to Union University in 1907) in Jackson—and this history's relationship to denominational founders and growing state universities. Perceptions of the declining fortunes of some church colleges and the supposed secularization of others inspired many religious leaders to call for more explicit respect for Christianity in the public schools and greater public scrutiny of state university officers.

Much like their concern for the education of youth, evangelical activity in the temperance and Prohibition campaigns signified a new era and level of social engagement by Tennessee Christians. Furthermore, Evangelicals' experiences with the mixed success of the Prohibition crusade—at its heart an attempt to control social behavior—reinforced the perception of the need to shape future citizens' morals and behavior through the public schools. As chapter 4 details, many adults opposed and openly violated Prohibition laws and consequently led many Evangelicals to concentrate their efforts on raising a generation of Tennesseans with the internal morality (learned in the school, not left to chance in the home) to resist alcohol and to support prosecuting their fellow citizens who disobeyed the law. In the Prohibition campaigns, evangelical leaders rehearsed many of the arguments they would later utilize in the early twentieth century to advocate daily Bible reading and to oppose the teaching of evolution in the public schools.

Chapter 5 picks up the narrative begun in chapter 2, examining the changing relationship of religion and public education during the first decades of the twentieth century. At the turn of the century, state evangelical leaders went from simply accommodating the public schools to actively endorsing and promoting them. Tennessee's public school campaigns took on the flavor of religious revivals and enjoyed wide support from the pulpit and in the religious press. The success of the Progressive-era school campaigns had several unintended consequences; most important, state school officials effectively dismantled the home rule compromise as they expanded public education to include high schools and colleges and centralized school control in the hands of a bureaucracy. Religious parents and church leaders saw the new, centrally organized schools as both a threat to traditional sources of authority and a new vehicle for spreading religion. Beginning as early as 1903 and picking up speed during and after World War I, many Methodists and Baptists argued for moral and even specifically religious instruction—especially in the form of required daily

Bible reading—in the public schools. These religious leaders no longer evaded constitutional questions as Fitzgerald had done a generation before; instead, the new Evangelicals boldly proclaimed that religion in the public school was a question of majority rule. America was a "Christian nation," the Bible was "nonsectarian," and they were exercising a "citizen's right" in demanding its use in the schools.

Religious arguments in favor of Bible reading in the public schools laid the groundwork for the campaigns, a decade later, to ban the teaching of evolution in Tennessee public schools. Chapter 6 explores the role of white Tennessee Methodists and Baptists in passing and enforcing Tennessee's 1925 antievolution law. Following World War I, Darwin's theory of evolution became the most potent symbol of materialistic secular science challenging religious orthodoxy and sapping religious and moral fervor in Germany and potentially in the United States as well. Perceiving a decline in youth religion, the majority of Tennessee evangelical leaders eagerly supported William Jennings Bryan's campaign against evolution and cheered on the 1925 prosecution of John T. Scopes at Dayton.

Writing in March 1881, Fitzgerald presented what he believed should be the "true policy for the South." Much like the earlier admonitions of his Baptist counterpart, Graves, Fitzgerald considered both earthly and divine goals in his plans. The "true policy," Fitzgerald asserted, should be to "build cotton factories and school-houses, reclaim the wasted lands, stay at home, and cling to the God of our fathers."[16] Religion, in the minds of Fitzgerald and his contemporaries, pervaded southern life, in homes and schools as much as in industry and government. As government grew and as isolated individuals and families increasingly became part of larger and more interrelated social and political networks, Evangelicals expressed their beliefs in more formal and political arenas. Through campaigns against alcohol and in favor of religious study in public education and through attempts to demonstrate the South's superior morality, Tennessee Evangelicals blurred the lines between church and state in an effort to realize their apotheosized vision of a particularly religious South.

2. *Reading, Writing, and Religion*

Evangelicals and the Creation of Public Education

Addressing a convention of county public school superintendents in the summer of 1887, southern Methodist clergyman and editor Oscar Fitzgerald praised their efforts in rebuilding Tennessee's society since the end of the Civil War. Stating that "everything was broken to pieces in that great convulsion," Fitzgerald hyperbolized, "Nothing in all the history of this world equals the progress made by the South in the two decades extending from 1867 to 1887." Such progress was remarkable, he continued, because it came in spite of the interference of "repressing and disturbing influences from abroad." Fitzgerald came to the convention to extol the educators' efforts as well as to offer direction for their future activities. While lauding the role of education in rebuilding the South, he insisted on properly situating schools within the larger realm of southern culture and society. The success (from a southern point of view) of Reconstruction "would have been . . . impossible . . . had you not had the elements of a Christian civilization so inwrought into the thought, conscience, and aspirations of the people that nothing short of their annihilation could destroy it."[1] This "Christian civilization" was the only thing that had saved the South so far, Fitzgerald intimated, and must not be ignored in continuing efforts to rebuild the region.

Fitzgerald and most of his contemporaries saw education not merely as a matter of learning the basic skills of reading, writing, and arithmetic. Education was instead the whole process of transmitting culture from one generation to the next. As such, education was not confined to school buildings and lesson plans but was interwoven with a myriad of cultural events and processes. Schoolteachers and officials had an important role to play in education, but parents, pastors, and community leaders were equal partners in this great responsibility of perpetuating a distinctive southern culture. But all of these parties did not necessarily agree on what parts of that culture should be passed on to the new generation or, even more importantly, who should decide such questions.

Before the Civil War, education in Tennessee, as in most of the antebellum South, was an informal process carried on primarily in the home, in the church, and in everyday social interactions. What formal education existed was decidedly ad hoc, consisting of tutors to wealthy families, subscription schools in some communities, scattered denominational "colleges" and "seminaries," and, in the late antebellum period, a few city schools for orphans and pauper children. In the twenty postbellum years Fitzgerald was reviewing, the Tennessee legislature had created, dismantled, and then re-created two systems of public education— one for white children and a conspicuously inferior one for black children. In making elementary schools a regular state government concern, Tennessee's postbellum educational advocates were attempting to institutionalize education. With the formalization of education in the public schools, contests emerged over the control of the new schools and over what was taught. Parents and church leaders at first saw the new schools as unallowable threats but gradually came to see schools as powerful allies in efforts to perpetuate local and Christian culture.

Efforts to establish a system of public education unleashed debates in Tennessee and throughout the South about the role of parents and religion in the New South. Above all, Fitzgerald and his religious contemporaries wanted to ensure that the region's "Christian civilization" would be reproduced in the rising generation of Tennesseans. The inauguration and growth of public education threatened the cultural authority of ministers and even parents as increasingly formalized elementary education became a recognized government function. Efforts to create and centralize a public educational system in Tennessee forced citizens to reexamine this emerging notion of the secular state and their role and that of religion in the state.

"The relation of the State to [the] Schools" was, as concerned Nashville minister Collins D. Elliott exclaimed in the 1880s, "the greatest problem of our times."[2] What families and churches thought about public education can reveal much about their understanding of the proper role of government in the New South. But, even more importantly, their concerns for maintaining a "Christian civilization" led them increasingly to embrace a social role for religion in Tennessee. Ultimately concerned about the spiritual health of their children, devout Tennesseans wanted to ensure that the new schools would not be inimical to religion. In so doing, such citizens began to expand the scope of the church's work in the world, recognizing that they could and should work to affect society as a whole, not just the souls of individual sinners.

The Concept of the Especially Religious South

When Fitzgerald addressed the school superintendents in 1887, the South was defeated, struggling in the throes of racial, economic, and social realignments. Yet he and his audience could readily agree on the importance of the region's Christian heritage. The South had long recognized itself as the country's Bible Belt, with Tennessee near the proverbial buckle because of its proximity to the genesis of the 1800 southern revival in nearby areas of Kentucky as well as the large number of southern denominations headquartered in Nashville, the so-called Protestant Vatican. Fitzgerald and other postbellum southerners cultivated the image of the especially religious South to fit their cultural agendas but did not create the image out of whole cloth. This image had some basis in reality but had long been inflated to fit southern white conservatives' political, social, and cultural needs.

Antebellum Tennessee Evangelicals never faced the problems of an established church as did their neighbors to the east, but they were nonetheless inheritors of a dissenter tradition and tended to identify most strongly with their local church communities. White Baptists had been some of the area's earliest settlers, followed near the end of the American Revolution by a smaller number of Methodists. But both nascent denominations trailed the Presbyterians in numbers and influence among the first settlers and in the early society. However, the three denominations, despite their aggressive proselytizing, could claim only about 5 percent of the population as formal members when Tennessee became a state in 1796.[3] These conditions changed quickly when the Great Revival began near the Kentucky and Tennessee border in 1800 and radiated throughout the state and the rest of the South. Although the revivalism had peaked by 1805, the intensity of those five years greatly increased Methodist and Baptist membership in the state. At the same time, the Presbyterians, who had been the original leaders of the revival, split over the propriety of revival methods. Alexander Campbell's Reformers and Barton Stone's Christians rounded out the majority of Tennessee's religious adherents after the first decades of the nineteenth century.[4]

By the time of the Civil War, white Tennessee Baptists and Methodists had moved from a position of religious and social dissent to form part of an evangelical social and cultural establishment and believed themselves to be living in a particularly religious society.[5] According to the 1850 federal census, Methodists had 861 churches in Tennessee, estimated at a value of $381,711 and with a seating capacity of 249,000. Baptists followed with 646 churches, 195,315 seats, and property worth $271,899.[6] "No institution save the family loomed larger" than the churches did in the everyday lives of religious Tennesseans on the eve of secession.[7]

Part of the antebellum Evangelicals' success in gaining converts and social status came through a silencing of their potential for social criticism, especially with regard to the institution of slavery. Tennessee Evangelicalism, born of the revivals at Cane Ridge and spread throughout the state by continued revivalism, focused far more on the condition of the individual human soul than on society. As John Boles explains about the antebellum church, "the conversion emphasis was not one to elicit social criticism. Instead, the tendency of southern religion was toward an acceptance of the existing social arrangements."[8] Indeed, a number of white Tennessee Evangelicals in the early 1800s supported the peaceful abolition of slavery, noting that "it is an evil" but refusing to endorse any particular strategy for ending the institution. Some East Tennessee Baptists joined manumission societies in the 1810s and 1820s but, like most of their southern counterparts, grew more reticent as northern abolitionism increasingly emphasized immediatism. Tennessee Baptist editor R. B. C. Howell dismissed an 1840 proabolition circular as nothing but "rant, nonsense, mis-statements, and fanaticism." Arguing that "Southern Christians and Southern people are the only true friends of the black race," Howell and other southern Evangelicals pronounced biblical defenses of slavery and endorsed slavery as a means for civilizing Africans. Early Tennessee Methodists likewise agitated over the slavery question, although by 1820 the Tennessee Conference (covering Middle Tennessee only) "was decidedly under proslavery control."[9]

Although some Tennessee Baptists and Methodists defended slavery less forcefully than did the surrounding white society and even pointed out problems within the peculiar institution, these relative moderates nonetheless joined ranks with other religious groups to, in effect, sanctify the existing society and culture.[10] The endorsement of southern society as particularly religious and the justification of slavery as an evangelistic tool to civilize and Christianize Africans enabled Confederate leaders to further legitimate the separate southern nation as divinely favored. As Drew Gilpin Faust suggests, the creation of Confederate nationalism involved "more than simply establishing a new political status for the South; it required the location of the Confederacy not only within the world but within eternity, as an instrumental part of God's designs."[11] The Confederacy was, in the words of Episcopal Bishop Stephen Elliott, "the nation to do His work on earth."[12] Once this image of the South as a religious society had been established, it did not disappear easily from the minds of religious leaders or even common southerners.

Confederate defeat doomed evangelical hopes for a separate, religious nation based on Christian slaveholding. But instead of causing southern Evangelicals to doubt their chosen status, the horrors of war reinforced their conception of the South as a particularly religious region. [13] Indeed, as Gardiner Shattuck Jr. argues, "most [white] southern Protestants were well prepared *theologically* to meet the challenge Appomattox presented." The task of postwar southern religion was to provide an explanation for the Confederate defeat; most southern clergy accomplished this task by reaffirming white southerners as God's chosen people. Presbyterian Robert Louis Dabney of Virginia explained that "temporal good and the exemption from temporal evil" were not signs of God's favor; white southerners should instead find solace in "the darkness of mysterious suffering." [14] As sociologist Peter Berger suggests, theodicy, or the theological explanation of evil, involves a certain element of "masochistic liberation"—a surrender of the self (and in this case the Confederate nation) to a larger, divine reality. [15] Such immersion in the faith blunted the questions about where God's favor really lay that could arise out of defeat. Abraham Lincoln had suggested in his second inaugural address that both northern and southern partisans prayed to the same God but that neither could have their prayers fully answered. Lest the Union military victors make exclusive claims on divine support of their effort, southern Christian apologists such as Elliott and Dabney retreated from cocksure antebellum expressions of divine favor to chastened reminders of the inscrutable nature of divine will. Religious reassurance in defeat, Berger explains, resulted from religion's alienating power, which obscured the southern faithful's realization that their society—including its facets that had led to the recent war—and their religion were to some degree their own constructions. This alienating power of religious belief provided a welcome relief from the potentially anomic situation of defeat with a divinely stable legitimating force to order and explain the world.

In his study of the southern religious response to Confederate defeat, Charles Reagan Wilson suggests that cultural and religious leaders developed a new civil religion of the Lost Cause. Citing anthropologist Anthony F. C. Wallace, Wilson notes that "religion originates 'in situations of social and cultural stress' " and points out that following the Civil War, the South was in distress, suffering from poverty as well as disillusionment, disorder, and a perceived loss of meaning—a state of communal anomie. Using Clifford Geertz's conception of religion, Wilson explains how the religious response to disorder is "the creation of symbols 'of such a genuine order of the world which will account for, and even celebrate, the perceived ambiguities, puzzles, and paradoxes in human experience.' " Wilson sees this response embodied in the rituals of the Lost Cause, a distinctively southern civil religion that was a "revivalistic movement, aiming . . . 'to restore a golden age believed to have existed in the society's past' "—an attempt to res-urrect the culture and values of the Old South.[16] Putting aside questions about the existence of the especially religious Old South, this concept of the South as a particularly religious society nonetheless carried enormous cultural capital, not just for conservative Democratic politicians but for religious leaders as well. Denominational leaders utilized the images of the Old South as particularly religious to spur on southern Christians (both within and outside of the leaders' particular denominations). These defeated southerners attempted to assuage their grief by redoubling their efforts to make the New South a sacred society. Elliott admonished his flock even in the humiliation of defeat to "forget not that you are Christ's servants, bound to do His work in the church militant upon earth, and to advance His kingdom wherever He may spread the banner of the Cross. Instead of permitting suffering to overcome your faith, let it rather lead you on to perfection."[17]

Following the charge of Bishop Elliott and many others, white Tennessee Protestants sought to continue and strengthen southerners' religion. Leaders sought to rebuild their own particular denominations as well as to add to them. Indeed, as Fitzgerald admonished his audience of school superintendents two decades after the war, only a "Christian civilization" had saved the South through the war and Reconstruction; educators, in turn, should now strive to continue and perfect that civilization in the rising generations.

White Baptists and Methodists answered this charge in part by increasing their missionary efforts among the recently emancipated slaves. During and soon after the war, most white leaders had opposed the exodus of black members from what had been biracial churches. Asserting that they were "the best friends the black man ever had, or will have," the ministers of the Memphis Annual Conference of the southern Methodist church hoped to maintain religious as well as cultural and political control over black church members.[18] Most white denominations declared that their black coreligionists could not sustain proper interpretations of the Gospel without the continued influence of their former white religious leaders or, even worse, could fall under the influence of northern missionaries who might upset southern cultural, racial, and political hierarchies. Failing to keep blacks within their churches—black Tennessee membership in the Methodist Episcopal Church, South declined from 12,676 in 1860 to a mere 17 in 1877—white leaders hoped either to provide white ministers for the blacks or to train black ministers and to keep black Christians under the oversight of white denominational leaders. White religious leaders ultimately had to admit defeat, with the southern Methodists helping to create the Colored (later Christian) Methodist Church with a black hierarchy, but even it paled in numerical comparison to separate black-led religious organizations such as the African Methodist Episcopal (AME) and AME Zion churches.[19]

When such efforts to control blacks' religious and social organizations were largely frustrated by individual black agency and desires for religious self-determination, white Tennessee religious leaders mostly settled for retaining at least some limited contact with their black counterparts while enhancing efforts to shore up white society's religion and morality. These leaders' first priority was increasing membership and reestablishing the denominational institutions that had been greatly disrupted by the years of warfare and disorganization. Individual Baptist and Methodist churches reconnected with similar churches throughout the state to reestablish denominational structures in 1865 and 1866. Tennessee Baptists, who had long been divided into separate general associations in the state's three geographical regions, resumed their antebellum efforts at union soon after the war, eventually forming the Tennessee Baptist Convention in 1874.[20] Methodist denominational leaders and enterprising Baptist ministers and laymen resumed editing and printing religious newspapers in Memphis, Nashville, and Chattanooga, aiding in the spread of religious and secular news throughout the state. Both denominations resumed missionary efforts at home and abroad, seeking to spread the Gospel and to add to their numbers.

An even more important component of Tennessee Baptists' and Methodists' religious reconstruction was the strengthening of their existing membership and taking measures to provide for the religious education of the rising generation. Denominational leaders accomplished this, in part, by establishing or reopening colleges under the sponsorship and supervision of the denominations. (A closer examination of two such schools—Southwestern Baptist University in Jackson and the Methodists' Vanderbilt University in Nashville—appears in chapter 3.) But recognizing that no matter how low the tuition, denominational colleges could serve only a small percentage of church members, religious leaders sought to strengthen the faith of the rising generation through the institution of the Sunday school. Like the individual churches and denominational organizations, most Sunday schools had suffered great disorganization during the war. West Tennessee Baptists lamented in 1866 that "the large majority of the Churches" in their bounds were "without schools." Baptist leaders in Middle Tennessee likewise complained in 1865 that few churches outside the cities had Sunday schools and recorded the "painful fact that too many christian parents take no interest in the Sabbath Schools—a large number of our country churches have none at all."[21]

Tennessee Evangelicals saw the education of their children as the greatest opportunity for strengthening the religious hold on southern society. Baptists in West Tennessee supported the expansion of the Sunday schools as "a most efficient means of instilling moral and religious sentiments into the minds of children, and properly training the rising generations for the momentous responsibilities which must soon devolve upon them as members of society and of the church of God."[22] Not only would children learn the particular tenets of Baptist or Methodist faith and thus hopefully be led to conversion and salvation, but denominational leaders further hoped that children could be trained to lead pious lives on earth and thereafter, spreading the Gospel and increasing church membership. In his excellent account of what he calls the "religious reconstruction" of the South, Daniel W. Stowell argues that southern Christians valued education highly because "they understood that the perpetuation of their distinctive religious identity depended on their success at transmitting cultural ideals to the next generation." Stowell explains the efforts of southern denominations to rebuild antebellum institutions such as Sunday schools and denominational colleges as expressions of the desire to maintain a hold on young minds.[23] The histories of institutions such as Vanderbilt and Southwestern Baptist are certainly revealing, but this concentration on strictly religious enterprises overlooks the fact that few Tennessee Evangelicals were willing simply to surrender other means of education to the state. "The future of the land we love," warned Tennessee religious educator Elizabeth Denty Abernethy early in the twentieth century, "depends upon what we make of our public school system."[24] When Reconstruction and Redeemer state legislators formalized a system of public elementary education in the state, denominational leaders endeavored to ensure that such schools would further or at least not oppose religious goals.

The Emergence of Public Education

Nineteenth-century Tennessee, both before and after the Civil War, was a predominantly rural society. Formal schooling was a rarity most rural children experienced for only a month or so, if at all, during any given year.[25] But this did not mean that the children were uneducated; they were instead taught—raised and influenced—by their families, churches, and broad communities. As educational historian David B. Tyack explains, formal "schooling—which farmers usually associated with book learning—was only a small, and to many, an incidental part of the total education the community provided." Instead of focusing narrowly on literacy skills, Tyack suggests that in rural societies like that of nineteenth-century Tennessee, "the child acquired his values and skills from his family and from neighbors of all ages and conditions." Education did not come only in *McGuffey's Eclectic Reader,* in Webster's blue-backed speller, or from practicing "figuring"; rather, "a child growing up in such a community could see work-family-religion-recreation-school as an organically related system of human relationships" and education.[26]

Education reformers of the late nineteenth and early twentieth centuries fetishized literacy statistics as a clear indication of a community's level of education. By such standards, antebellum Tennesseans were obviously deficient, with roughly one-quarter of the white population unable to read or write at the time of the 1850 census. Reformers pointed to the remarkable improvements in the last antebellum decade, noting that white Tennesseans' rate of illiteracy had dropped to 19.7 percent by 1860. Imagine the further success, they seemed to imply, had the terrible disruption of war and Reconstruction not intervened.[27] Late-nineteenth-century American education reformers found local community control of education the greatest hindrance to school reform. They, like their antebellum counterparts, urged increasingly formalized schooling in publicly funded schools under centralized bureaucratic control as the key to state unity and progress.[28]

Formal instruction in publicly owned schoolhouses funded by taxation had developed slowly in antebellum Tennessee, as in most of the South. Most formal educational opportunities were confined to academies, local subscription schools, and colleges or seminaries loosely affiliated with various religious denominations.[29] Despite frequent efforts by some antebellum statesmen to provide for common schools like those in the northeastern states, state funding remained very limited, taxation for schools was practically nonexistent, and popular support was divided by class and region.

The earliest schools in Tennessee (some even predating statehood) were connected at least informally with religious bodies. Denominations and ministers created several schools in the late antebellum era, most of them "mainly offering educational opportunities on primary and secondary levels with a limited attempt at college work." Presbyterian minister Samuel Doak, a graduate of the College of New Jersey (later Princeton University), simultaneously founded congregations and schools as one of the first settlers of the eastern parts of what would become Tennessee. Tennessee Baptists built several colleges in the antebellum era, the most prominent of them Union University in Murfreesboro in 1841, Mossy Creek Baptist Seminary in Mossy Creek (the town was later renamed Jefferson City and the school Carson College) in 1851, and the Tennessee Baptist Female Institute (formally rechartered as Mary Sharp College in 1857) in Winchester in 1851. In addition to these central institutions, Baptist leaders encouraged local churches and associations to sponsor male and female academies. In the 1820s, Tennessee Methodists cooperated in the establish-ment of colleges in nearby Kentucky (Bethel Academy) and north Alabama (La Grange in 1828).[30] In the later antebellum period, these Methodists increased their efforts to found schools for both men and women, but few of the schools came under the direct control or ownership of the denomination. Some were directly linked to Methodism in name—Tennessee Conference Female Institute in Jackson and the Tennessee Conference Male High School in Spring Hill, for example—but most, like the Nashville Female Academy, were linked to the church through their choice of managers and placement of advertising. Collins D. Elliott, a Methodist minister who would long remain active in Tennessee's postwar educational debates, taught at La Grange College before joining the Nashville girls' school in 1839 and managing it from 1844 until 1866.[31]

Antebellum education in Tennessee reflected and perpetuated the state's class divisions. Academies were usually frequented by wealthier Tennesseans who could afford tuition. From his analysis of the surveys completed by Ten-nessee Confederate Veterans, Fred A. Bailey has determined that "academy attendance was concentrated in those sections of the state with slaves and af-fluence."[32] Parents who could afford to do so sent their children to academies, hired private tutors, or banded together with other neighbors to pay for private subscription schools. Legislative votes on public funds for education usually divided along sectional lines, with upcountry East Tennesseans usually favoring the common schools while Middle and West Tennesseans, who were more likely to own slaves, usually opposed the increased taxation.[33] Although some variety of semiformal public schooling existed in most of the populated parts of the state by the 1850s, these schools operated for only short periods of time, usually in abysmal buildings, and often were taught by less-than-inspiring teachers. Conditions were typified by one student's description of attending school in a "Sorry little log hut and poorly furnished" for only "a month or so" with "Verry [*sic*] common and Sorry Teachers."[34] In part, the lack of educational oppor-tunities reflected the antebellum Tennessee political culture's unwillingness to expend (and thus have to gather) great amounts of tax revenue. Conversely, the rarity of school opportunities was mostly in keeping with the realities of the predominantly rural society, in which farmer parents were reluctant or unable to spare their children's labor. A Bedford County veteran observed that children "were not made to go [to school], besides there was work to do"; another former soldier noted that his father had allowed him to attend school only for about a month a year when the family was "not making crops."[35]

Tennessee's 1796 Constitution made no specific provision for public educa-tion, and little funding was available for schools until just before the Civil War.

A portion of proceeds from federal land sales after 1806 was supposed to be dedicated to education, but only a small percentage of the anticipated funds materialized, and they were dedicated to supporting semiprivate, tuition-charging secondary academies. After the War of 1812, the legislature attempted to support more widespread education, but the wording of the act targeted the funding at "those poor orphans who have no property to support and educate them, and whose fathers were killed or have died in the service of their country in the late war."[36] Whatever the legislators' good intentions, identifying the public schools with poor relief unfortunately branded the new institutions as pauper schools and thus to be avoided by any self-respecting Jacksonian individualist. The revised Constitution of 1834 reassigned the land sale monies to the Common School Fund, and the succeeding sessions of the General Assembly created the Board of Common School Commissioners (in 1836) on the state level and established district school commissioners (in 1838) on the local level. Unfortunately, the financial downturn of the period, combined with confusingly overlapping land claims, meant that the new school fund amounted to far less than had been anticipated. Allegations that the first state superintendent of schools was guilty of embezzlement and financial mismanagement further derailed efforts to establish common schools and left a lingering distrust of state bureaucratic involvement in education. Though some cities established common-school systems in this period, state funding remained limited, even after Governor Andrew Johnson convinced the legislature to provide at least some public funds for schools out of tax revenue in 1854.[37]

Educational historian Robert Hiram White summarizes the antebellum development of public education in Tennessee in these satirically optimistic terms: "Without adequate funds, deprived of any centralized supervising authority, subjected to the economic and social handicaps imposed by slavery, and bereft of any militant public sentiment, the challenging fact was that the common schools were able to be even in existence at all at the advent of the Civil War." The disruptions of 1861–65 were not likely to ameliorate this situation. In fact, schools received no state funds during the war. The legislature, when it could meet, focused exclusively on items of immediate importance to the war effort. The school funds, which had been deposited in the Bank of Tennessee, disappeared when the bank dissolved at the end of the war, leaving the state with only a fictional "permanent school fund" on which the General Assembly promised to pay 6 percent interest to public schools annually.[38]

Tennessee remained occupied territory for much of the war, with former Governor Andrew Johnson serving as military governor before moving to Washington to become vice president in 1865 and giving way to Republican civilian governor William G. "Parson" Brownlow. In 1865, Brownlow's Republican-controlled General Assembly began to debate new legislation that would provide for centralization, funding, and control of the school system. One proponent of the measure proclaimed that "the common schools of Tennessee should be declared as free as the air we breathe, to every child of the proper age to participate in their benefits, and their support should be made a charge upon the whole property of the state." In opposition, a conservative senator from Shelby County warned that "the bill levies enormous taxes to pay a swarm of new and unheard of officers, and . . . the people are ill prepared to submit to onerous taxes, when they have just emerged from a long and desolate war." Such legislation, though it might bring some temporary blessings, "eventually will end in ruin, destruction, and a subversion of the rights and liberties of the people." Despite such fears, the legislature passed the bill.[39] The Reconstruction government appropriated taxes for the schools and appointed General John Eaton to survey and organize the state's school system. But Brownlow's unabashed disgust for the former rebels, the provision of schools and social services for blacks, and the appointment of a northerner and former Freedman's Bureau official as state superintendent of schools meant that the school system would have trouble when conservative Tennesseans regained control of the government in 1869. The Redeemer legislature quickly dismantled much of the state school system, eliminating the position of state superintendent and leaving only a fifty-cent poll tax for education.[40]

An 1873 survey of public education in Tennessee, paid for by concerned teachers with support of funds from northern philanthropist George F. Peabody's Education Fund to improve southern schools and teacher education, revealed that less than 20 percent of Tennessee's school-age population had access to schools, "nor were there any efforts being made by the citizens to remedy the deficiency."[41] Joseph B. Killebrew, a prominent Tennessee New South visionary, authored the report and pronounced more widespread public schooling a panacea for the state's problems. He ended with some predictions:

> It is also believed that a large amount can be saved from what is now expended for
> the prosecution of crime; that a considerable portion can be realized by increasing
> the productive capacity of the people, by education; that greater security will be
> given to life and property; that society will be elevated, improved and dignified;
> that intelligent men and women will be attracted to the State by making the State
> attractive with public schools; that the price of property will be increased; that a
> steady development of our native resources will be assured; that our industries and
> products will be greatly diversified; and that the State of Tennessee, so glorious

in the memories of the past, will rise from her depressed condition, and take her place among the galaxy of States, shining with no uncertain splendor in the light of knowledge, truth, civilization and patriotism. [42]

Following Killebrew's report and the State Teachers Association's intensive lobbying efforts, the Tennessee General Assembly in 1873 reenacted virtually the same 1867 school legislation that had been repealed in 1870.

Passing school legislation was not easy, but funding and putting into operation the newly created system of schools proved even more difficult in a Tennessee still struggling with the dramatic changes in society, economics, and government following the Civil War. The 1873 school legislation passed as Tennessee was enjoying a brief financial recovery; that fall, the state and the rest of the country fell into a deep financial panic that lasted the better part of the next decade. Funding for the schools remained slight, and many schools shortened their terms or failed to open at all, as one county superintendent reported in 1885, "on account of money being short." State Superintendent Leon Trousdale recorded the reluctance of many rural parents to spare the labor of their children, even for the short school term: "The financial pressure prevented many from enrollment who would otherwise have attended. The short crop of 1873 created an absolute necessity for every available hand on the farms in the subsequent year. Absolute poverty and want thus cut off attendance." [43] The country's financial problems exacerbated Tennessee's postwar financial crisis, and politicians and taxpayers seemed leery of further encumbering the tax system.

State funding for education was limited by the looming presence of the state debt as well as by the anticipation of private philanthropic money and new federal funds for public schools. The initial Common School Fund had been created out of federal land sales, and many Tennesseans continued to look for outside assistance for the schools. The Peabody Education Fund had underwritten Killebrew's survey and report that led to the passage of the 1873 school laws, and Peabody continued to pour money into Tennessee education, funding schools and teacher training institutes and eventually a large-scale normal school in Nashville early in the twentieth century. Other northern philanthropies donated funds to improve education for both white and black Tennesseans as Tennessee's mounting debt continued to overshadow its educational expenditures. As late as 1899, the state owed more than $540,000 per year in interest on its debt, more than three times the amount spent on education. [44]

Many public school advocates found inviting the prospect of federal funding for public education, but racial politics eventually derailed any opportunity to secure federal funds for Tennessee schools. Many white Tennesseans vehemently objected to providing schools for former slaves: some county school officials reported being warned at gunpoint not to include blacks in the school census, and Eaton recorded sixty-seven African American schools burned between 1865 and 1869. Opponents feared that federally funded and controlled education would require racially integrated schools, which Tennessee's Reconstruction and Redeemer governments opposed and which Tennessee's 1870 Constitution prohibited.[45] In the 1870s and 1880s, various congressmen attempted to appropriate federal funds for state schools. Tennessee Republican Representative William F. Prosser offered a bill in 1870 to create a national system of education and was defeated in his reelection bid later that year. The problem with Prosser's bill, as well as with a similar proposal by Massachusetts Republican George Hoar, was that many conservatives feared both the expense and the new opportunities for political patronage and corruption. But the real opposition to such bills—strongest in the South but by no means absent in the North—arose from fears of racially integrated schools. While Congress debated bills to aid in funding state schools, Massachusetts Senator Charles Sumner openly argued for racially integrated schools in the District of Columbia. Although Sumner's bill was defeated, "from then on, mixed schools and federal involvement in public education were inseparably linked." Later attempts at federal funding, most notably the Blair bill in the 1880s, eventually foundered because opponents could always raise the "bogey man of mixed schools."[46]

Postbellum Tennessee school superintendents realized that the racial integration of the state's public schools would result in "the almost instantaneous death of the present school system." Tennessee citizens, explained Superintendent John Fleming in an 1874 protest against the pending federal civil rights bill's potential consequences for the state's system of segregated schools, "could not be brought to regard schools as merely civil organizations, subject only to political government; the school is too close to the family circle not to be subject in a great degree to social laws and influences."[47] Beyond his and white citizens' racial fears, Fleming's comments offer an important clue about why Tennesseans of all races, religions, and political affiliations became so interested in the creation, operation, and control of the public schools. Much of the previously informal educational efforts were picked up by the new public schools—not just instruction in reading, writing, and arithmetic but also an emphasis on morality and citizenship—thus, to a degree, formalizing the process of education. But conversely, the schoolhouse, which, by its existence, limited the effects of previous sources of largely informal education, would increasingly play a profound role in shaping the future of the state and its citizens. Cultural transmission, previously diffused through families, churches, and communities, would now be controlled and centralized in the public schoolhouse. Therefore, people and groups with differing conceptions of what kind of culture they thought important to continue or change began to recognize the public schools and curricula as a powerful ally for or enemy of their plans.

Evangelical Opposition to Public Education

In April 1873, southern Methodist minister and educator W. G. F. Cunnyngham wrote a series of three articles giving his "Thoughts on Education" for the *Nashville Christian Advocate.* Cunnyngham was at the time a professor at Martha Washington College in Abingdon, Virginia, and a frequent contributor of articles and book reviews for the religious newspaper. In his first article, Cunnyngham made a case to his coreligionists for the importance of popular—even tax-supported—education and the necessity of the southern Methodist church being involved in its control. Stipulating first that the "mind governs the world" and reasoning that "education forms the mind," Cunnyngham argued that "no scheme which proposes permanently to reform the world can succeed unless it is able to control the education of mankind." He argued that Methodism—in its most popular forms a religion of the heart aiming to reform individual souls—should also concentrate on education as a means to both sow the seeds for future converts and to reshape society in keeping with Christian principles. [48]

Cunnyngham's prescriptions that his fellow Methodists be diligent about educating their children reveal something of the importance nineteenth-century Tennesseans—religious or otherwise—placed on education. As educator G. R. Shields noted, "the citizens of today is [*sic*] the child of yesterday, and that a school is another name for shaping, what tomorrow, will be society, and state." Children would eventually grow to be adults and, as such, would usually reflect their education. East Tennessee Baptists pronounced concern for future citizens, warning, "Whether these children and their descendents be religious, moral, industrious, and benevolent—or irreligious, immoral, intemperate, profane and Godless, depends much upon what Christianity does" about education. [49]

Tennesseans of the 1870s, whether particularly religious or not, recognized that education was a process of broad cultural transmission that extended beyond the few weeks of formal schooling each year. Trousdale agreed that today's children would be tomorrow's adult citizens, but even he recognized that what children became as adults depended on more than just what they learned in the schoolhouse. The "character" of an adult, Trousdale explained, "has been impressed on him by minute, continued and elaborate manipulations of masters, tutors, philosophers, parents and pastors, in the family, the church and the school, exercised during the period when the mind is most easily formed and bent."[50] Likewise, Collins D. Elliott argued that children were not formed by school alone but were instead "something else, below, above, and within all" the influences from family, church, and community.[51] Children were, in Trousdale's words, "human clay" waiting to be molded by various influences.[52]

If children were clay to be shaped through education into cultured adults and citizens, then control of that education could mean control of society's future. "Those who educate the present generation of children in these United States will hold the reins of power when they are grown," argued Fitzgerald. He further warned the readers of the *Nashville Christian Advocate,* "If we turn over the education of our children to others, we renounce our hold upon the future."[53] In part, Fitzgerald was worried about training children in the specific theological tenets of the southern Methodist church. But Fitzgerald's larger concern, which he shared with many of his fellow evangelical leaders, was that the rapidly expanding system of public education that removed the primary responsibility for educating children from the realm of parents and churches to the impersonal state school machinery threatened to estrange children from the faith and culture of their parents. Consequently, Fitzgerald and others believed, religious groups needed to closely monitor and influence the new public school system. Over the next decade, however, Tennessee Baptists and Methodists would gradually grow to accept public schools for the elementary education of children in the state, and by the 1880s these religious denominations began to see public schools as allies in the mission to Christianize the South.

Parents, public school advocates, and religious leaders agreed on the necessity of education for children but could not agree on its object or specific curricula. Some school boosters saw purely secular and material aims for the schools, arguing that expanded education would create more lawful citizens, reduce poverty, and build up southern industry and wealth. Proponents of this view saw education's highest aim as strengthening the state itself. Some religious leaders feared that such education, if divorced from religious influences, could increase crime and weaken the influence of religion as children were taught to prioritize material knowledge, wealth, and responsibility. Education, these men argued, should be both moral and material and should simultaneously strengthen children, the church, and the state.

The great expansion of suffrage to freedmen following the Civil War, complicated by the existing high rate of illiteracy among white Tennesseans, made a powerful argument for the necessity of better popular education in the 1870s. Leon Trousdale, speaking to the Alumni Association of East Tennessee University in 1875, titled his address, "A Plea for Universal Education by the State, as the Correlative of Citizenship." It was "the whole business of the State," argued Trousdale, "to educate its citizens and thus prevent crime." Crime resulted from "the want of proper training or education," he argued, and instead of spending so much on prisons and punishing crime, the state should educate children to read and understand the law and not to transgress it. As school reformer G. R. Shields argued, educators should "put into the child" today what they wanted to see in the state tomorrow. Trousdale and many other public school advocates also saw in state education "the sure preventative of pauperism [and] bankruptcy." Stating that "industry and education are handmaidens," school promoters described children as "resources" to fuel the state's economic and industrial growth and argued that money spent on education would be returned manifold through the growth of southern industry.[54]

The largely secular aims espoused by such spokesmen for expanded popular education worried other Tennesseans who prioritized religious objectives for education. During the Civil War, Edward S. Joynes, later an original faculty member at the Methodists' Vanderbilt University in 1875, wrote an essay for the *Southern Literary Messenger* speculating on the state of "Education after the War." He predicted that the conflict would encourage the late antebellum trend toward expanding education, but he feared that one "effect of the war" would be an emphasis on "materialism" and a "spirit of utilitarianism" in that education. Collins D. Elliott likewise criticized the aims of the new public school system and its leaders, who "assume in educating children that the chief end of man is to get money and that which money may buy for him." Elliott called on his fellow southern Protestants to unite in "opposition to this merely and only this Worldism of this New England System" of education. He believed that religious southerners were still God's chosen people, set apart for a special work of preserving a culture free from the materialism and infidelity of the rest of the world. As Joynes had argued in his wartime essay, the "safety and future glory" of the South lay in "a *right* and *wise* education" that focused more on religion and morality than on material aims.[55]

The first reaction of many Baptists and Methodists to the establishment of public schools was to denounce them as necessarily "godless" institutions. Bishop Holland McTyeire, the first president of Vanderbilt University, worried that the "ultimate tendency" of a "a public-school system . . . will be a godless institution."[56] In part, religious leaders were motivated by a desire to protect the struggling denominational institutions of learning that were just beginning to rebuild after the Civil War. Even if the public schools were not godless, they probably could not teach denominationally specific religion.[57] In a religious marketplace crowded with competing evangelical denominations, Baptist and Methodist leaders feared losing any opportunity to impress the faith on any member of the rising generation.

To a large extent, white evangelical Tennesseans' fears that religion would be banned from the public schools represented more a reaction to controversies elsewhere in the country than an accurate assessment of the current climate in Tennessee. State religious newspapers carried stories from Boston, New York, Cincinnati, and other parts of the country where Catholics and Protestants were locking horns over the place of the Bible in the public schools. The so-called Cincinnati Bible War, arising from Catholic charges that public schools favored Protestant faiths and ending with the Ohio Supreme Court upholding a ban on Bible reading in the city schools, set in motion waves of fear and anger of a supposed Catholic conspiracy to either destroy public education or make it unpalatably irreligious.[58] Though Tennessee was overwhelmingly Protestant and not likely to be subject to similar opposition from the small numbers of Catholics, Jews, or other nonevangelical Christians, many Baptists and Methodists nonetheless feared a future secularization of Tennessee's public schools. Indeed, opposition to religion in the public schools was not unheard of: during the General Assembly debates regarding the 1873 school bill, a representative had introduced an amendment forbidding the use of any religious text in the state's public schools.[59] William Witcher warned his fellow Methodists, "May we not look next for the legislature to be asked to forbid religious exercises in the opening of schools?"[60]

Tennessee's religious leaders reminded their flocks and state politicians of the necessity of religious public education. The *Memphis Baptist,* one of the most influential Baptist papers in Tennessee and the South, warned school officials that "religion is so interwoven with morality, and morality so essential to good citizenship, that Christian people will never consent to exclude the ethics of religion from the public schools."[61] As Robert Louis Dabney had written in his opposition to the creation of public schools in Virginia in the 1860s, schoolteachers needed to "add the awakening and elevating force of Christian principles" to have "a true education—a hundredfold more true, more suitable, more useful, than the communication of certain literary arts."[62] Tennessee religious leaders did not oppose education but did fear that public schooling devoid of the religious influence that had permeated previous sources of informal education could end only in disaster for society.

Tennessee Evangelicals questioned public school boosters' claims that expanded common-school education would by itself lower crime. While public education advocates suggested that widespread education would reduce vice, some Tennessee Evangelicals countered that education in the "three Rs" alone would be insufficient to prevent crime: "Does any man believe that crime would disappear from the United States if every person over ten years of age could read and write?"[63] Others warned that "Education is no panacea for crime and sin. There is no necessary relation between mere knowledge and moral goodness." In fact, cautioned Fitzgerald in his *Nashville Christian Advocate,* "godless education" or the "mere sharpening of the intellect without moral culture, will only result in making its recipients more powerful agents for evil."[64] Collins Elliott was so convinced of the necessity of religion in education that he even admitted that the state's current informal systems of education left more children illiterate in Tennessee than in other states. But by comparing literacy, crime, and poverty statistics from Tennessee and Massachusetts, the supposed epitome of common-school education, Elliott argued that "fewer of [Tennessee's] illiterates will be in the poor-house and in the prison, than of the *literates*" of the New England common-school system. In short, Elliott claimed that his statistics proved that with the religious influence of Tennessee education, "Tennessee illiterates" were "better citizens than Massachusetts' literates."[65]

Believing as they did that the state public school system would necessarily be godless, many Evangelicals saw no option but to keep their children in schools under church control. Because these religious leaders believed, as Methodist editor Thomas Summers Sr. succinctly put it, that "there can be no education without religion," they felt that Christian parents had no option but to eschew public schools. Summers believed that church members should "pay our taxes to the Church, and let her manage the business" of education. "We would have some control over it then." Methodists and Baptists alike planned and opened many local church schools as "the only antidote to that godless feature in the public schools which ignores the Holy Scriptures in the training of youth."[66] If the public schools were to concentrate on training of either the head or the heart alone, Tennessee Evangelicals could see no recourse but to found schools where they could train both the head and the heart.

The vast majority of public school officials were not irreligious; like most Tennessee Evangelicals, school bureaucrats saw the necessity of a moral component in education. Both groups could agree with Fitzgerald that "learning and religion must go hand in hand on their beneficent mission to the millions" of American children. State superintendent Trousdale said in 1875 that the "only firm and lasting base" of security for the state "can be the virtue and intelligence of the people" secured through the broad education of all citizens. Believing that theirs was a "Christian nation," both the preachers and the pedagogues could agree that public education in Tennessee should and would be at least broadly religious if not denominationally specific. The 1873 State Teachers Association convention called for teachers in the public schools who have "religion free from degrading superstition on the one hand, and from the evils of excessive sectarianism on the other."[67] But this apparent agreement on the need for religion in education masked a second question that would trouble parents, school superintendents, legislators, and religious leaders for the next fifty years and beyond. Who exactly would be in charge of children, the schools, and their curricula?

For the most part, such questions were left to be resolved at the local level. Although Collins D. Elliott denounced Republican proposals to appropriate as much as $15 million a year to the southern states as a "theological abomination," many other Tennesseans of the 1870s and 1880s supported the idea of federal money for southern education while rejecting any suggestion of consequent federal control.[68] Methodist leaders Fitzgerald and Atticus Haygood even signed an 1883 petition (which Fitzgerald reprinted in the *Nashville Christian Advocate*) memorializing Congress to apportion aid to the states on a basis of their illiteracy rates but with the condition that the money was to be distributed through existing systems of education.[69] Race explains much of the opposition to federal control of education, but there was also a further fear that an educational system controlled from faraway Washington or even from Nashville could threaten the ability of families and churches to direct the education of children as parents saw most appropriate.

Antebellum Tennessee's lack of public schools left the education of children primarily in the hands of individual families. Though the new public schools promised to provide opportunities for increased numbers of children, some parents and religious leaders feared that the new state systems would supplant family authority over children. The advantage of the antebellum Tennessee system of education, argued Collins Elliott, was that it recognized that "the family is the chief power, and thus the family educates." According to the 1834 Constitution, Elliott explained, the role of the state in education was to "promote," "encourage," and "foster" and "thus to help the 'Family.' " Even as the *Nashville Christian Advocate* moved to support an expansion of public education in the 1880s, the newspaper warned school officials not to push aside the "divine institution" of the family, which constituted "the basis of all social, civil, moral, and religious institutions. Destroy the integrity and purity of the family, and social order, civil government, public morality, civilization, and Christianity will be alike impossible."[70] Despite their original reaction to state-provided education as necessarily secular and therefore harmful, Tennessee religious leaders gradually moved toward an acceptance of public elementary schools in the late

1870s and 1880s, arguing that such schools would not have to be irreligious, only nonsectarian, and further that students would still receive moral and religious training contemporaneously at home, in Sunday school, and in church.

"The Principle of Home Rule": Evangelical Accommodation of Public Education

Soon after the General Assembly passed the sweeping 1873 education bill that laid the legal groundwork for a state-funded system of common schools, the bishops of the Methodist Episcopal Church, South, declared that they regarded "the education of the young as one of the leading functions of the Church" and warned "that she cannot abdicate in favor of the State without infidelity to her trust and irreparable damage to society."[71] The southern Methodist leaders, though more outspoken than many common citizens who protested by simply not sending their children to the schools, were not alone in their opposition to the new state role in education. Dr. Barnas Sears, the former president of Brown University and since 1867 director of the Peabody Education Fund, noted in an 1874 report on the state of education in Tennessee that at best "only about one-third of the population are decidedly friendly to free schools."[72]

However, the traditional Protestant emphasis on the importance of the individual believer being able to read, interpret, and accept the Scriptures gave Tennessee evangelical leaders little standing from which to criticize efforts to provide education and promote literacy. Baptist and Methodist newspapers routinely criticized Catholic objections to the Bible in the public schools as proof of a papist and clerical tyranny over individual believers.[73] How, then, could Protestants oppose state efforts to increase literacy? J. C. Brooks, the Jackson city school superintendent, criticized opponents of public education, asking "how any person claiming to be a christian can in any way oppose the great humanitarian and elevating principle of public education. It must go hand in hand with christianity, and second to it, only, in the elevation of mankind."[74]

Even as Tennessee Evangelicals continued to maintain that they were "fully persuaded that the salt of religious truth alone can preserve education from abuse and mischievous results," they quickly began to realize that, unaided, churches and families would be unable to educate the great numbers of children—white and black—coming of age.[75] "It is absolutely hopeless," concluded Haygood; "the Church cannot run the common schools" because it "has not the money." Realistic assessments such as Haygood's forced other Evangelicals to abandon their opposition to public education and search for a way to work with and through the state's growing educational system. East Tennessee Baptist minister

G. P. Faw urged his fellow Evangelicals to recognize the enormity of the task ahead of them: "I am a friend of our denominational institutions of learning, but when it is remembered that there are not enough Schools under Baptist control in the United States to accommodate the children of East Tennessee, nor enough such schools in the whole South to accommodate the scholastic population of Washington County, Tennessee, the question arises, what shall Baptists do to supply the pressing demands of the rising generation for an education[?] To my mind the only solution is, for us to foster the public schools of the country."[76] From the mid-1870s onward, Tennessee Baptists and Methodists began a process of a religious accommodation with state-supported education, and by the late 1880s, Wilbur F. Tillett, a leading Methodist educator, conceded that "the public schools system furnishes the amplest opportunities for primary education, so that it is needless for the Church to attempt" to duplicate its efforts.[77]

Thomas O. Summers Sr., an aging English-born Methodist and editor of the denomination's influential *Nashville Christian Advocate* since the Civil War, had been one of the chief religious critics of the new public schools in Tennessee during the 1860s, arguing that "the State has no business with education."[78] Summers, like many of his ministerial contemporaries, gradually recognized the impossibility of individual churches or denominations providing sufficient educational opportunities and grudgingly promoted limited public education.[79] Even more telling, however, is the Methodist General Conference's choice of his editorial successor. In 1878, when Summers joined the faculty of Vanderbilt University full time as a professor of systematic theology (he had been acting as both editor and professor since 1875), the southern Methodists replaced him with Oscar Penn Fitzgerald. A native of Virginia, Fitzgerald was a well-traveled minister and educator, working in North Carolina, Georgia, and Virginia before going to California as a missionary in 1855. There, Fitzgerald became the state superintendent of public instruction, edited a teachers' journal in San Francisco, and then assumed the presidency of Pacific Methodist College in 1875.[80]

From the start of his tenure at the *Nashville Christian Advocate,* Fitzgerald utilized the paper as a bully pulpit to promote education by both the church and the state. Fitzgerald quickly became an ardent supporter of the nascent Vanderbilt University and all other educational endeavors of the southern Methodist church. During his first week as editor, Fitzgerald added a regular column on education and even recruited Trousdale as a contributing editor to the column.

In the winter of 1882, Fitzgerald printed a pointed front-page editorial in which he sought to clarify the relationship between the church and the state's growing public school system. Fitzgerald delineated the roles of parents, churches, and school directors in education to benefit both church and society, endorsing both a system of public schools funded by taxation and subject to the control of local communities and church schools under denominational supervision and support. Titled simply "Education," the editorial began with the argument that popular democracy, especially in light of the recent "sudden and enormous extension of the suffrage," required "popular education." Fitzgerald then called for a truce between "those who deny altogether that education is a function of the State" and "those who would turn over its whole management to state authority." Arguing that proponents of both opinions would "have to make concessions or quarrel indefinitely," Fitzgerald proposed a compromise. The state could provide elementary education for all citizens but should leave any further schooling to parents and the churches. Fitzgerald's plan not only answered the question of who was in charge of children's education but also provided a blueprint for church, state, and family responsibilities for the proper training of the next generation. Churches should, therefore, concentrate on building up their secondary schools and colleges and otherwise assist parents in the religious education of children in the home and Sunday school. [81]

Fitzgerald's compromise plan described an educational division of labor that provided an avenue out of the constant bickering between partisans of education under exclusive church or state control. He wrote, "Let the State provide for the elements of an English education, and leave the rest to individual enterprise and to the Church. When a boy can 'read, write, and cipher' he has the tools with which to work his way onward, and is equipped for the ordinary duties of citizenship. State control of education will, we think, be confined within this limit." [82] Most Tennessee evangelical leaders seemed to approve Fitzgerald's compromise and agreed, as Bishop McTyeire wrote, that "States and municipal corporations should confine their work to common-school education, and that with colleges and universities they properly have nothing to do." [83]

Religious leaders' arguments that the state should stay out of higher education were in part motivated by the desires to protect denominational colleges from competition with tax-funded institutions. Taking notice of controversies in North and South Carolina during the 1880s regarding state plans to offer free tuition to public universities, Fitzgerald and others warned against similar state encroachment in Tennessee. [84] Tennessee's denominational schools of the time had only a precarious existence, surviving off of small endowments and low tuition payments and seemingly unlikely to withstand stiff competition from the state.

To stem the growth of state-supported higher education, several Tennessee evangelical leaders tapped into the state's growing populist antielitism. Support

for the public schools fit the democratic tendencies of the evangelical denominations' emphasis on the religion of the common person. In these leaders' minds,
"what is necessary for all should be free for all"; therefore, Tennessee evangelical
leaders could support popular elementary education funded by the state because
it gave everyone "the keys to get to the starting line on equal footing." McTyeire
painted state universities as elitist institutions and the practice of granting free
tuition as a "perversion of the public funds." Furthering his charges with an apt
gastronomical metaphor, McTyeire argued that although the "people must not
starve, . . . the public purse may not be drawn upon to feed them on turtle-soup
and plum-pudding."[85]

As their most powerful argument for why the state should stay out of the
business of higher education, Tennessee Evangelicals contended that church
academies and colleges were the only hope for the future morality of individual
students and were necessary for the future prosperity of the church, the state,
and the South. Calling readers' attention to advertisements in the *Christian
Advocate* for denominational schools in the fall of 1880, Fitzgerald instructed
parents to ask themselves, "Who shall educate my children?" As he explained,
"it is a question that involves their interest for both worlds, and ought to be
decided with reference to both."[86] Church schools, Tennessee Evangelicals
argued, would not just educate the intellect but would work actively to educate
the character and lead students toward conversion. Denominational leaders
continued to distinguish between state elementary and higher education—that
is, between acceptable and unacceptable public education. These religious officials recognized that the growth of public elementary schools would help the
denominational colleges, providing a larger pool of students qualified for and
eager to continue their education.[87] Faw did not want to leave anything to chance
and urged Baptists "to qualify themselves for Teachers, and then go out into
the country and seek positions in the public schools." The influence of Baptist
teachers would help the public schools while making those schools "feeders of
[Baptist] Colleges and High Schools under denominational control."[88] Though
willing to accommodate public elementary schools, most Tennessee Evangelicals remained adamant in their contentions that higher education should remain
the exclusive province of the churches.

Church leaders urged laymen and ministers to establish and strengthen denominational schools to pick up where the state elementary schools left off.
Noting that state "schools do not and cannot meet all the needs of education in
our country," Baptists and Methodists called for church members to support
denominational education.[89] Fitzgerald encouraged "Southern Methodists [to]
put more thought, labor, money, and prayer into denominational education"

because, he warned, "the Church that turns over its children to be educated by others gives a mortgage upon them with a strong probability of foreclosure."[90] But the church would also benefit from the education of children in denominational schools. Not only were children educated in denominational schools far more likely to stay in the religion of their parents, but the church also needed trained and intelligent leaders in both the pulpit and the pew. As Haygood asserted, "the Church cannot get on and do her work without educated men and women."[91]

In the absence of explicit religious control of elementary education, church leaders argued that the only security for the state was a strong system of denominational colleges that could educate heart and head together. Only with the moral leaven of Christian higher education, denominational leaders argued, could more widespread popular education be turned for the good of society. Christian institutions of higher education would allow students safely to explore the relationship between true science and true religion, proving the unity of one divine truth. As Cunnyngham warned, "If such men as [Charles] Darwin, [T. H.] Huxley, [John] Tyndal[l] & Co., have the training of our young men, it requires no prophetic ken to forsee what will be the moral and religious character of our educated men in the next generation."[92] Finally, religious higher education had the utmost importance for the future of Tennessee and southern society in general. Tennessee Evangelicals celebrated the fact that they had maintained a society free from the materialism and infidelity of the North.[93] Christian control of education was important because the South would "belong to those who educate its children. A godless education will turn it over to Satan as surely as effect follows cause. A Christian education is necessary to secure and perpetuate the blessings of a Christian civilization."[94]

Evangelical leaders, while arguing for the necessity of religious higher education, did not turn their backs on the public elementary schools. Like Fitzgerald in California, many Tennessee evangelical laymen and ministers became local, county, and state school officials. When the Jackson city schools needed a building and instructors for its male students in 1875 and 1876, it turned to the teachers and facilities of Southwestern Baptist University.[95]

Few Baptist or Methodist state leaders desired legal requirements for religious teaching in public schools, but both groups anticipated that individual schools would reflect the moral and religious background of their surrounding, predominantly Protestant, communities. But Tennessee's religious and educational leaders debated the propriety of using the Scriptures in the public classrooms, tackling the issue that had convulsed the nation for the past decade. Some religious leaders and educators argued that the use of the Bible in the classroom would constitute an unconstitutional state endorsement of religion, while others, including Fitzgerald, worried that the practice of non-Christian or immoral teachers reading from the Bible would be more harmful than excluding it altogether. Said Fitzgerald's *Nashville Christian Advocate,* "to force the Bible into all the public schools would be folly" because "no Christian parent would want any Bible-teaching of his child" by "infidel" teachers: "such a use as they would make of the Bible would in most cases be sacrilegious rather than religious."[96] Still others worried, however, that banning the Bible from the school would suggest to impressionable children that the book was somehow dangerous and should be avoided.

Fitzgerald again stepped into the fray, offering a compromise to supporters and opponents of the Bible in the public school and in the process further accommodating Tennessee Evangelicals to the existence of public elementary schools in general. "The solution" to the question of the Bible in public schools, Fitzgerald argued, "seems to be plain enough on the principle of home rule. Let the State keep hands off. No legislation is called for one way or the other." Fitzgerald, like most Tennessee Evangelicals, clearly favored some level of religious content in the public schools. But he also recognized that a diversity of opinion existed within Tennessee's various religious communities on the use of the Bible in the schools, and he could foresee that great "discord . . . would result from the compulsory use of the Bible in the public schools" in some communities. Though he did not state it explicitly, Fitzgerald seemed to recognize that passing a state law requiring Bible reading in the schools would not only cause some controversy among Protestants but might also be unconstitutional and would certainly draw protests from the state's non-Protestant minority. Believing as he did that the Bible was already widely used in most public schools, Fitzgerald feared that overt legislation could lead to an adverse legal ruling that would end the practice. But he called on local communities, which he assumed would be almost universally sympathetic to Protestant aims, to take an active part in the public schools and thereby ensure a respect for religion and morality in them: "A wrong bias will surely be given to the education of this country unless Christian men and women put their labor, their prayers, and their money into it."[97]

Fitzgerald's argument in favor of home rule relied on Protestant hegemony within state religious circles to guarantee that education in public schools would reflect the religion of the majority of the state's inhabitants. "Surely every community may be left to settle the question itself. Ought it not have the right to do so?" he asked rhetorically. Fitzgerald assumed that most communities in the state, except perhaps for a few pockets in the larger cities, were predominantly Protestant and would desire to continue using the Bible in schools. Tennessee

Evangelicals agreed with another essayist, W. M. Leftwich, who suggested that although the public schools could not teach denominational religion as each church might prefer, there were nonetheless "fundamental principles of morality and fundamental doctrines of Christianity upon which all Protestant Churches agree." Lessons, readings, and even textbooks based on this nonsectarian Protestantism "would be unobjectionable to the Christian people of the State and . . . might be thoroughly taught in our public schools."[98] Such arguments of course either ignored or blatantly dismissed the beliefs of the state's Jews and Catholics.

Although Fitzgerald had written his editorial in response to the specific issue of the use of the Bible in the public schools, his emphasis on the principle of home rule would be critical to Tennessee Protestants' acceptance of a public elementary school system. The state's Evangelicals recognized that children were influenced by many forces—families, churches, and communities as well as public schools—and that the character of a child was "usually the result of mixed forces operating silently, unobserved by the masses, [and] not the work of legislation or convention" or public common-school education alone.[99] Public schools close to every home and under the "special guidance and protection" of parents and local communities would be better for young children, who were easily impressionable and only just beginning to form their characters.[100] Furthermore, a Sunday school operating in every church would guarantee that children's education would be supplemented with denominational religious teaching.[101] Many Methodist and Baptist educators used this emphasis on the important role of parents, especially mothers, in supervising the moral and religious education of children to justify supporting denominational schools and colleges for women.[102]

Tennessee evangelical leaders, many of whom had opposed the expansion of public education in the 1860s and early 1870s as a challenge to religious cultural authority, were some of its strongest advocates by the end of the nineteenth century. Elijah E. Hoss, who took over editing the *Nashville Christian Advocate* in 1890 when Fitzgerald was elected bishop, pointedly defended state common schools in the spring of 1897:

> Once in awhile we hear a belated protest against popular education. It is generally based upon the fact that some boy or girl, after enjoying the advantage of the public schools, has turned out to be worthless. The only reply that needs to be made is that one swallow does not make a summer. Knowledge is better than ignorance. Even a limited and superficial discipline is to be preferred to none at all. The State provides for the instruction of all its citizens in self-defense. Without an open schoolhouse in every community, universal suffrage is a farce. Intelligence

is the basis of free government. The pleas that it is not just to tax one man to educate another man's children may properly be met by the counter statement that there is no other method of guaranteeing the safety of society.[103]

Noticeably absent is any mention of religion or its absence in the public common schools of Tennessee. Hoss would argue elsewhere that the public schools "stand on a good moral basis"; "though not distinctively religious, our public schools are not anti-religious."[104] Operating under Fitzgerald's principle of home rule to allow general religious teaching in most public schools and relying on parents, Sunday schools, and denominational colleges to provide denominationally specific supplemental education, Tennessee Evangelicals at the turn of the century could endorse the public schools wholeheartedly as allies of church efforts to bring up children to honor their parents' religion and region.

"Lay Up Knowledge": Public Education and Social Christianity

In the fall of 1898, inspired by the opening of a new school year, Baptist minister and longtime denominational leader John Boardman Hawthorne preached a sermon aimed at stimulating his congregation at Nashville's First Baptist Church "to a more earnest and practical support of the educational systems of our country." Hawthorne chose a short couplet from Proverbs for his text: "Wise men lay up knowledge, / but the mouth of the foolish is near destruction."[105] His message was a far cry from the earlier opposition of Robert Louis Dabney, Collins D. Elliott, and others religious leaders. All objections had not been completely driven from the field, but Hawthorne, a thirty-year veteran of the Baptist ministry and former president of the Southern Baptist Convention, was preaching from the pulpit of the largest Baptist church in the middle of Nashville, the organizational center of southern Baptism.[106] The sermon was silent on the subject of the state's role in higher education, but Hawthorne offered an unequivocal, ringing endorsement of the growing system of public elementary and secondary schools. Recognizing Baptist roots among the South's common, rural people, Hawthorne pleaded for Tennessee to "put the means of procuring an education within the reach of every family." Hawthorne's suggestions to help the population as a whole were supported by reasons calculated to appeal to his congregation at First Baptist, which included some of Nashville's wealthiest and most influential citizens. Expanded education, he argued, would decrease poverty, improve morality, clean up politics, and generally strengthen the South. Noting that "where education is general, poverty is the exception and not the rule," Hawthorne asked rhetorically, "is it desirable to lift the burden of poverty from a community?" Hawthorne's concern for the poor was by no means a radical departure for the church; charity had long been recognized as a legitimate function of religious organizations. But Hawthorne was speaking of more than simple charity for church members down on their luck or even the more systematic visiting of the city's poor. His endorsement of education as a means "to lift the burden of poverty" sounds more like a plan to teach fishing than to pass out fish to the hungry. With an implicit criticism of class-based opposition to public education, Hawthorne reminded his congregation of the Baptists' historical position as a church of the common people and of the necessity of moving the whole society forward together. "Ignorance," not poverty, he argued, was "the insuperable social barrier" keeping many Baptists from success in this world.

As a further endorsement of education, Hawthorne praised the public school as essential for promoting "morality, law, and order in society." In the post–Civil War era, which combined an expanded electorate with limited educational opportunities, southern politics was ripe with opportunities for manipulation by resourceful politicians capable of mobilizing voters under various banners. Like other southern states, Tennessee had drastically restricted suffrage to disenfranchise blacks and poor whites, but Hawthorne's congregation members no doubt remained chagrined that local ministers and reforming laymen's persistent efforts to banish alcohol from the city had come to naught when faced with the opposition of the local political machines.[107] Hawthorne proclaimed that education was the solution to the city's political problems: "the only way to dethrone the demagogue, either in politics or religion, is to banish ignorance." A morally and religiously sound education spread widely among all citizens, Hawthorne assumed, would elevate the principles of the electorate and sweep new—presumably less objectionable—leaders into public office. Finally, Hawthorne proclaimed that education would strengthen the nation as a whole. Looking back over the world conflicts of the previous half century, he surmised that as a rule, better-educated nations won wars. Eschewing references to the American Civil War (though his congregation may have drawn some implicit connections), Hawthorne credited France's defeat in the Franco-Prussian War to "the superior intellectual culture of Germany."

In addition to offering such material endorsements of expanded education, Hawthorne explained to his congregation that education could lead to great spiritual and religious gains. In response to some naysayers who warned that continued education would eventually lead to a loss of faith, Hawthorne argued the opposite: "every step that a man takes in intellectual progress prepares him for a loftier appreciation of the Christian religion." He was unconcerned that schools would necessarily be "godless," arguing instead that education would aid in the spread of religion, especially if popular education were infused with the religious values of local communities. Indeed, Hawthorne seemed to suggest widespread education as a premillennial requirement, proclaiming his belief "that before that day when 'the kingdoms of this world shall become the kingdoms of our Lord and his Christ,' and when righteousness reigns from shore to shore and from pole to pole, education will be universal." Hawthorne was not departing radically from the earlier views of his fellow Tennessee Baptists, who had resolved in 1883 that "the future prosperity of church and state, as well as the advancement of Christ's Kingdom, is dependent upon the Christian education of the youth of our land."[108]

An experienced orator, Hawthorne sought to answer any potential objections before they were raised. Predicting the usual objection from theological conservatives that anything beyond a goal of individual conversion and salvation fell outside the mission of the church, Hawthorne described education as instrumental to that goal. Interjecting a voice of opposition, Hawthorne asked himself rhetorically, "Do you not teach that Christianity is the great regenerator and elevator of society?" Seeking to reassure his audience, he professed his wholehearted agreement with such a summary of evangelical theology. But he then opened the door a bit wider to recognize a social mission of Christianity, arguing that "in regenerating society, [Christianity] acts in concert with a thousand other helpful agencies and influences." Conspicuous among such agencies, Hawthorne suggested, education was the chief "ally of religion" in its earthly mission.

Hawthorne referred explicitly to "regenerating society," not simply to individuals. He greatly expanded what historian Samuel S. Hill describes as the limitations of southern Protestantism's traditional overriding concern, "the salvation of the individual."[109] Traditional southern Protestantism, Hill explains, concerned itself primarily with the vertical relationship between humans and God, focusing on converting the individual sinner. But Hawthorne's address on the importance of education demonstrates a different focus for at least some southern Evangelicals. Hawthorne began his sermon with the explicit proclamation that "Christianity concerns itself with everything that concerns the welfare of mankind." It was certainly no departure from Hill's "central theme" of southern evangelical individualism for Hawthorne to proclaim Christianity's mission to prepare people "for blessedness and glory in the limitless hereafter." Hawthorne's address is most striking, however, because of his focus on the improvement of individuals and society on earth. The purpose of Christianity,

Hawthorne proclaimed, was "to promote man's development and progress, to prepare him for a career of usefulness, honor and happiness here" in this lifetime, as well as in the next.

Hawthorne specifically cited education as one of the agencies the church should endorse as furthering its earthly and heavenly mission. "Conspicuous among the influences which contribute to the welfare of men and advance the world towards the ideal state revealed in the sacred Scriptures," he proclaimed, "is education." Hawthorne's endorsement of the importance of education was nothing new for Tennessee Evangelicals. Cunnyngham had argued as early as 1873 that "no scheme which proposes permanently to reform the world can succeed unless it is able to control the education of mankind."[110] Popular education was not to be opposed as undermining the church or to be ignored as outside the church's concerns; rather, education was vital to the church's earthly and eternal missions.

Not all Tennessee Evangelicals would necessarily have endorsed Hawthorne's explicit linkage of public education with an expanded mission of social Christianity, but the widespread acceptance and endorsement of state-funded elementary education by the end of the nineteenth century suggests white Evangelicals' growing social concern centered on the public school. Concerns about the religious content of public education suggest an evangelical acknowledgment of the school's role in shaping the future southern society and a desire to influence that society for both temporal and eternal aims. Whether or not they recognized present social—as opposed to individual and spiritual—reformation as a legitimate goal of religion, most of Tennessee's evangelical leaders could agree with Hawthorne's concluding endorsement of education: "I am proud of our public school system. As the years go by and we advance in material wealth, let us enlarge it and improve it, until every American boy and girl can find, at a convenient distance from home, a comfortable school house and a competent school teacher."

At its 1899 annual meeting, the Tennessee Baptist Convention's Committee on Education adopted a resolution expressing, in effect, its general concurrence with the themes and argument of Hawthorne's sermon. Noting first that "the church is not an institution that flourishes in the ignorance and superstition of people" and further observing the biblical admonition for "people to get wisdom, to submit to instruction and gain knowledge," the Baptists declared that education was "a handmaid to Christianity."[111] That education would come in many forms—from parents, from the pulpit, and from professors in denominational colleges. But the most important source of education—and increasingly, the one most accessible to nearly every child—was the state's public school system. Despite their original opposition to the growth of public schools, by 1900 Tennessee Evangelicals could admit that "the common school system has come to stay. It is imbedded in State constitutions and entrenched in the convictions of the people. Nothing is gained by descanting against it." Instead of complaining about the public schools, religious leaders realized that they should embrace, support, and subtly assert some control over public education.[112]

In accommodating themselves to the public common schools, denominational leaders left a heavy burden on parents, teachers, local churches, and denominational colleges. Religious officials accepted the nonsectarian character of public schools but warned that they could not be irreligious. Baptist and Methodist leaders accepted state responsibility for elementary instruction as long as schools were staffed with Christian teachers and as long as parents and churches supplemented public education with moral and Christian teachings in the home. Church officials delegated the ultimate decision on the role of the Bible in the classroom to local communities, believing that most would guarantee an honored place for the Scriptures. Finally, these leaders expected Sunday schools and then church colleges to formally unite the education of heart and head, teach youths particular denominational tenets, and provide a legion of educated and converted ministers and laymen to lead the expansion of the church throughout the state, South, nation, and world. If any of these groups failed to live up to such expectations—if parents did not teach their children to read the Bible and pray, if Sunday school attendance fell, if immoral teachers ran the schools, if local communities lost control of the schools to a rigid state bureaucracy, if church colleges strayed from the denominations that founded them, or if the public schools were to adopt an antireligious posture—how could Tennessee Evangelicals continue to endorse the public schools?

Events in the early twentieth century suggested to many Tennessee Evangelicals that all of these groups were failing in their obligations and that Fitzgerald's home rule compromise would no longer suffice. Increasingly alarmed over what religious officials perceived as the alienation of education from their own moral and cultural standards, evangelical leaders would escalate campaigns to legislate their beliefs into the schools and thus into future generations of Tennesseans. With the eclipse or at least weakening of previous informal means of education, early-twentieth-century Tennesseans would struggle for control of the curriculum and management of formalized education in the public schools.

3. *Educating Ministers and Citizens*

Denominational Colleges and Universities, 1870–1925

Explaining how "the family, the state, and the churches are in a great measure influenced for good or evil by the educational institutions which they maintain and patronize," the Big Hatchie Baptist Association urged West Tennessee Baptists in 1878 to closely consider education in the new era of state-funded common schools. "To mould the character and control the conduct of communities and states," Evangelicals would have to both take an interest in the new public schools and "establish and control" colleges of their own. At the end of the nineteenth century, Tennessee Evangelicals recognized that the growth of public elementary education made denominational colleges more important than ever before. As more of the state's citizens attained a higher "standard of culture" and knowledge, churches would have to produce better-educated ministers to expand membership. As the Big Hatchie Baptists concluded, "General education is being disseminated throughout the land. Important country communities and all towns and cities are rapidly attaining to a standard of culture which renders a considerable fund of general information necessary upon the part of him who would preach to their edification. It is necessary."[1]

Looking through the lens of the history of Vanderbilt University and South-western Baptist University (renamed Union University in 1907), this chapter examines the role of higher education in both denominational self-preservation and efforts to evangelize the surrounding society. The rise of state control of public education in the late nineteenth century threatened the extent to which denominations could directly control the formal education of younger students. But both Methodists and Baptists took refuge in a belief that religious deficiencies in the common schools could be overcome by proper religious training in the home and Sunday school during the elementary years. After that, denominational institutions of higher education would provide safe learning environments for students forced to leave home to secure education. Further, such schools would provide leaders for the denomination and society as well as add a certain moral leaven to the affairs of the state. Institutions of higher education were, as Baptist educator H. E. Watters explained, "The hope of our Zion." But their continued uncertain existence and competition with the state universities by the 1920s only increased many evangelical Tennesseans' concerns about the content and direction of public education as a whole. [2]

Early Denominational Higher Education

Tennessee's Baptists and Methodists emerged from the Civil War with a history of numerous small, local educational institutions roughly connected to the churches but with few financial or intellectual resources. Both denominations possessed evangelical roots, and neither had an institutional tradition stressing higher education to the extent of the Presbyterians or Episcopalians, although the Baptists and Methodists had fostered several academies and so-called colleges during the antebellum period. Most of these schools were barely distinguishable from other subscription schools except perhaps for their explicit endorsement of a particular denomination in the hopes of thereby securing more student patronage. Few were financially well endowed, if they were endowed at all; they depended primarily on tuition to pay salaries and expenses.

The roots of both Vanderbilt and Southwestern Baptist stretch into antebellum Tennessee, but neither existed in its present location or charter until the 1870s. After some discussion in church newspapers and at the quadrennial General Conference held at Nashville in 1858, the southern Methodists secured a charter for the Central University of the General Conference of the Methodist Episcopal Church, South, in January 1859, but this endeavor amounted to little before the Civil War disrupted the church and the South. [3] The 1871 Tennessee Annual Conference adopted a resolution calling for cooperation with several neighboring annual conferences in "the establishment and endowment of a Methodist university of high grade and large endowment." [4] Largely through the efforts of Bishop Holland N. McTyeire, the school received a donation of five hundred thousand dollars from Commodore Cornelius Vanderbilt, a New York shipping and railroad tycoon whose wife was a Methodist and a distant relative of the bishop. The Board of Trust quickly accepted the gift, changed the school's name to Vanderbilt University, and thus secured a great advantage over many other southern denominational schools of the period: a stable and productive endowment. [5] Though many decades would pass before the school embodied the idealistic hopes of some of its earliest proponents, the dividends from the endowment (supplemented by further gifts from the Vanderbilt family) gave the board a steady, if yet limited, income to facilitate growth.

Like their Methodist brethren, antebellum Tennessee Baptists recognized "that it is the duty of the Baptists of Tennessee no longer to remain supine on the subject of general education, but that we owe it to ourselves, to our State and the Cause, to take the place which our numbers and position in society assign us in the education of the rising generation."[6] As a result of such resolutions and the tireless efforts of Rev. Joseph Eaton and others, they established Union University (not much more than an academy, really) at Murfreesboro in 1848.[7] Like many similar institutions, it was nearly devastated by the Civil War; its buildings were occupied by federal troops and its meager endowment was rendered practically worthless by the financial disruptions that followed. It struggled to reopen after the war, only to be forced to close in 1873 as a result of a lack of finances and a crippling regional cholera epidemic.

Plans for a new university grew out of a desire to unite all of Tennessee's Baptists into a single state convention. In 1870, the state's Baptists were still divided by geography into general associations in the eastern, middle, and western portions of the state. In an 1874 conference in Murfreesboro, Baptists from all three sections resolved to combine their efforts because they believed it was "of vital importance to the denominational interests of the Baptists of the State, to establish within or near the borders of Tennessee, a well-endowed thoroughly equipped University, of the highest order."[8] Meeting to discuss denominational unity, the Baptist leaders believed the new university would be a potent symbol of their united purpose and a training ground for their future leaders. Tennessee Baptists elected to locate the new university in Jackson, in the west-central section of the state, accepting the town's offer of the existing buildings and endowment (forty thousand dollars in state bonds) of West Tennessee College provided that the Baptists could raise an additional three hundred thousand dollars in ten years.

Supporters presented several reasons why denominations should help fund church colleges. First, higher education by the church constituted an irreplaceable part of efforts to Christianize society by providing for trained leaders (both lay and ministerial) to spread the word as widely and as well as possible. Further, church colleges were valuable tools in the competition between denominations; the schools would provide for a replication of each denomination's peculiar theological tenets in the next generation as well as prestige that could attract new members. Finally, denominational education was the answer to secularizing trends in modern education, reassuring believers of the truth of divine revelation even in the wake of biblical criticism and scientific naturalism.

Some of the strongest support for both Vanderbilt and Southwestern Baptist came from advocates of ministerial education. Nineteenth-century Tennessee was overwhelmingly Protestant and evangelical but was nonetheless home to many varying groups. In addition to competition among Baptists, Methodists, and other denominations, most faced rivals within their theological traditions. Furthermore, both southern Baptists and Methodists saw theological threats lurking around every corner: from the growth of the Cumberland Presbyterians, from the persistence of Presbyterians and Episcopalians, and from the supposed machinations of Catholics and Mormons. The answer to all of these threats, some believers asserted, was a better-trained ministry, strongly versed in the peculiar tenets of the denomination and armed with sufficiently trained intellect to refute the erroneous claims of other orders. As a committee of East Tennessee Baptists reported to the group's 1873 convention, "Other denominations are educating more thoroughly than heretofore their ministry. . . . Such a course is commendable and worthy of imitation. Romanism in various forms is making inroads upon us, and unless we do more for the education and support of our ministry, the consequences may be disastrous."[9] West Tennessee Baptists answered in like fashion, urging better ministerial education "To *cope with* the champions of *rival denominations*" and "To *repel the attacks* of speculative philosophy and answer the *criticism* of physical science."[10]

Appeals for a better-educated ministry did not always elicit unanimous consent, however. Southern Methodists had a particularly acrimonious debate over establishing a theological school at the church's 1866 and 1870 quadrennial conventions and in the pages of the *Nashville Christian Advocate* and other denominational papers. Beginning in the 1860s, the debate reached a new level when it was joined by two of the bishops of the church, with the elder George F. Pierce publicly confronting McTyeire, an educational advocate and first president of the Vanderbilt Board of Trust, in the spring of 1872. Reasoning that "Gaining knowledge is a good thing—saving souls is better," Bishop Pierce argued that "Our greatest preachers, intellectually considered, are not our most useful men. We are beginning, I fear, to deify talent, and talk too much about the 'age' and 'progress' and the demand of the times, for the simplicity of our faith, or the safety of the Church."[11] McTyeire was quick to point out that he did not believe a theological education could replace a divine call to the ministry, explaining that the goal of ministerial education was "not to make preachers, or to anticipate the Lord in making them, but to 'improve the junior preachers'—not to educate men for the ministry, but in the ministry."[12] But he nonetheless argued for a more up-to-date Methodism that could appeal to both the masses and to the better-educated members of southern society.[13] David Kelley, who in 1867 had warned that requiring theological training would result in a "rigid, fixed, and forbidding formalism" antithetic to the traditionally enthusiastic Methodist style of preaching, nonetheless saw a grand opportunity for the church to shape its native South through university education.[14] Now clearly behind the proposed Central University, he came to McTyeire's aid in the discussion, arguing that "questions are on us now which were unknown to Wesley"; therefore, "to attempt to confine our theological culture to the standards prepared more than a half century ago, is blindness extreme." Kelley realized that southern society was changing. To establish itself in the growing cities and among the region's wealthier citizens, he implied, Methodism would need more educated and cultured ministers for its urban pulpits.[15]

Despite some early opposition, ministerial education would prove to be one of the most cited reasons why Baptists and Methodists should support their respective schools. Both Vanderbilt and Southwestern Baptist offered free tuition to ministerial students, while both denominations attempted to pay future ministers' living expenses. In its reports to the Tennessee Conference Board of Education, Vanderbilt officials usually calculated the amount of aid (in terms of lost tuition fees) given by the school for ministerial education.[16] In later years, both schools would boast of the number of ministers supported.[17] Southwestern Baptist/Union University supporters reported on the ministerial students' activities, even using a full-page advertisement in the *Nashville Baptist and Reflector* to document 1,523 conversions and 1,186 baptisms performed by the school's minister-students during 1917.[18] Financially, ministerial education would prove to be both a benefit and hindrance to the two schools. Efforts to educate young preachers usually elicited the support, however small, of denominational adherents. But in an age when schools depended on tuition fees to meet expenses, tuition-free ministers proved a heavy burden on already strained budgets.

In 1875, its first year of operation, Vanderbilt's Biblical Department offered training in systematic theology, hermeneutics, homiletics, and pastoral theology, but the vast majority of the ministerial students were in such need of a literary education that theological discussions frequently passed well over their heads. As a committee reported to the Vanderbilt Board of Trust in 1885, "a considerable proportion" of the school's ministerial students lacked even the "rudiments of a common English education" and "have been totally unfit for the work assigned them." Many students were forced to withdraw but were nonetheless reported to their annual conferences as former students of Vanderbilt. Such poor advertising caused the board great concern.[19] Resolving that "a literary training without the theological is better than a theological without the literary," the board changed the admission standards for the department, requiring at least the same entrance standards as the university's other departments.[20] Southwestern Baptist University had similar problems. Its executive committee expressed concern in May 1880 about the large number of students claiming free tuition as licentiate ministers in training and displayed even more distress about students who stayed only for a few months or a couple of years yet went "forth as students of the university to the discredit of their teachers and of the institution."[21]

Both Baptists and Methodists had reputations as being churches of the common and rural population, but they also harbored aspirations of ministering to more affluent and worldly urban dwellers.[22] Rising standards of public education threatened the position of the ministry as the most educated class in any community, and both denominations urged improved ministerial education as a means of keeping present members and expanding into other parts of the cities: "An educated membership demands an educated ministry; and it is very doubtful whether an educated laity would long remain in a Church that should be served by an uneducated ministry."[23] Improved opportunities for common-school education would eventually mean that potential ministers would begin with a better educational foundation, but in the short term the expansion of education meant that the old-style frontier exhorters would have increasing difficulty gathering new members to the flock. Methodist editor Elijah E. Hoss warned that "No Church can exist, much less prosper, in this age that is not constantly seeking to improve the intellectual status of its ministry and laity."[24]

Arguments for denominational education extended far beyond the training of ministers, and both Baptists and Methodists urged educating the laity as a means of reproducing the denomination in the rising generation. Baptist editor and steadfast promoter of Southwestern Baptist University James R. Graves echoed these sentiments, noting, "we owe it to our sons" to provide for a school under Baptist control. Rejecting the possibility of "keep[ing] them in ignorance at home, which our duty to them will not allow us to do," Graves presented two options: "We must secure a first-class school for our sons, or send them away from home to be subjected to influences unfriendly to the faith of their fathers."[25] Schooling at home or in the local community could be closely watched, and the religious training of children would remain under the careful supervision of parents and the local church or Sunday school. When children had exhausted the educational opportunities of the local schools, however, evangelical leaders worried that exposure to other faiths could lure children away from their parents' denominations.

In the early years of both Vanderbilt and Southwestern Baptist, most educators and church leaders assumed that "Christian education means denominational education." Although this would later become a more contentious issue, late-nineteenth-century evangelical leaders agreed on the importance of strict denominational control of higher education. Tennessee Baptists believed that theirs was the uniquely correct understanding of Christianity. As the Big Hatchie Association explained, "But the great necessity and importance of education in this respect will appear more strictly perhaps when it is remembered that to us as the church of Christ has been delivered the glorious and blessed truth and gospel of God to be kept in its purity, to be defended against its enemies, and to be given to every creature."[26]

Leaders in both denominations argued that education for the ministry would trickle down through society, suggesting that "the learning of the ministry in a great measure determines for good or evil the character of the whole education, public and private, of a State."[27] Not only did the colleges provide a means for improving the general intellectual and moral tone of southern society, but the new institutions could also be missionary endeavors and great evangelistic tools. As a supporter of Southwestern Baptist put it, "Make the University what it ought to be, and in twenty-five or fifty years, its alumni will be filling the most responsible positions in society. The ministers, the lawyers, the judges, physicians, teachers, presidents of colleges, merchant princes, and successful farmers will prize the University as their alma mater, and will be the friends and supporters of the denomination whose foresight and liberality provided generously for their education and advancement. Baptists should think of these things. Their future is identified with their institutions of learning."[28]

One of the further purposes of establishing denominational schools for higher education, their founders believed, was the need for a Christian answer to the growing skepticism of late-nineteenth-century America. Because many Evangelicals feared that "the State schools both in the United States and in Europe are hotbeds of skepticism and infidelity," the Vanderbilt board promoted the university as "a bulwark for the defense of Truth, in every department of human knowledge. In its maintenance of the truth, they expect it to vindicate the existence of a perfect harmony between a sound philosophy and a true religion." Christian institutions such as Vanderbilt and Southwestern Baptist would provide a safe environment in which to find the harmonious meeting place of science and religion; therefore, the only hope for society was the continuation and improvement of denominational colleges.[29]

Having founded colleges with a goal of replicating the faith of the fathers in the next generation, many Baptists and Methodists objected to competition from a state-funded and -endorsed university. Overcoming their early opposition to public primary education, evangelical religious leaders nevertheless continued to criticize state efforts to provide academy and college education. Admitting that "Primary education is the duty of the State," they reasoned that the state could and should "teach the three R's, 'reading, 'riting, and 'rithmetic,' " because "Every citizen ought to be able to read his ballot and a civil warrant." But the state should not go beyond the basic necessities in education. Fearing that state universities would compete directly with religious institutions, Oscar Fitzgerald asked "what right has the State to tax the poor, and the religious people who prefer religious schools, in order to provide colleges and universities for the children of rich men who are too godless to patronize a religious institution?"[30]

As long as children stayed near home, informal moral and cultural education from the family and church would provide sufficient supplements for the secular education of the public common schools. Hoss explained that "under existing conditions the primary education of our children must be obtained in the public schools, which, though not anti-religious, never give religious instruction. This lack is supplied by Sunday school and home instruction." But sending children away to state colleges—away from the supposed moral safety net of the home and local religious community—could result in moral disaster. Fitzgerald was only one of the many religious educators repeating the charges that state higher education, "however complete, when it shall have reached perfection or its ultimate tendency, will be a godless institution." Thus, religious leaders constantly called for better support of denominational higher education as the only possible answer to the threat of "godless education."[31]

It is noteworthy that at their foundings, denominational schools were not really being crushed by state institutions of higher education but were at least equal competitors in a wide-open field. Only limited state funding for higher education existed in nineteenth-century Tennessee, and East Tennessee University (later the University of Tennessee–Knoxville) existed largely on funds secured under the federal Morill land grant act. State legislators were unconvinced of the state's role in providing more than a common-school education for citizens, especially while Tennessee was burdened by an imposing state debt contracted during the Civil War and Reconstruction.[32] Supporters of denominational education would often criticize state efforts at higher education in an attempt to garner more patronage for church schools, but in the early 1870s at least, church and state schools were engaged in an even fight for visibility, student patronage, and financial support.

Detractors maligned the moral environment of the school in Knoxville, with one even suggesting that "the quickest way to prepare a boy for a 'Devilish life . . . was by [way of] College Hill,' " the site of the early state university.[33] Despite sectarian protests to the contrary, the early state university was not an antireligious institution: the school's minister-presidents required students regularly to attend university chapel. Nevertheless, the state university differed markedly from the church schools in its lack of affiliation with or oversight by any particular denomination. As Hoss explained in 1900, state universities were not "godless in themselves" but were "so circumscribed that, notwithstanding the personal piety of professors and tutors, they cannot in their capacity as teachers take any active part in religious instruction in the school-room."[34] Hoss took a surprisingly moderate tone by not arguing that such schools were antireligious. The problem, he asserted, was that because instruction could not be denominational, state schools could not serve any useful function for Methodists. Graves was likewise concerned about the large percentage of Presbyterians and Episcopalians represented on the faculty of the state university:

> A correspondent informs us of the fact, that although the Baptist have a membership of about 120,000 in the State, and the Episcopalians only about 4000, the State University is completely under the control of the Episcopalians. There is not a Baptist Professor connected with the Faculty. Every important Chair in the University is occupied by an Episcopalian. The President, Professors of Mathematics, Chemistry, Ancient Languages, Belles-lettres, Agriculture, Modern Languages, and English Literature, are all Episcopalians. Now, it does seem to me that Baptists should remonstrate against this monstrous abuse of State patronage by the smallest and most objectionable denomination, except the Roman Catholics, in the State.[35]

Unconcerned with modern conceptions of academic qualifications for the positions, Graves apparently viewed professorships in Knoxville as yet another form of political patronage to be distributed evenly among the state's population groups.

Religious leaders voiced scattered complaints about state higher education, but the opposition in Tennessee in the 1870s and 1880s was not anywhere close to the bitter wrangling in neighboring North Carolina during the period.[36] Only in the twentieth century, as state funding for the University of Tennessee increased and financial resources for denominational colleges became more scarce, did the Knoxville school become the target of religious criticism.

Moral and Religious Standards of the Church College

Though their later history would find Vanderbilt and Southwestern Baptist/ Union universities on vastly different trajectories, both at first aspired to become full-scale universities encompassing undergraduate, professional, and theological education.[37] Vanderbilt began operation with law and medical programs inherited from the University of Nashville, while Southwestern Baptist proposed such departments several times but with little success. The planned opening of Southwestern's medical school in Memphis in 1878 was postponed because of a terrible yellow fever epidemic. The law department was proposed several times and should have succeeded because Jackson's was the location of both state and federal courts, but plans never bore fruit. But both schools began with college and preparatory courses little different from those at most other colleges of the time. With a lack of public high schools outside of the largest cities and only a few high-quality preparatory schools or academies, there was simply a lack of sufficiently trained students to fill the early collegiate classes at either school.[38]

From the beginning, both schools stressed their importance as Christian and denominational institutions—Southwestern Baptist by its name and Vanderbilt by its original moniker, the Central University of the Methodist Episcopal Church, South, although this name was quickly forgotten.[39] Although state higher education as yet remained only a distant threat to the prosperity of these schools, supporters of denominational education tried from the beginning to enunciate what made such institutions different and better. "In the first place," Landon Garland stressed in his inaugural address as Vanderbilt's first chancellor, "this is a Xn.[Christian] Institution."[40] Garland expanded on this explanation fifteen years later, reporting to the Board of Trust, "We never cease to impress upon students the fact that the great object of education is the formation of a high moral character based upon an acceptance of the principles of Christianity—and that without this, mere intellectual culture is as patent for evil as for good."[41]

Proper education, Baptist and Methodist educators agreed, involved the training of both heart and mind, spirit and intellect. In their efforts to persuade parents and denominational leaders to entrust their children to the care of these schools, presidents and boards took great pains in the selection of faculty members and in attempting to guard the institutions' moral, religious, and social atmosphere. The lengthy correspondence between Garland and McTyeire laying the plans for Vanderbilt's campus, faculty, and curriculum reveals the two men's aspirations for academic respectability but also their even greater determination to remain morally and theologically safe. "Above all things," urged Garland in February 1874, "let us secure modest Christian gentlemen of fine capacity, good foundation and laborious habits of business."[42]

The early faculties of both schools were notoriously underpaid and overworked, often teaching far afield of their academic specialties at short notice and holding many responsibilities outside of the lecture rooms. The faculty and, in particular, school presidents were instrumental in presenting the institutions' interests to the denominations in the hope of securing student patronage and financial assistance. "The future life and financial prosperity of the University," recorded the trustees of Southwestern Baptist, "depends upon the election by your Board of an able and competent President whose character and reputation will command the confidence and respect of the whole denomination."[43] Southwestern Baptist had perennial difficulties meeting the promised salaries of officers and instructors, and in 1881 the board finally codified what had been its position from the beginning, clarifying that if the funds from the limited endowment "together with fees of tuition is not sufficient to pay the [promised] amounts, then the amount of money received is to be prorated in proportion to each salary and it is further understood that this is all the money they are to receive and further that this Board of Trustees are not to be held liable for any deficiency whatever."[44]

George W. Griffin, a Baptist minister from West Tennessee, was one of Southwestern Baptist University's early boosters. In the winter of 1877–78, Griffin began traveling the territory of the Big Hatchie Baptist Association in West Tennessee, collecting cash and pledges to endow a chair for the university. After Griffin had worked in this capacity for the better part of a year, traveling constantly and writing several articles for the *Memphis Baptist,* the university trustees elected him to fill that chair as soon as they felt there was money enough to pay his salary.[45] Although the board reasoned that it was "wise economy to use his services in the University at such seasons as are unpropitious for his agency work," Griffin apparently did no teaching during the 1878–79 academic year. The board reported in July 1879 that it did not have the money to pay Griffin and thus had not employed him in the classroom because he could not raise money in the field if he were teaching. The next day, however, the finance committee recommended that Griffin assume the chair of "Logic and Moral Philosophy" and draw the salary of eight hundred dollars for ten months. The catch was that this salary was "to be paid out of the interest accruing on the notes, bonds and subscriptions subscribed for the endowment of the Chair of Philosophy or by donations for his salary and Dr. Griffin is to look to this source alone for his salary."[46] Thus, Griffin was left hoping that the subscriptions he had secured to fund his chair could be collected.

If the account of Griffin's predicament of being forced to take to the field to raise his own salary is somewhat comedic, the situation of Edward Joynes's dismissal from Vanderbilt is considerably more tragic yet nonetheless reveals the professional standards and expectations of the early church universities. Joynes, a graduate of the University of Virginia and the University of Berlin, was elected to the chair of modern languages of the original faculty. Although he "proved the most popular professor at the early Vanderbilt," Joynes ran afoul of the university's strict moral standards, a victim of Vanderbilt officials' concern with securing the confidence of their southern Methodist constituency.[47]

An Episcopalian at a Methodist school, Joynes's troubles began in his first year as rumors surfaced that he was not a total stranger to the bottle. With its general emphasis on personal piety and strong temperance tradition, the southern Methodist church frowned on even occasional or social drinking. As McTyeire later explained, "From Mississippi, Alabama, Georgia, and elsewhere we learned that it was being said—The Vanderbilt University had a drunken professor in one of the principal chairs."[48] After hearing such rumors, the Board of Trust in 1876 exacted a pledge from Joynes to "abstain from such injurious practice and unbecoming and disastrous example."[49] Expressing concern in 1877 that the rumors of Joynes's indiscretion had not subsided, the board considered dismissing Joynes but postponed action with the hope that he would soon resign of his own accord.[50] When he failed to leave at the end of the school year, McTyeire had the board move to vacate Joynes's chair. McTyeire then wrote to Joynes, who refused to go quietly, justifying the professor's termination because "The Church and the public look to us not only for able teachers, in all departments of learning, but we are, if possible, under a still higher pledge— that no immoral influence shall be installed or sanctioned here." Furthermore, McTyeire explained, "no brilliancy of talent, no personal popularity of a professor can be allowed to condone for practices or habits or principles that would corrupt or mislead the youth who are entrusted to our care."[51]

By all accounts Joynes was an able professor and would find future academic success at the state university in Knoxville.[52] But his drinking—real or rumored, it did not really matter to McTyeire and the board—harmed the university's aspirations to attract the patronage of southern Methodists. University officials, mindful of the need to clearly distinguish church schools from secular educational institutions, emphasized the moral soundness of their campus and governance.

The Church College in a Changing World

Having laid foundations in the 1870s for educational institutions to serve both their respective denominations and the South, Tennessee Baptists and Methodists anticipated increasing influence and respectability. Despite confident predictions, the faith of denominational and university leaders was tested constantly throughout the ensuing quarter century as both schools struggled to live up to their founders' grand expectations.[53] In the process of creating great universities, educational leaders stretched the old conceptions of the denominational college and precipitated intrachurch debates about the role of religion in higher education. It was "the age of the university": what then was the fate of the denominational college?

The late nineteenth and early twentieth centuries witnessed sweeping changes nationally in academic standards for colleges and universities; these changes were slowly but nonetheless surely infiltrating the South, including its church colleges. Although both Vanderbilt and Southwestern Baptist refused to bend on moral standards for faculty, the schools found from the beginning a shortage within their denominations of officers who were fully qualified academically. As Vanderbilt's Chancellor Garland lamented even before the school opened, "It will not be possible to bring large experience and wide reputation into all our chairs. The Ch[urch] has not the men."[54] From its opening Vanderbilt had non-Methodists on the faculty, and Garland hoped to strike a delicate balance between avoiding charges of narrow sectarianism and avoiding alienating southern Methodists.[55] Southwestern Baptist adhered more closely than Vanderbilt to a strict denominational test for officers, but both schools increasingly recognized the need to elevate academic standards to compete with other schools in attracting students. In making his annual recommendations to the board to fill faculty vacancies, Southwestern Baptist's chairman of the faculty (president in all but title), George Jarman, strongly urged the candidacy of J. W. Gore for the chair of natural science. Jarman gave both academic and character references for Gore, citing his education at Richmond College (a Baptist school) and the University of Virginia and further noting that he was "a Fellow of two years standing in the John Hopkins University" and "has the endorsement of some of the most distinguished educators of the land." But such academic qualifications would not be enough, so Jarman concluded in Gore's favor that "besides his very superior educational advantages, he is roundly commended for exalted moral and Christian worth."[56]

Both Vanderbilt and Southwestern Baptist worked to elevate the region's late-nineteenth-century educational standards. Vanderbilt has often been credited with raising the standards for college admission, and several early officers of the school were instrumental in the organization of the Association of Colleges and Preparatory Schools of the South (later the Southern Association of Colleges and Schools).[57] Within the first decade of Vanderbilt's existence, Garland warily observed the growing number of preparatory students at the university and suggested that the problem could be fixed by enacting higher standards of admission, which would, in turn, raise the standards of the preparatory schools.[58] James Hampton Kirkland, a German-trained Ph.D. who succeeded Garland as

Vanderbilt's chancellor in 1893, spoke out often in favor of setting rigid standards for degree-granting institutions. In his inaugural address, Kirkland argued that "In educational institutions what we need now above all things is not quantity, but quality."[59]

While good for the region in the end, elevated standards for both public education and college admission would cut into Vanderbilt and Southwestern Baptist's preparatory departments, which had, especially during the early years, served a large percentage of the student populations. As the Jackson city schools improved, the Southwestern Baptist trustees noted the declining number of preparatory students. Although the trustees suggested that this change represented only "a temporary inconvenience, and that in the years to come the public school will be a constant feeder to the University," they were still concerned by the loss of revenue and the possible misperception that declining enrollment figures signaled a dying university.[60]

Modern college and university instruction required not only instructors and students but increasingly scientific apparatus, books and journals, and dedicated laboratory rooms and buildings. The commodore's generous gift enabled the Vanderbilt trustees to send an instructor to Europe to purchase seven thousand dollars worth of scientific equipment (which Bishop McTyeire estimated would have cost between ten and twelve thousand dollars in the United States) and commissioned an English bibliophile to acquire a library of "about 5000 volumes, at a cost of nearly $3500."[61] Southwestern Baptist was not nearly as fortunate, having inherited the deteriorating buildings of the old West Tennessee College. An 1878 memorial from the faculty cited "the poorly furnished condition of our chemical and philosophical laboratory" and asked the board to build a new science building. The petition continued, "Our entire outfit in this department is not worth one hundred and fifty dollars. . . . [W]e are not furnished with apparatus necessary for preparing the most trifling experiments."[62] Apparently these conditions did not soon improve, for as a student from the early 1880s later recalled, "The equipment was practically nil."[63]

All of these conditions—the elevation of academic standards for faculty and students, the growth of public education, the increased expectation of scientific apparatus and library holdings—kept coming back to the same basic need of colleges and aspiring universities: money. Vanderbilt certainly had an edge over Southwestern Baptist because of the continued patronage of the Vanderbilt family, but both schools looked to their denominations for financial assistance and students. Despite the Vanderbilts' gifts of more than one million dollars, the Methodist school remained concerned about finances. The early history of Southwestern Baptist reveals honest efforts by dedicated officers and agents but nonetheless a long series of financial blunders and embarrassments. First, deteriorating West Tennessee agricultural conditions in the late nineteenth century made it hard for Southwestern's agents to secure financial pledges and even harder to collect on them. The executive committee reported in 1879 that "Our experience in agency work is not encouraging. . . . To employ an agent to obtain subscriptions and another to collect them, consumes the whole and leaves nothing for the treasury."[64] The school was unfortunate in that it had to compete with other Baptist schools throughout the state—Carson-Newman remained the favorite of East Tennessee Baptists, while Hall-Moody Institute in nearby Martin competed for students and financial assistance—and with the Memphis Conference Female Institute, a Methodist women's school in Jackson that later became Lambuth University.[65] These church schools also had to compete with the numerous local academies that claimed to be colleges. The problem with such "shams and frauds," explained E. E. Hoss, was that when the presidents of real colleges appealed to the state conventions for money to increase the endowments, "the delegates would often only give small sums, having been convinced that the glorified high-schools in their districts really [were] colleges, and thus there [was] no need to support the far-off institution."[66] Contributions of cash and children overwhelmingly favored local schools, which parents and churches could more easily monitor.

Both Vanderbilt and Southwestern Baptist constantly appealed to their denominations for money and made special efforts to solicit contributions to correspond with the opening of the twentieth century. These efforts to secure denominational aid instigated renewed efforts to justify church maintenance of schools. When denominational sources seemed unwilling or unable to support the schools, college officials began to look elsewhere for funding. But outside money, some denominational leaders worried, threatened to alienate school from church. This search for funds ultimately led Vanderbilt and Southwestern Baptist/Union in very different directions, eventually including Vanderbilt's acrimonious divorce from the southern Methodist church in 1914.

Church college leaders' appeals for support came at the same time that church editors and opinion shapers were muting their attacks on the state universities. Mostly picking up on accounts from other states, Methodist and Baptist editors had previously criticized state institutions as necessarily godless places so dangerous to morality and faith that Christian parents could not afford to send their children there.[67] But Tennessee Evangelicals gradually softened their criticisms of the state university; YMCA secretary John P. Mott offered a backhanded endorsement in 1892, noting that "the condition of the religious life in the University of Tennessee is unquestionably far better than it was three years ago." Tennessee religious commentators distinguished between southern state universities and those in other parts of the country, suggesting that the Knoxville school was "better than . . . a majority of the State institutions of the country. . . . Its religious life will compare very favorably with that of the denominational colleges—in fact, with that of a majority of them."[68] But many denominational leaders found unsettling this apparent approval of state higher education, which raised a critical question: if state higher education in Tennessee was not morally and religiously threatening, why should the churches continue to support denominational institutions?

Tennessee Evangelicals answered this question by eschewing criticisms of the state university but appealing anew for the denominational colleges as superior to the state institution. Methodist Bishop W. B. Murrah conceded that "the State School is here, and it is here to stay," but he reminded readers that such an education was only part of what was needed: only church schools could provide the necessary education for both heart and head. "Abandon denominational colleges," Murrah warned, "and you do away with education in its true and highest sense."[69] J. W. Conger, the president of Union University between 1907 and 1909, tried to convince Tennessee Baptists of the "fundamental" difference between schools run by the state and the church. "The *secular* school cannot have in its curriculum any courses that deal with religion as a primary object; the religious school must have such courses if it subserves the purpose of its creation." Conger argued that denominational schools could continue only if they offered every bit as good an education intellectually as other schools and then went the extra but necessary mile to provide real religious education. As he explained, "No amount of religious zeal can alone [compensate] for low standards of admission and graduation. There must be no substitute in the way of piety or religious conformity for low ideals of scholarship and broad culture."[70] At the same time, religious schools had to be decidedly religious, as S. E. Jones, president of Carson-Newman College, explained: "A Baptist institution of learning ought to mean more than literary and arts courses under teachers who are Baptists." Jones advocated denominationally specific courses of Bible study in all Baptist schools because "We want our people educated, it is true, in Latin and Greek and English and mathematics and so on, but it is vastly more important that they go out from our colleges well versed in the Holy Scriptures. Any thing short of that is hardly denominational education."[71]

Despite the increasing efforts to better distinguish between state and church colleges, disagreement grew over the standards and criteria used in judging schools. As Tennessee Evangelicals began to admit that education in the state university was broadly Christian or at the very least not unfriendly to Christianity, many of them renewed efforts to ensure that church colleges were not just Christian but, more importantly, denominational. Hoss argued, "It is not possible to defend the planting, endowing, and maintaining of Church schools upon any ground except this, that they are specially designed to foster the spirit of religion" and further the interests of their founding churches.[72] He urged Methodists to contribute money and students to church schools but warned college officials that the only way to deserve those gifts was to "frankly keep themselves in perfect harmony with the Church."[73]

This question of denominational loyalty of schools became an increasingly divisive issue in the southern Methodist church at the beginning of the twentieth century. As editor of the *Nashville Christian Advocate,* Hoss had substantial influence on the flow of information to and the thinking of southern Methodists. From his editor's desk just down the street from the Vanderbilt campus, Hoss waged a lengthy battle with Chancellor Kirkland and the majority of the Board of Trust, criticizing them for a lack of denominational loyalty and for the public misbehavior of students.[74] Chancellor Kirkland, though a Methodist layman, envisioned religious education as a broadly Christian endeavor. As he explained in his 1900 address commemorating the twenty-fifth anniversary of Vanderbilt's opening, he proposed "to be forever true to our position as a Christian institution. We shall follow this high ideal in the same spirit that has controlled us in the past—a spirit of enlightened patriotism and broad Christianity."[75] While Kirkland called for broad Christianity, Methodist bishop and Vanderbilt board member Warren A. Candler introduced a resolution to the board's 1901 annual meeting "that in filling the vacancies in the board of instruction . . . preference be given to Methodists, other things being equal."[76] Candler remained a thorn in Kirkland's side, opposing a 1904 effort to promote two non-Methodists within the faculty. Angered especially by the appointment of Dr. Frederick W. Moore, a devout Baptist, as academic dean, Candler presented a lengthy protest to the board. After counting up the number of non-Methodists in the faculty, Candler warned that "this is out of all proportion, and must necessarily tend to estrange the University from the Church and the Church from the University."[77] Candler, Hoss, and a large number of the Methodist rank and file who followed the two men's lead feared that nondenominational "broad Christianity" was only a very short step away from completely secular education.

Thus, by the first years of the twentieth century, some Methodist leaders argued that the only justification for church support of higher education was to further denominational goals. This did not represent a departure from the ideas of many of the founders of the church colleges. But part of the problem, particularly in the case of Vanderbilt, was, as Bishop Eugene R. Hendrix, a trustee and avid supporter of the school and its policies, pointed out, that rigid theological tests might be appropriate for a denominational college, but Vanderbilt was meant to be a university.[78] The other problem was that the exact relationship between the southern Methodist church and the school had never really been legally clear. One northern millionaire had been required to found the school, and another would be needed to bring the lingering uncertainties to a head.

When Andrew Carnegie announced in 1905 the creation of a foundation to provide pensions to college teachers, he raised many southern schools' hopes for firm financial footing. They could attract better faculty through a promise of more comfortable compensation, even in retirement. But those hopes were soon dashed as Dr. Henry Pritchett, the director of the fund, explained that Carnegie's policy was not to aid any "sectarian" institutions. Pritchett and the foundation made a close inspection of the manner of control of schools applying for aid; in response, the churches soon engaged in the same task. The Methodists in particular sought "to define closely and carefully [their] attitude toward educational institutions and determine definite tests by which an institution should be recognized as under the control of the church."[79] Methodists in Virginia and Maryland became especially agitated in 1908 about the Carnegie Foundation's acceptance of Randolph-Macon Woman's College into the pension program. Debates regarding the school's relationship to the church and to the foundation filled denominational papers for nearly five years (1906–11).[80] The repercussions of the controversy over church control of Randolph-Macon served as a catalyst for the questions that had been swirling around Vanderbilt since the 1890s. Certain denominational leaders—Hoss and Candler chief among them—were determined to clarify the church's legal relationship to the Nashville university.

Chancellor Kirkland was likewise interested in clearly defining Vanderbilt's relationship to the Methodist Episcopal Church, South. From the beginning of his tenure at Vanderbilt, he had ambitious plans for expansion, plans that would require a great increase in buildings, equipment, faculty, and, most important, funding. In his 1899 report to the board he urged greater contributions from "our own people and by our own church."[81] He was encouraged when the Southern Methodist General Conference promised to raise three hundred thousand dollars for religious education at Vanderbilt through its Twentieth Century Education Fund. Dean Wilbur F. Tillett of the Vanderbilt Biblical Department was head of the fund-raising effort in the Tennessee Conference, but even with his tireless campaigning, most contributions went to smaller, local aims, and Vanderbilt received only a small percentage of the projected funds.[82] Early in the twentieth century, Kirkland reported to the board the "meagre results" from the church's plan "to increase the endowment of the University."[83] This failure clarified any doubts in Kirkland's mind about the potential financial support from within the church and led him to cast a widening net in his search for funding.

Kirkland's efforts led him to downplay the school's relationship to the Methodist Episcopal Church, South, except when speaking about the Biblical Department. His interest in making Vanderbilt a "genuine university, broad & liberal & free," attracted the interest of northern donors, including officials of the Carnegie Foundation, the Rockefellers' General Education Board, and the Peabody Fund. In a private 1904 letter to a potential benefactor, Kirkland avowed that "outside its Theological Department we do not wish it to be the exponent of any sect or any creed, save such as belongs to our common Christianity."[84] Kirkland's efforts to promote a "broad & liberal" Vanderbilt that emphasized "common Christianity" ran directly counter to the thoughts of other Methodist factions that could justify church colleges only as active promoters of specific denominational interests. Although Hoss had softened his criticisms of the state university after realizing that it was at least broadly Christian, he was left to wonder how Kirkland's plans for Vanderbilt were any different.

Questions about Vanderbilt's relationship to the Methodist Episcopal Church, South, moved from a discussion of broad themes related to the purposes of higher education by the church to tightly contested legal battles over the specific powers of the church's governing General Conference, the bishops, and the Vanderbilt University Board of Trust.[85] As Kirkland sought to emphasize Vanderbilt University's espousal of a nonsectarian approach, he worried about the large and ever-growing number of Methodist bishops on the Board of Trust. Through an 1895 bylaw, the Vanderbilt Board of Trust made church bishops ex officio board members. The original measure had been calculated to increase Methodist interest in the school. But when the 1902 General Conference increased the number of bishops to thirteen and the 1906 General Conference seemed poised to vote for even more additions, Kirkland feared that the bishops would soon have a commanding majority of the thirty-three-member board. Wanting to remain connected to the church but not under the thumb of the Methodist episcopacy, Kirkland proposed and the Board of Trust revoked the 1895 bylaw at the 1905 annual meeting. In place of a blanket membership for all bishops, the board elected the five senior active bishops as full members. Also at Kirkland's urging, the board voted to secure a new, standard charter from the state of Tennessee to replace the original charter from the 1870s. The original charter was somewhat irregular, but most alarming to Kirkland's plans was its provision that the bishops could act as a board of supervisors, overseeing the business of the Board of Trust. Kirkland did not want to disavow all connection with the church, but he did want to assure himself—and potential donors—of the Board of Trust's absolute autonomy.[86]

Hoss, by 1905 a bishop of the church and therefore an ex officio member of the Vanderbilt board, missed the June meetings because he was overseeing church affairs in Brazil. When he returned, he learned that he was no longer considered a board member. As one of Kirkland's longest-standing critics, he could see the bylaw changes only as a subtle and underhanded scheme to remove him from the board. Hoss's reaction was anything but subtle, and he immediately protested to Kirkland, the other bishops, and the southern Methodist church at large. Hoss reacted, in Paul Conkin's words, "like a bull in a china shop" and remained on the offensive against Kirkland's supposed machinations and usurpation for at least a decade.[87]

Bishop Hoss asked how effectively the southern Methodist church could control the school by nominating or confirming trustees and exercising the bishops' supposed visitorial rights under the original charter. He put his editorial talents to work, stirring up opposition to Kirkland and the board majority and forcing the issue at the quadrennial General Conferences of 1906 and 1910. The 1906 conference appointed a committee of lawyers to examine the charter and report on the exact relations between the church and the university. The Vanderbilt Commission's report, issued in 1907, assigned extensive powers to the church. Arguing that an 1895 Tennessee statute provided religious bodies that established and were "maintaining and patronizing" educational institutions the right to appoint trustees and otherwise supervise those schools, the report became a strong weapon in Hoss's arsenal as he continued his campaign for strict denominational control of Vanderbilt.[88]

The 1910 General Conference acted on its newly discovered rights and, at the urging of Hoss and his partisans, elected three trustees to the Vanderbilt board. Depicting the church's actions as an attempt to revert "his" Vanderbilt to a narrowly sectarian institution, Chancellor Kirkland convinced a majority of the board to refuse to seat the "gentlemen" selected by the General Conference and "claiming membership in this board." In response, Hoss and his faction of the bishops sued to stop the Board of Trust from seating three trustees of its own choosing and to force compliance with the findings of the Vanderbilt Commission. After a 1913 ruling favorable to the advocates of strict church control, the majority members of the Board of Trust appealed the case to the Tennessee Supreme Court.[89]

The court decided in March 1914 that the members of the Vanderbilt University Board of Trust could elect their successors, but any elections would be subject to confirmation by the church. It was, more or less, the relationship that had been followed since the university's founding, but Hoss and other opinion makers decried the decision, claiming that it left them with no real control over Vanderbilt; therefore, they argued, they would be better off severing all connections and turning their attention to establishing schools under clear Methodist control. Thomas N. Ivey, who had become editor of the *Nashville Christian Advocate* in 1910 and who had consistently worked to marshal public opinion against the university, declared the amount of control left to the church practically meaningless and urged a total separation.[90]

Some scattered voices within the church and especially in Tennessee favored a continued relationship with the school, but denominational leaders quickly turned their attention to new universities—Southern Methodist University in Dallas and Emory University in Atlanta. Supporters of continuing the connection praised Vanderbilt's broadly Christian loyalty and the fact that it offered Methodists the "opportunity to touch the intellectual development of the South with the religious spirit which no other church has." Continued affiliation with the school, these advocates argued, was "a matter of vital concern for the entire religious life of the South."[91] Tillett expressed his fears that he could not "conceive of a more unwise act" than for the church to wholly abandon Vanderbilt, noting that the "itinerant ranks of the Southern Methodist Church to-day" are filled with "eight hundred and twenty-five former Vanderbilt students, more than one in every nine" of the ministers of the Methodist Episcopal Church, South. Tillett urged the church at least to hold onto the school of theology.[92]

Such voices were not popular among denominational leaders and were only rarely allowed into official church papers. President R. E. Blackwell of Randolph-Macon wrote to Tillett, complimenting him on his article in the *Nashville Advocate* and agreeing with Tillett's call for a continued church-Vanderbilt relationship. Blackwell hoped that the article would elicit support from a hitherto unheard majority within the denomination "who have not bowed their intellects to the Episcopal boards." The problem, he explained, was that Hoss's minions had control of the denominational press; Blackwell wrote that he had received information from a "prominent minister in your part of the world who holds your views, but who writes me that he has made three attempts to get into the Advocate, but in vain."[93]

Tennessee's Baptists did not fail to notice the controversies over the interpretation of the Vanderbilt charter and over the university's specific relationship to the southern Methodist church.[94] In truth, Southwestern Baptist/Union had never drifted far from most of the ideals of its founding denomination. Though blessed with fairly competent leadership, Southwestern had also been firmly under the direction of Baptist ministers and dedicated laymen.[95] Money was also certainly important, and one could argue that Vanderbilt's early wealth raised expectations and created a frequent and seemingly insatiable desire for expansion, growth that after the failure of the Twentieth Century Education Fund drive seemed possible only with contributions garnered from outside the church. Southwestern also had financial needs, running as it did on only a small endowment and a large deficit, but the school operated on a much lower financial scale and became accustomed to program maintenance rather than growth. Also, by the dawn of the new century, Southwestern Baptist trustees and school boosters recognized that their school was not necessarily the great southern university the founders had predicted.[96] It was, however, clearly a church college and an arm of the denomination. When a fire destroyed the main buildings in January 1912, the board addressed appeals to Baptist philanthropist John Rockefeller's General Education Board as well as to Andrew Carnegie, soliciting challenge grants to help in the rebuilding. These actions would have occasioned a firestorm of criticism from the sensitive Methodist press, but the state Baptist papers supported the fund-raising and did not even mention the appeal to Carnegie.[97]

Perhaps the greatest difference between Union and Vanderbilt can be found in a broader comparison of ideologies of the two denominations. Whereas Bishops Robert K. Hargrove, Eugene R. Hendrix, Oscar P. Fitzgerald and many other supporters of Kirkland and the majority of the Vanderbilt board's actions actively engaged in and strongly supported national and worldwide ecumenical movements, Tennessee Baptists still held to many Landmarkist principles that promoted Baptists as the only true inheritors and interpreters of the authentic Gospel message.[98] Reflecting the legacy of James R. Graves, an early and prominent Southwestern Baptist University supporter, most Tennessee Baptists inside and outside of the school could consider it only a denominational agency for training the church's lay and ministerial leaders.[99] While Kirkland advocated a "broad Christianity," Tennessee Baptist educators worried that ecumenically "Christian" education was inseparable from church unionism and the decline of distinctive Baptist beliefs: " 'Christian education' will more and more entangle Baptists in the net of denominational affiliation which, if it means anything, means the side-tracking of some vital doctrinal point or points, or a very unnecessary and unsafe mixing of the Truth with error." [100]

The Vanderbilt unrest raised doubts among some Baptists about the future of their schools, but the denomination's educational leaders used the agitation surrounding Vanderbilt to their benefit, taking the opportunity to reassure Baptists of their schools' loyalty. Southwestern Baptist's president, P. T. Hale, picked the opportune moment of the spring of 1906—just when Hoss was canvassing the state to stir up resentment against Vanderbilt and to call for greater church control of the school—to begin a new campaign for funding the Baptist school. Hale emphasized Southwestern's close connection to the church, explaining that its trustees were elected by the Tennessee Baptist Convention and that their actions were "reviewed by the controlling power, which is the denomination."[101] Not willing to be left leaning only on historical ties or rhetorical pledges of affiliation, however, the Tennessee Baptist Convention appointed an educational committee in 1902 to clarify the relation between church and school. After the Vanderbilt case had gone to the courts, the convention in 1911 created a committee "authorized to . . . work out a plan which will stand the test of the courts, so that all our educational institutions shall be for all time under organized Baptist control."[102] The Baptists eventually chartered the Education Board of the Tennessee Baptist Convention, which was to raise funds for all of the state's Baptist colleges, making a contract with each school guaranteeing certain rights of supervision by the denomination and holding a first mortgage on all property and endowment funds.[103] If the schools ever deviated from denominational wishes, the Education Board, through the contract, could get back any investment, plus interest.

Christian Education for Church and State

The bitterness of Vanderbilt's split from the Methodist church had broader implications not just for Methodists but for all Tennessee Protestants. The apparent "loss" of Vanderbilt undermined many Tennesseans' faith in the permanence of church colleges and caused the state's Evangelicals to take a greater interest in the specific religious content of all levels of public education.

World War I would profoundly affect higher education in the United States in both church and state colleges. Military spending brought a wealth of students to both Vanderbilt and Union during the war years and greatly increased attendance thereafter. A conservative resurgence during and following the conflict led denominational leaders both to promote their schools as vastly superior and morally safer than the state institutions and to argue for greater oversight of the state schools. Bishop Candler urged Methodist education as a missionary enterprise, explaining the unique position of the southern church and its responsibility to the nation and the world: "The degenerate forms of rationalistic religion have never been able to take root in our section. Southern Churches, therefore, can make evangelical institutions of learning more easily than can the Churches of other sections." Candler had been one of the chief critics of the policies of the Vanderbilt Board of Trust, and as the first president of the rechartered Emory University he made sure to publicize and safeguard the close relationship between the school and the church. As an early Emory advertisement in the *Nashville Christian Advocate* proclaimed, the university was *"an institution founded, owned, and controlled by the Methodist Episcopal Church, South."* Only through such close denominational ties, Candler warned, could southern colleges save the world from error. [104]

Advocates of denominational education quickly took advantage of America's anti-German hysteria. Tennessee's Baptists especially emphasized the relationship between German state systems of public education and the Prussian militarism that was sweeping Europe. An overstated, full-page *Baptist and Reflector* advertisement explained that the "absence in the German Empire of Baptist, and other denominational colleges enjoying the freedom which these institutions possess in America, accounts for the present world war." [105] Ivey urged diligence and a "Counter 'Watch on the Rhine,' " warning that "Christian thought is not yet free of the toils of the German schools" and urging Methodists to "see that our educational systems are free from the poison of German rationalism and the German military spirit." [106]

Both Baptists and Methodists inaugurated ambitious postwar fund-raising efforts. Buoyed by the sacrifice they saw poured out for the war effort, denominational fund-raisers called for a similar show of "patriotism" for the church. At the end of the war, Baptists urged members to donate their Liberty Bonds to relieve the debt of the church's colleges. A massive campaign followed, with the goal of raising seventy-five million dollars over five years for education, missions, and other church causes. Methodist educators launched the Christian Education Movement to aid all levels of education by the church but called for special assistance for colleges. In January 1921, the leaders of the Christian Education Movement initiated a massive advertising campaign, using a full page on the back cover of each week's *Nashville Christian Advocate.* Warning that "The Church Must Educate or Die," one representative advertisement explained that Christian education was for the good of the denomination and the country: "It means the saving of Methodist education to the nation and the production of those Christian leaders, now lacking, who alone can lead the blinded world aright. . . . It ultimately means life or death for the M. E. Church, South; it means moral character and stable government for the nation." [107] Other advertisements promised parents contemplating sending daughters to school, "She'll Be Safe at the Christian College." [108] Still others reminded parents that "Christian Education is Complete Education" because it "trains head and heart together." [109] Further, Christians could help "Banish the Bolshevik" by supporting Methodist colleges because "the best protection against anarchy, Bolshevism, radicalism, I.W.W'ism, [and] red revolution is Christian Education. It lays the foundation of society upon the Rock of Ages—upon righteousness, law and order, cooperation and unselfishness."[110]

Such advertising was intended to increase support for denominational schools, but Tennessee Evangelicals also undertook an increased effort to supervise education by the state. Some Baptists and Methodists had discussed of the need to minister to students at the state universities, but the Vanderbilt controversy, combined with the nagging realization that church colleges simply could not keep up with the demands of the increasing numbers of people seeking higher education, gave new impetus to plans for ministering to students at the state schools and to the movement to exercise greater oversight of the public education system. Asserting that "considerably more than half of our Methodist young men and women who are in college are being educated in State colleges and universities," one writer urged parents, ministers, and local churches to take a greater interest in the students and faculty of the state universities.[111] Some correspondents urged the appointment of ministers to college students, while other writers called for more intrusive investigation of the officers of and instruction at the state schools.[112]

Tennessee Governor John Calvin Brown, speaking at the laying of the cornerstone of Vanderbilt University in 1874, had praised the prospects of the Methodist university, which, "dedicated to the living God, . . . will send forth an army of evangelists, drilled, disciplined, and armed, to meet and overthrow the swelling bands of infidelity."[113] But in the twentieth century, when questions arose about just what kind of army Vanderbilt was producing, a great many Tennessee Protestants were called to defend the old faith. Many Tennesseans saw the "theft" of Vanderbilt as a potent symbol of the encroachment of secular culture on their Zion. Fearing that denominational colleges would no longer provide sufficient guarantees of piety and morality within the state, many Evangelicals increasingly came to advocate greater religious oversight of public education on all levels. If the orthodoxy of the religious colleges and universities was not dependable, then ensuring that public common schools promulgated and defended the basics of evangelical Christianity became more important.

4. From Temperance to Prohibition

Tennessee Evangelicals and the Legislation of Morality

Addressing the readers of the *Nashville Christian Advocate* on the first Fourth of July of the twentieth century, Methodist editor and outspoken prohibitionist Elijah E. Hoss crafted a lengthy editorial on the responsibility of the church and its members for the welfare not just of other church members but of the whole society. Noting that his denomination was represented "in almost every community from the Potomac to the Rio Grande, and from the Ohio River to Key West," Hoss challenged any "intelligent man [to] deny" that "the moral and religious welfare of these Southern States is largely committed into the hands of the Methodist Church." In part, Hoss was repeating the missionary charge that had first sent Methodist ministers out to such disparate points on the map to preach the gospel and call individual sinners to repentance. But Hoss also saw his and the church's mission as societal as well as individual: "The future of great commonwealths, as well as the immortal destiny of millions of souls, depends on the manner in which we discharge the obligations that God has imposed upon us."[1]

Tennessee Methodists and Baptists acted on this charge, taking an active interest in the education of youth as a means for individual conversion and salvation that would, by extension, shape the future society and state. Propelled by a missionary call to further Christianize the South and reassure southerners of their status as God's chosen people, late-nineteenth-century Tennessee Evangelicals sought a voice in determining the curriculum and control of the state's growing public education system. This interest in public education in part paralleled but also lagged behind Tennessee Evangelicals' more prominent engagement with their surrounding society, the battles to eradicate alcohol.

Prohibition and education intersect in several places in Tennessee history, so much so, in fact, that historian Eric R. Lacy describes the state's dry crusade as a battle of "Schoolhouse versus saloon." After several failed legislative attempts to secure a local-option Prohibition law, an 1877 state statute forbade liquor sales within four miles of chartered schools outside of incorporated towns. After the defeat of other, more direct legislative measures to ban the manufacture, sale, and consumption of alcohol, Prohibition forces dried up the state by gradually extending the Four Mile Law and applying it to all schools—public and private—and in all parts of the state, so that the schoolhouse became "a weapon with which to fight the saloon."[2] Although the efforts to banish alcohol from the Volunteer State included a variety of interests, Methodist and Baptist ministers and editors, especially Edgar Estes Folk of the *Nashville Baptist and Reflector* and Hoss of the *Nashville Christian Advocate,* were the crusade's chief standard-bearers and publicists.

The Evangelicals' Prohibition campaign, much like their growing concern about public education, represented a new era of broader social concern on the part of southern white Christians. Although they continued to make the most of preaching the Gospel and converting individual sinners, Tennessee Evangelicals increasingly understood theirs as a divine mission with both earthly and heavenly goals. As the individuals, the churches, the state of Tennessee, and the nation began a new century, Hoss insisted that "There never was a time when it was more important to assert the absoluteness of God's authority over the individual, the family, the community, [and] the nation." While charging southern Methodists to work for the spread of religion and "keep alive in the minds of men the sense of eternal things," Hoss reminded church members and others of "the absoluteness of God's authority" on earth and in heaven.[3] Hoss is an important transitional figure in the history of Tennessee Evangelicals: though he remained a theologically conservative voice in church councils and gained prominence as the church's chief prosecutor in its efforts to keep Vanderbilt University on the denominational straight and narrow, he also became one of Tennessee's leading Prohibition advocates. Hoss most clearly articulated his changed conception of the church in his Prohibition campaigns. No longer a separate community of believers at odds with the surrounding society, Hoss's religious community and its moral order extended to and embraced all people in the state of Tennessee, whether or not they recognized the church's authority.

Not surprisingly, Prohibition activities by individual church members and denominational bodies invited vigorous protest from liquor interests. But church actions in the fight against alcohol also raised serious questions within denominations about the proper relationship between the church and the state and the place of preachers and moral concerns in public civic and political life. The debates that occurred in church councils and appeared in the pages of denominational and secular newspapers offer a window through which to observe the changing nature of southern Christianity. In pursuing a moral crusade against alcohol, Tennessee Evangelicals radically expanded the church's temporal and earthly mission and by the end of the nineteenth century demonstrated the extent to which religious leaders believed that the church had become coterminous with the surrounding society.

The Slow Growth of Prohibition Sentiment and Activism

By the early twentieth century, most Tennesseans—whether or not they were church members—would have recognized state Baptist and Methodist preachers and officials at the head of the antiliquor phalanx. With editors Hoss and Folk leading the Prohibition charge not only in church papers but as heads of the Local Option League and later the state branch of the Anti-Saloon League, white Tennessee Methodists and Baptists appeared united in their push to dry up the Volunteer State. The southern Methodists' Memphis Annual Conference, meeting in Martin in 1913, rejoiced that it had, "from the beginning . . . insisted upon the complete separation of our people from the manufacture and use of intoxicating liquors."[4] Such unified Prohibition support had not always marked Tennessee's Evangelicals, however. In fact, support for strict legislative Prohibition was slow to develop among nineteenth-century evangelical leaders and rank-and-file church members. A long history of moderate social consumption of alcohol marked southern lives in the more established societies east of the Appalachians as well as on Tennessee's early southwestern frontier. Many individual Tennessee Methodists and Baptists advocated abstinence from alcohol, and some even encouraged legislative appeals to limit the sale and distribution of spirits in antebellum years. But after rigid prohibitionism became associated with abolitionism and other forms of political preaching in the late antebellum period, at least as many Tennessee Evangelicals eschewed as supported the movement. The Civil War and Reconstruction in part reinforced southern evangelical tendencies to forgo explicit political action, but simultaneous desires to re-create the especially religious South motivated a slow growth of evangelical sentiment in favor of securing wider application of religious morality throughout southern society.

Alcohol, especially simple whiskey made from corn, was one of the earliest improved products of Tennessee agriculture. More profitable to transport eastward over the mountains or down the Cumberland and Mississippi Rivers than unprocessed corn, whiskey was a common product in the Old Southwest. Not exclusively an export product, alcohol was commonly consumed in the state by all classes. As a general rule, early pioneer Methodist and Baptist ministers in Tennessee did not condemn moderate drinking by church members or by the clergy, although churches commonly disciplined members for drunkenness. Alcohol consumption was so prevalent in early Tennessee that when Methodist circuit rider Peter Cartwright first entered his ministry in Middle Tennessee, he noted in his journal that he "found 20 talented local preachers, all whiskey drinkers." When he attempted to bring church charges against one of them for drinking too frequently, he found it difficult to secure a trial "committee what were not dram-drinkers themselves." Some Methodist circuit riders and local preachers apparently supplemented their meager incomes by making whiskey and selling it as they traveled.[5] Tennessee Methodists did not drink alone; the Baptist clergy and laity likewise imbibed, "sometimes even at church gatherings."[6] The *Tennessee Baptist* newspaper reported in June 1836 on the low number of teetotalers and larger numbers of Baptists who "owned distilleries, distilled whisky, and sold it by the gallon." Baptist minister Josiah Rucks of Smith and Wilson Counties humorously commented on his coreligionists' propensity to drink, claiming that "The Methodists cry, Fire, fire! The Presbyterians cry Order, order! The Baptists cry, Water, water! but mix a little whisky with it."[7]

Though willing to accept some drinking, both the Baptists and the Methodists did, however, condemn drunkenness among the clergy and laity, gradually moving toward total abstinence when many members were found unable to drink only in moderation. Tennessee Methodist minister James Axley pressed the 1812 General Convention (the national body of Methodists) to forbid pastors to sell liquor, securing the measure's passage in 1816. At the urging of pioneering minister William McKendree, the members of the Tennessee Conference of Methodists resolved in 1833 to abstain from using alcohol and to encourage their families, friends, and communities to do likewise. Middle Tennessee Baptist minister R. B. C. Howell, founder and longtime editor of the *Tennessee Baptist,* strongly advocated temperance from the pulpit and most effectively through the pages of his weekly paper. With leadership from Howell and outspoken teetotalers such as fellow Baptist Robert W. January, several state Baptist associations passed temperance resolutions, verbally attacked alcohol sale and consumption, and even pressed the Baptist General Association of Tennessee to petition the legislature in favor of prohibitory laws. But these actions often caused trouble, even within Baptist ranks. Several members balked when January made total abstinence a test for membership at Mill Creek Church. While admitting that some of their number had become "too unguarded in taking their drams, forgetting that they ought to abstain from all appearance of evil," some Baptists nonetheless recoiled from Howell and January's strict teetotalism.

Primitive Baptist John M. Watson asked, "Shall we leave the Church of God and go into a temperance society for the cultivation of temperance, because the human institution is more holy?" He further criticized the temperance societies for "insist[ing] on a higher order of abstinence than did the Saviour himself."[8]

In addition to denominational bodies' efforts to curb the consumption of alcohol by their members and clergy, several temperance organizations emerged in antebellum Tennessee. This voluntary movement, part of a larger national organization most prominent among Quakers and Evangelicals of the mid-Atlantic and New England states in the 1820s, gained limited but not unified support in the South. Some ardent evangelical advocates of temperance criticized the societies because they were not strongly enough pro-temperance. Despite his outspoken claims to be "an original—aye an *ultra* Temperance man," East Tennessee Methodist circuit rider turned local preacher and Whig politician William G. "Parson" Brownlow in 1842 explained his failure to join a temperance society "but for no other reason, than that we were not willing that it should be inferred therefrom, that we regarded our rule of [the Methodist *Book of*] *Discipline* on that subject, as wanting in efficiency." Nevertheless, much like their counterparts in Virginia and the Carolinas, many Tennessee Evangelicals found their way to the leadership of the temperance societies.[9]

Despite the misgivings of some evangelical leaders and apparently many of their denominational constituents regarding the wisdom of increased temperance, abstinence, and even Prohibition activism, Tennessee's Methodist and Baptist leaders stepped up their verbal, disciplinary, and legal attacks on demon rum in the late antebellum years. During the 1850s, both the *Tennessee Baptist* and the *Nashville Christian Advocate* published tracts "advocating the legal prohibition of liquor." After temperance forces secured an 1838 law banning the sale of spirits in any quantity less than a quart (an attempt to close down taverns), Baptists and Methodists kept a watch on the succeeding legislature and urged it not to weaken the law. Calling it the "Magna Charta of Morality" and the "most salutory [*sic*] and efficient measure ever yet adopted by legislative authority to promote and advance the cause of virtue and good order," representatives of both denominations urged the Tennessee General Assembly not to repeal the measure.[10]

Anne Loveland explains southern Baptists', Methodists', and Presbyterians' increasing support for "legal suasion" to curtail the liquor trade as an outgrowth of antebellum southern temperance societies. Seeing the societies and their aims as more "worldly," religious leaders felt free to attempt political action through such groups. As a general rule, prior to 1831, when abolitionism provoked southern religious proslavery arguments, southern clergymen avoided political involvement, at least as long as politics concerned questions only of policy or party. However, as Mitchell Snay describes, southern clergymen did claim a voice "if any political issue was perceived as possessing any kind of moral or religious significance. . . . Morality thus became the main criterion for determining religious involvement in politics." Even as Tennessee Evangelicals such as R. B. C. Howell and John McFerrin claimed a right to speak out on what they perceived as the moral issue of regulating or eliminating alcohol, larger issues of sectional politics made several other evangelical ministers and members uneasy about political entanglement. Much of this desire to distance the church proper from explicit participation in politics likely resulted from increased agitation by northern, religious abolitionists; southern Evangelicals roundly criticized the northerners as political preachers, even as the southerners amplified their moral and political proslavery arguments.[11]

In the wake of the antislavery crisis, some southern ministers denounced the legal temperance campaigns by raising the specter of abolitionism. Criticizing a proposal by the New York Conference to add a more stringent abstinence clause to the Methodist Episcopal Church's General Rules, editor William Capers of the *Southern Christian Advocate* warned that the change was not based on any scriptural directive and was instead an effort to substitute human for divine law. "If one arbitrary law, why not another? When you have loosed from the Bible, whither may you not be carried?" Capers inquired, implying the relationship between the abstinence plank and a contemporaneous effort by the New England Conference to add a rule against slaveholding. Tennessee temperance advocates achieved only sporadic and short-lived legislative success prior to the war. Soured on the prospects of legally enforceable abstinence, most southern Evangelicals reverted to an emphasis on moral suasion and an explanation that individual conversion was the only sure cure for the drink habit.[12]

Despite the efforts of Brownlow, McFerrin, and other temperance leaders, the movement to adopt a "Maine liquor law"—named for that state's prohibition on the manufacture or sale of liquor in any quantity except for "medicinal and mechanical purposes"—failed to persuade Tennessee's political leadership. In his successful 1855 gubernatorial campaign, Andrew Johnson opposed the adoption of such a law because it would be, he explained, not only contrary to the Tennessee constitution but also "incompatible with the rights and privileges of freemen."[13] Unlike many other Confederate states, Tennessee did not enact a temporary Prohibition law during the Civil War and so emerged with its relatively loose prewar laws regarding the manufacture and sale of liquor.[14] But there was an important difference: Brownlow, a vituperative Whig turned

Know-Nothing turned Republican politician, sometime Methodist preacher, outspoken Unionist, critic of the Confederacy and a fervent supporter of the Sons of Temperance, became the state's first Reconstruction governor after Johnson, the military governor, became U.S. vice president in 1865. Parson Brownlow continued his antebellum attacks on demon rum but now had the larger stage of the governor's office and the increased power of a strong governorship and a mostly accommodating Reconstruction legislature.[15]

From his earliest messages to the legislature, Brownlow urged action against an enemy he labeled "King Alcohol." Citing the harmful effects of intemperance on the armies during the war, Brownlow warned that liquor "is now transferring its baneful influence to the walks of civil life, demoralizing the young and rising generations and sending to premature graves many of our best and most useful citizens." In response to the continued threat of alcohol, Brownlow urged the General Assembly to "dry up" the state. As governor, Brownlow aligned himself with Congressional Reconstruction and against the more conservative policies of his old Tennessee political opponent, Johnson, by now serving as U.S. president. Brownlow's support for legislative temperance and Prohibition gained him some favor among antebellum temperance advocates, but his political position as head of the state's Radicals and subsequent endorsement of black social and political rights did little to remove old accusations about the linkages between temperance and abolition.[16]

Political tensions took on heightened significance when grafted onto the pressing questions of the relationship between northern and southern branches of great evangelical bodies such as the Methodists, Baptists, and Presbyterians, which, unlike their political counterparts, were not institutionally reunited by the war's conclusion. Although he had been an ardent antebellum defender of slavery, Brownlow was best known among southern Evangelicals as a zealous Unionist, the leader of Tennessee's Radical Republican administration, and a supporter of the northern Methodist Episcopal Church. In the fall of 1865, as Brownlow was becoming Tennessee's first postwar civil governor, senior southern Methodist bishops addressed to their ministers and congregants a letter expressing "apprehension that a large proportion, if not a majority of northern Methodists have become incurably radical." Charging that members of the northern wing of the church had "incorporated social dogmas and political tests into their church creeds," the southern bishops admitted that they could "anticipate no good result from even entertaining the subject of re-union with them."[17]

Eastern Tennessee, which harbored far more Unionist sentiment than the other two-thirds of the state and, not surprisingly, formed Brownlow's political power base, also witnessed the continuing strength of the northern Methodists throughout Reconstruction and postbellum years. Middle Tennessee's southern Methodists purposefully positioned themselves in opposition to northern Methodists such as Brownlow, who, the southerners charged, were unable to separate religious and political questions. Wishing to avoid even the appearance of meddling in political questions, the Tennessee Annual Conference membership in 1874 voted by a ratio of three to one against a proposal to add total abstinence to the list of General Rules to be observed by all ministers and members. [18]

Although antebellum Tennessee Methodists and Baptists had begun to take a stand not just against drunkenness but against any use of alcohol, the political climate of the sectional crisis, Civil War, and Reconstruction sapped southern denominational support for explicit political and legal action by churches to limit or ban alcohol sale and consumption. Brownlow's support for temperance legislation did little to diminish conservatives' connection of temperance with radicalism, but the decline of open political strife following Tennessee's "redemption" by conservative Democrats in 1869 would create a fertile atmosphere for the growth of temperance sentiment among southern Evangelicals. Although southern churches and citizens remained divided on the proper role of religion and preachers in politics, temperance and then Prohibition sentiment increased perceptibly in the closing decades of the nineteenth century and opening years of the twentieth.

From Temperance to Prohibition within Church and State

In the first two decades following the Civil War and the restoration of native southern Democrats to political control in 1869, temperance forces gained power in both civic and religious assemblies but repeatedly came up short in their crusades for a dry Tennessee. Emerging following Reconstruction was a social, cultural, and political climate that privileged white males' individual liberty and encouraged loyalty to the conservative Democratic Party. Because state liquor interests allied themselves with the Democrats, antidrink advocates faced enormous obstacles to legislative Prohibition. Evangelical leaders likewise struggled to differentiate themselves from the northern wings of their denominations while still claiming relevance to a southern society greatly disrupted by the war and its accompanying social upheavals. Temperance activities grew out of the continuing sectional tensions that followed the Civil War, as southern Evangelicals attempted to reassure themselves of their status as God's chosen nation—even after defeat—by re-creating the especially religious southern society that they claimed had existed before the war. Efforts to resanctify southern society led many postbellum Tennessee Evangelicals first to increase discipline within their ranks and then to move beyond church boundaries to preach morality—or at least temperance—to Tennesseans as a whole.

Although he had shifted with the political winds from his antebellum defense of slavery to an outspoken advocacy of the Radical social and political agenda, Brownlow used the bully pulpit of the governor's office to resume his old campaign against the sale and consumption of alcohol. He made explicit his temperance beliefs and Prohibition desires in each of his biennial messages to the Tennessee General Assembly, calling on the legislature to enact high taxes on liquor to drive it from the state or, at the very least, to prohibit its sale or consumption near chartered schools. Despite the General Assembly's usual Reconstruction-era support for Brownlow, the legislature rebuffed all the governor's antialcohol proposals.[19] A few similar though likewise unsuccessful bills were initiated in the General Assembly, suggesting that antidrink forces had at least some support there.[20]

After Reconstruction, civil antialcohol forces moved along two fronts, voluntary societies and legal petitions to the legislature. On the voluntary front, state branches of the Sons of Temperance, the Order of Good Templars, the Cadets of Temperance, the Friends of Temperance, and some local and women's groups, including local chapters of the Women's Christian Temperance Union after 1882, pushed Tennesseans to pledge abstinence, pressured saloonkeepers to close their shops, and worked to create what one organization termed "a healthy temperance sentiment" throughout the state. While the voluntary societies urged individual Tennesseans to pledge abstinence, other reformers petitioned the legislature in favor of more stringent legal restrictions on the manufacture, sale, and use of alcohol. Like crusaders elsewhere in the nation, most southern legal efforts centered on securing local-option legislation that would allow counties or local communities to prohibit the sale of alcohol within their bounds. After a failed attempt to include a local-option Prohibition clause in Tennessee's 1870 constitution, antialcohol forces deluged the General Assembly with petitions in favor of a bill empowering local citizens to vote for or against a license for each potential saloonkeeper. This "act to provide against the evils resulting from the sale of intoxicating liquors in the state" passed both houses but was vetoed by Governor John C. Brown, who cited two problems, one narrowly procedural, the other constitutional. The most important long-term legacy of Brown's veto was his assertion that local-option laws, which, by their nature, appealed to the people in a given district, were an unconstitutional delegation of legislative power by the General Assembly. (Less important was the procedural problem: the bill presented for Brown's signature had originated in the Senate but was transmitted to the House and adopted in place of a similar measure that had originated there. Because the Senate bill had not been read and passed on three different days in the House, Brown argued, it was invalid.)[21] Although future legislators would introduce local-option laws, the anti-Prohibition forces benefited from the legal and constitutional doubt surrounding such measures. Many opponents argued that prohibitory laws were a waste of legislative effort, thereby easily stymieing antialcohol laws in a state low on funds and suspicious of excessive governance.

Efforts in the 1870s to separate schools from saloons set a precedent for legislative Prohibition. George R. Fairbanks, business manager, tireless promoter, and early historian of the University of the South, an Episcopal college in Sewanee, on the Cumberland plateau in rural southeastern Tennessee, responded to "the attempts of vicious and willful parties to establish . . . grog shops" near the university by imploring his state legislator to introduce a bill providing for a dry zone surrounding the school. After several failed attempts, Fairbanks secured passage of an 1877 law prohibiting "the sale of all intoxicating beverages within four miles of any chartered institution of learning outside an incorporated town." Fairbanks had sought to establish Prohibition only in Sewanee, but since the 1870 state constitution required all laws to be general, the Four Mile Law applied to all private chartered schools not in chartered cities. The law's rural limitation suggests the reason for its passage: Fairbanks explained that because the law did "not affect the cities and incorporated towns, the liquor dealers [had] no direct interest in having it repealed."[22]

Although the Four Mile Law effectively eliminated alcohol from the Tennessee countryside, adamant prohibitionists wanted a more effective ban that would cover the whole state. Many of the voluntary associations as well as the newly formed state chapter of the Women's Christian Temperance Union banded together in the Tennessee Temperance Alliance to agitate for a prohibitory constitutional amendment. The proposal, which would allow the General Assembly to pass laws and set fines for the manufacture or sale of "any intoxicating liquors whatever, including wine, ale, and beer," was passed by the legislatures of 1885 and 1887. A fall 1887 statewide referendum resulted in 135,197 votes against the amendment and 117,504 in favor, a strong showing but a defeat nonetheless for the Prohibition forces.[23] Antisaloon forces responded by turning their attention back to local-option laws and extending the effective range of the Four Mile Law to all schools and to successively larger cities until by the early twentieth century it applied to the whole state, rural and urban.

Tennessee Evangelicals provided strong support for the 1887 Prohibition referendum, but the continuing legacies of the Civil War and Reconstruction made it difficult for any of the southern churches to speak with one voice on temperance and Prohibition. Tennessee Evangelicals took an increasingly hard line against church members involved with alcohol in any capacity. Through the last decades of the nineteenth century, many Tennessee Methodist and Baptist churches began to recognize the interconnected nature of the New South society and sought to ease the burden on individual church members to resist alcohol by removing the temptation from their surroundings. More and more identifying the boundaries and moral standards of the church with those of the larger society, many state Evangelicals led and joined the campaigns for effective prohibitory legislation in Tennessee and became the principal spokespeople for the unsuccessful 1887 referendum.

Postwar Tennessee Evangelicals continued their antebellum practices of church discipline of members suspected of moral offenses. Stephen V. Ash notes that Middle Tennessee congregations supervised the behavior of members "with renewed energy and determination" following the war. Although several studies of southern religion suggest a decline in the postwar practice of church discipline, an increase occurred in the scope of alcohol-related offenses that could incur the sanctions of church discipline. Whereas antebellum church trials disciplined members for drunkenness or for operating saloons, postbellum churches increasingly chastised members for any involvement in the manufacture, sale, transport, or consumption of alcohol.[24] *Tennessee Baptist* editor James R. Graves appears to have been more strict than some of his brethren in this matter: while Virginia's *Richmond Religious Herald* defended grocers who sold spirits as no more culpable than "the farmer who grew the grain," the "cooper who manufactured the barrel," or the "mechanic who made the still," Graves argued that anyone associated with the manufacture or sale of liquor should come under church censure.[25]

Baptist and Methodist associations throughout the South struggled internally with Prohibition questions in the late nineteenth century. Several Methodists led a charge for Wesleyan perfectionism and urged higher standards of human behavior and moral accountability within the church, while other church members continued to argue for a prohibition only of drunkenness, not moderate use of alcohol. *Nashville Christian Advocate* editor Thomas Summers Sr. warned both factions that such agitation could only harm the church and urged a return to the church's "great business [of] saving souls—everything else must be made tributary to this."[26] Nevertheless, the antialcohol agitation continued, including a successful push for church laws sanctioning members or clergy in any way involved in the manufacture, sale, transport, or consumption of alcohol.

The Baptists' congregational heritage and organizational structure made the top-down tactics favored by the Methodists difficult, but various state conventions and finally the Southern Baptist Convention passed resolutions strongly encouraging member churches and organizations not to retain "in the fellowship of a Baptist church" any person "who engages in the manufacture or sale of alcoholic liquors." But instead of stopping there, a position most southern Baptists had held at least since the 1850s, the new resolution also included an advisement to exclude any member "who invests his money in the manufacture or sale of a[l]coholic liquors, or who rents his property to be used for distilleries, wholesale liquor houses, or saloons" as well as "any member who drinks intoxicating liquors as a beverage, or visits saloons or drinking places for the purpose of such indulgence."[27] Demonstrating the difficulty encountered by Baptist associations attempting to dictate rules to member churches, the 1890 gathering of the Union Association of Baptists in rural Middle Tennessee revised its temperance resolution, amending from a requirement to a recommendation the clause requiring churches to disfellowship members who used, manufactured, or sold alcohol.[28]

Despite churches' apparently firmer stance against alcohol during the late 1800s, the frequency of church discipline, even for drinking offenses, seems to have declined. Ted Owenby suggests several explanations for this apparent contradiction. Dismissing explanations that either church members had learned to control their behavior or the churches had "made peace with their culture" and "no longer felt the need or ability to judge each other's behavior," Owenby argues that southern Evangelicals had broadened their vision and the scope of the churches' authority to include all of the surrounding society. Citing the increase in civic moral legislation endorsed by Evangelicals, Owenby proposes that "as churches were losing interest in disciplining the behavior of their members, they were trying to reform the behavior of all Southerners. . . . [E]vangelicals were not giving in to the world but redefining their place in it."[29] However persuasive Owenby's explanation may be, it remains unsatisfying on a number of fronts. In addition to his smoothing of intrachurch tensions over the process of more clearly embracing a social mission, his explanation begs the question of why and how southern Evangelicals came to embrace a social mission when they did after most had so adamantly opposed one in the immediate postwar years.

The question of timing and motivation suggests a combination of at least three different explanations. First, evangelical Tennesseans' growing acceptance of an extension of church moral and disciplinary standards to the larger society was part of a larger Lost Cause effort to sanctify society and re-create the antebellum southern apologists' notion of the especially religious South.

Second, the movement toward a social mission represented a further outgrowth of the competition both between the northern and southern wings of the major denominations and among the various southern denominations—an evangelical desire constantly to increase the membership of each church that led nineteenth-century church officials repeatedly to call for the church to justify its relevance to the newly emerging society. Finally, increased church interest in the larger society resulted from the post-Reconstruction decline of outside pressure on the southern church to remain apolitical in an effort to distinguish itself from the abolitionism and radical social and racial ideas of northern Evangelicals.

One part of the explanation has to be the post–Civil War social, religious, and cultural phenomenon of the Lost Cause ideology that put such a premium on the idea of an especially religious antebellum South. This was, in part, a continuation of the sectional war, with words replacing guns as the weapons of choice. Southern ministers, noting the increase of drunkenness following the Civil War, argued that the "liquor interests were Northern based, and thus an alien, corrupting force," an argument somewhat hard to sustain in bourbon- and whiskey-rich Tennessee and Kentucky. Nevertheless, southern ministers such as H. A. Scomp argued that the southern armies had drunk less than any previous forces and canonized Stonewall Jackson and Robert E. Lee as "models of sobriety." Furthermore, when northern reformers sought to claim credit for postwar southern temperance and Prohibition campaigns, Scomp and others pointed proudly to temperance efforts of the 1830s and 1840s as further proof of southern sanctity.[30] In their efforts to understand and accept military defeat, southern evangelical apologists preached that the South was still God's chosen region. As key historians of the Lost Cause movement have pointed out, various social and political classes appropriated the Lost Cause rhetoric and ideology in support of racial, political, and social agendas, but that ideology had an important religious dimension as well.[31] Perversely interpreting Confederate defeat and the ordeal of Reconstruction as signs of God's favor (in the sense of an immanent God who acted in the world and cared enough to punish his chosen people for certain moral shortcomings and as a challenge to more ambitious evangelism), white Tennessee Evangelicals were motivated to take new efforts to spread the Gospel and attempt to evangelize society however possible.

Interpreting a growing membership list as a sign of a healthy (that is, God-approved) church, several denominational leaders stressed the importance of the church appearing relevant to modern society and not falling behind in either spiritual or physical affairs. Bristling at the growth of secular temperance and social relief organizations, O. P. Fitzgerald warned that the "Church must reassert her divine commission and resume her temporal function, in feeding the hungry, clothing the naked, visiting the sick and those that are in prison"; otherwise, the church must "be prepared for the most disastrous results. . . . If she will devolve this work upon other organizations, she must be content to let them take her place in the hearts of mankind." A correspondent made the implications of Fitzgerald's argument clear, warning that "the religion, by whatever name it may be called, and whatever pretensions it may make, that does not concern itself for the physical welfare of suffering humanity, will not be believed when it expresses great concern for the salvation of souls."[32] Good works would increase the stature of the church and might garner new members.

A third possible explanation for the growth of temperance activism within Tennessee Methodist and Baptist churches begins with an acknowledgment of the lingering sectional tensions but also stresses how the end of Reconstruction to some degree lessened the outside pressure on the southern churches. With little incentive to appear different from the northern, radical, political churches, southern Evangelicals could more safely enter politics on the side of moral questions.[33] Proliquor spokesmen still criticized preachers for straying out of their supposed proper realm, but the charge was no longer as potent as it had been during the crisis of abolitionism or Radical Reconstruction and the rule of Parson Brownlow.[34] In an interesting reversal of metaphors, prohibitionists often spoke of their campaigns as aimed at throwing off "slavery" to alcohol. The Tennessee Baptist Convention of 1901, after a lengthy harangue against the saloon as the root of all evil and a thoroughly un-American institution, concluded, "As it was with slavery, so shall it be with the saloon."[35]

Tennessee Evangelicals of the late nineteenth century did not just move toward stronger standards of individual temperance within the churches but also urged temperance and self-restraint among the larger public. Evangelicals lent moral and physical support as well as membership to the state's many voluntary temperance organizations while striving to make their churches strong temperance societies. Far more public were the efforts of various itinerant revivalists—most notably the flamboyant Methodist Sam Jones—to convert Tennessee sinners, drinkers, and whiskey peddlers. Jones, a revivalist from Georgia and self-professed former drunkard, made several appearances in Nashville and other cities to lead revivals emphasizing individual responsibility and morality. With endorsements from Knoxville and Nashville ministers as well as strong support from Fitzgerald in his *Nashville Christian Advocate,* Jones repeatedly returned to Tennessee to spread his temperance and revival messages.[36] Boastfully denouncing tavern keepers and liquor dealers as "wallowing hogs" and "puking dogs," Jones set up his Gospel tent right on Broad Street, just up the hill from Nashville's thriving saloon district. Captain Thomas G. Ryman, Jones's most famous convert of the Nashville meetings, banned the transport or sale of liquor on his extensive fleet of steamboats, closed up his Nashville saloon, named one of his ships the *Sam Jones,* and spearheaded a movement to build Nashville's Union Gospel Tabernacle (later renamed the Ryman Auditorium), where Jones could hold future revivals. A group of Nashvillians were so enthusiastic about Jones's beneficial effects on the town that they raised a subscription of funds and offered Jones and his wife a nice house if they would relocate.[37]

Though far from united on the subject, some Tennessee Evangelicals began calling for legal sanctions against alcohol in the early 1870s and became leaders in the civic campaigns against demon rum by the century's last decades. Methodist David C. Kelley, who was also active in the founding and growth of Vanderbilt University, addressed an 1872 temperance sermon to the Tennessee General Assembly, calling on the legislators to notice the great number of crimes caused by alcohol and to "make liquor dealers responsible for the legitimate results of their iniquitous trade." Several correspondents wrote to the denominational papers favoring local-option laws. Proclaiming its democratic principles, one Baptist association resolved that the state should "Let the voice of the people rule in everything, and say whether liquor shall be sold in their county or not."[38]

While several individuals advocated temperance activism, the editorial leadership of the state's religious papers was at first reluctant to fully endorse the movement. Graves frequently wrote in his *Memphis Baptist* of the need for individual abstinence and church supervision of members' discipline, calling for churches to charge members associated in any way with the liquor trade with "grossly unchristian conduct—aiding and abetting drunkenness."[39] But he was equally adamant that churches should not invite Prohibition Party meetings within their doors, especially not on Sundays. Many churches apparently followed Graves's advice, for when Rev. A. B. Wright, the circuit-riding chairman of a local branch of the Tennessee Temperance Alliance, arrived at the Baptist Church in Sunbright, Morgan County, he found that the Baptist preacher had "locked us out" and forced Wright to find another place for the temperance meeting.[40] Nevertheless, many Tennessee Baptist associations advocated more direct political action than did Graves. The Union Association, centered in rural Middle Tennessee, recorded in 1886 "that we favor total prohibition [and] will support no man for the Legislature who does not favor prohibition."[41] That same year the Tennessee Baptist Convention expressed similar sentiments, calling for the election of representatives who would favor the submission of Prohibition to a referendum of the state's voters.[42] Rev. Folk, Graves's successor at the Baptist newspaper (renamed the *Baptist and Reflector* when it moved to Nashville in 1889), would become a much more outspoken advocate of personal temperance and legal Prohibition, using the paper as a strong antialcohol information network.

As in the realm of education, Fitzgerald proved an important transitional figure in Tennessee Evangelicals' relationship to alcohol and politics. Though a strong advocate of personal restraint, individual abstinence, and even church activism to encourage temperance among others, Fitzgerald warned his readers about letting their temperance activism overshadow or obscure what he described as the church's true mission. In his first years at the editor's desk, Fitzgerald followed the theologically conservative tone set by his predecessor, Summers, who had argued for the importance of conversion and the ineffectiveness of laws to combat liquor: "Laws, however salutary the precepts, and just and summarily executed the penalties, will not effect a radical cure. Society must be regenerated by the power of the Holy Ghost."[43] Fitzgerald called for other reformers to have patience and "let the Church do its own work in its own way." That way, he explained, was the indirect method of social reformation, saving individuals and stirring up a desire for moral laws in society: "When the Church shall have created a Christian conscience in the community, it will be an easy matter to embody its judgment on moral question in suitable civil statutes."[44] The southern Methodist church, Fitzgerald explained, was not only "the divinely-appointed agency for the salvation of men" but also "adequate to its purpose. When Christians forget this, and direct their time, their enthusiasm, and their money into other channels, they sacrifice the higher for the lower, the stronger for the weaker, the divine for the human."[45]

While warning the church to concentrate more on individual salvation, Fitzgerald claimed for himself and other church spokesmen the right to comment when civil and political issues were particularly moral in nature.[46] Specifically, Fitzgerald supported temperance activism, gradually taking stronger and stronger stands in the *Christian Advocate* on the need for individual church members to take an active interest in the campaigns. Justifying his and the paper's entry into politics and attempting to head off criticism, Fitzgerald explained, "As long as the protest against this murderous work [alcohol sale] expressed itself only in praying, preaching, weeping, and passing condemnatory resolutions, the Whisky Devil laughed. Moral suasion, though a good thing, did not succeed in persuading him to spare an outraged and suffering humanity."[47] Writing a religious and political reflection on the Fourth of July 1886, he called Tennessee Methodists to action for an upcoming election that would determine the fate of the proposed state Prohibition amendment. Arguing that "Christian citizens cannot sit in cushioned pews and sing of heaven, and leave it to others to grapple with the deadly evils that threaten the destruction of social order and the moral life of the nation," Fitzgerald reminded his churchly readers of their responsibility to act in the world. [48]

The cause of temperance and social morality drew Tennessee's religious editors into a clear enunciation of the concept of Christian citizenship. An unsigned editorial in the *Memphis Baptist* explained that

> members of churches hold important relations to government as citizens, and these relations create certain political and civil obligations and duties. While a Christian man looks to the good order, purity, and integrity of his church, he is equally bound to look to the good order, purity and moral healthfulness of the society in which he lives. The State has claims upon him which he cannot rightfully ignore. In his political sphere he is a law-maker, and he is responsible to God and to conscience for the laws he makes.
>
> It is in view of these facts that we urge the Baptists of Tennessee, as good, Christian citizens, to put themselves on record as the friends and supporters of the proposed Local Option Law. [49]

The immediate purpose of the editorial was to encourage readers to support a local-option law to be proposed during the upcoming legislative session. The more lasting implications would be felt in the coming decades as many Tennessee Evangelicals endorsed Christian citizens' duty to employ legislation for supposedly moral ends—requiring Bible reading and banning the teaching of evolution in the state's schools.

From Preachers in Politics to Political Preachers

Although Tennessee's Baptists and Methodists remained internally divided over the proper limits of religious participation in politics, by 1887 the two denominations had nonetheless come a long way toward a broader embrace of southern society and were becoming increasingly militant in asserting their place not just in its culture but in its governance as well. In that year, Tennessee's evangelical leaders organized to support a constitutional Prohibition referendum, forcing them to adopt political methods to achieve what they saw as the moral imperative of drying up the state. The 1887 amendment campaigns failed, and the backlash from those efforts combined with other disturbances surrounding the 1890 gubernatorial election to force teetotaling Evangelicals to work through internal denominational dissension, ultimately clearing the way for more united Prohibition campaigns after the turn of the century.

Under pressure from the Tennessee Temperance Alliance, the state's General Assembly passed resolutions in 1885 and 1887 calling for a statewide vote on an amendment to the state constitution that stated, "No person shall sell, or keep for sale as a beverage any intoxicating liquors whatever." Having succeeded in getting the question onto the ballot, the civil and religious organizations that comprised the Tennessee Temperance Alliance mounted massive campaigns urging Prohibition supporters to turn out to vote for the measure.[50] Tennessee's Baptist and Methodist newspapers moved beyond moral suasion and calls for individual abstinence to adopt a political tone as the special election neared. The *Nashville Baptist and Reflector* called for divine sanctions against its opponents, predicting that "the man who refuses to vote, or the man who votes for the vile traffic with its fruits, will have the curse of God upon him and his family while his generations bear his name." In addition to moral arguments for Prohibition, the Methodist paper read like an old-time political manager in the weeks leading up to the election, calling on readers to take up face-to-face canvassing of voters and to beware of political tricks by antiprohibitionists.[51]

But when the votes were tallied, the prohibitionists lost. In an unusually large turnout, the people voted 145,000 to 118,000 against Prohibition. The Tennessee Annual Conference of the Methodist Episcopal Church, South, explained away the vote as "a temporary and trifling defeat at which we are in nowise surprised" and reminded members that "victory is assured to the right, and every step in the battle is a triumph, however else named by the world." In this explanation, electoral defeat of the Prohibition amendment "was a splendid triumph" and "a necessary step in the education and crystallization of a sentiment of tireless and ceaseless opposition to the saloon iniquity."[52] Fitzgerald echoed this sentiment, claiming to celebrate defeat because the strong showing by the prohibitionists showed the saloon forces that their days were numbered. The Tennessee Baptist Convention reacted similarly at its annual session in Jonesboro just after the election, noting the defeat but calling on Baptists to continue their agitation for personal temperance, the continuation and extension of the Four Mile Law, and the enactment of local-option laws that would encompass incorporated towns and cities.[53]

The 1887 campaigns caused some dissent within the churches about their too explicit involvement in politics and opened the door for critics both within and outside of official church circles. Proliquor attorney and Democratic politician John J. Vertrees mounted an impressive campaign to discredit the prohibitionists, marshalling political, racial, and gendered arguments to support his case. The Prohibition effort, he warned, might be led by "true prohibitionists and political Methodist priests" marching under "banners . . . blazoned with the legend of God," but they were only fronts for "the Republican, the ambitious place hunter, the woman's rights shrieker, the fanatic, and the independent."[54] In

addition to appeals to Democratic (white-solidarity) loyalty, the antiprohibitionists dredged up old sectional animosities. Reminding readers of the supposed
connections of Prohibition with abolition, opponents suggested a connection
with the other products of northern radicalism and attempted to make Prohibition guilty by association with "free loveism, woman's suffrage, infidelity,
etc."[55] Vertrees criticized the political actions of Methodists Fitzgerald, Warren
Candler, and Kelley, asking rhetorically, "Shall religion control politics? Shall
the political preacher hereafter be a factor in the politics of Tennessee?"[56]

In the wake of their 1887 referendum defeat, Prohibition advocates found
themselves under attack not just from liquor mouthpieces such as Vertrees but
from some less expected sources as well. David Lipscomb, editor of the Church
of Christ's Nashville-based journal, the *Gospel Advocate,* suggested that "where
the preachers and women most fully took charge of the canvass, the defeat has
been most decided." Lipscomb's charges must be taken with some caution, but
it is important to note that he was not arguing in favor of alcohol as much as he
was making a point that using civil authority "to enforce morality and religion is
a crime against God and man, and embodies all the elements of religion by law;
which is persecution for religious opinion."[57] Both Lipscomb's Christians and
the southern Presbyterians had been cautious in the campaigns leading up to
the 1887 referendum, declining to engage political power, even for supposedly
moral ends. Lipscomb was indeed interested in the importance of individual
responsibility in morality and conversion, practiced total abstinence himself,
and argued that alcohol users did not belong in the church, but he nonetheless
refused to endorse the prohibitory campaigns. Christian churches, even more
than their Baptist cousins, practiced congregational autonomy. A number of
local churches apparently supported Prohibition, but Lipscomb's refusal to let
the *Gospel Advocate* become a Prohibition organ left the churches without a
strong voice in favor of Prohibition.[58]

Answering the charges of Lipscomb, Vertrees, and others that prohibitionists
were advocating an unholy "union of church and state," religious advocates of
banning alcohol attempted to justify their political actions. In warning about
the "solidarity of evil parties" against morality and good government, Fitzgerald
attempted to refocus the arguments over a union of church and state. "Let no
man say we advocate a union of Church and State. We abhor such an unholy
marriage; but we more vehemently, if possible, protest against a divorcement of
the State and moral principle. We reject political atheism as we do any and all
other forms of atheism. We do not ask that Christianity be established by law, but
we demand that it shall not be defeated by law." Elaborating on this argument,
Candler clothed the religious prohibitionists' arguments with a powerful histor-

ical mantle, explaining that in their position on the necessity of moral legislation, he and Fitzgerald were "strictly in line with the founders of our government."[59]

Other than charges that the prohibitionists were advocating a "union of church and state," the most damning accusation Vertrees and other political antiprohibitionists could muster was that the Temperance Alliance threatened the ruling Democratic Party. In the mostly one-party post-Reconstruction South, white loyalty to the Democratic Party involved multiple layers of allegiance not just to party but to race, region, and even manhood as well. As historian Paul Harvey notes, southern white Baptist ministers played an important role in shoring up Democratic rule in the 1860s and 1870s by preaching "the political ideology of white supremacy from the pulpit." They clothed the "redeeming" Democratic Party with the fabric of moral and racial purity that would retain a strong hold on the postbellum South.[60] So when Tennessee Democrats became clear opponents of Prohibition, denominational leaders had to carefully word their attacks on alcohol.

Recognizing the political and social power of the Democratic Party, Prohibition advocates were reticent to tie their moral campaign to an opposing party and desired instead to work within the existing party structure to secure their goal. In frequently admonishing church members not to vote blindly for a party but to vote their consciences on moral issues, state Baptist and Methodist leaders were not attempting to overthrow the Democratic Party but rather to force it to adopt their Prohibition program. But Tennessee was also a politically divided state, with considerable Republican strength in the east and in some larger cities. The 1887 referendum had shown East Tennessee Republicans' tendency to vote more heavily in favor of Prohibition, foreshadowing the possibility of a political revolt if the prohibitionists took a more partisan approach. Former Tennessee Supreme Court justice T. J. Freeman, himself a strong proponent of Prohibition, warned Democrats not to identify themselves too closely with liquor, prophesying that Vertrees's efforts to save liquor by linking it to the Democratic Party would eventually lead to the party's defeat, along with that of alcohol. The moral issue, Freeman explained, was more powerful than the political, and the "Christian element of the state" would rather bolt the party than associate with alcohol-peddling sinners.[61]

The powerful pull of party loyalty came into sharp relief in Tennessee in 1890, when Methodist clergyman David Kelley put his moral crusade squarely into politics by running as the Prohibition Party candidate for governor. Though easily defeated at the polls, the resounding debates inside the churches and in the larger public arena forced state religious leaders and editors into a new round of justifying political action for moral ends. The Prohibition Party never really threatened Democratic Party loyalty, but the 1890 election provided a model for a future electoral defection that would eventually split the Democratic Party and sweep Baptist, prohibitionist, and Republican Governor Benjamin W. Hooper into office in the early twentieth century.

Kelley had been active in promoting efforts at legal Prohibition as early as 1872 and accepted the Prohibition Party's 1890 gubernatorial nomination. With neither of the major parties coming out strongly for Prohibition, Kelley received the endorsement and campaign support of the Nashville-based Prohibition paper, the *Issue*. As a regular minister of the southern Methodist church, Kelley attempted to receive the consent of his supervising bishop before leaving his pastoral duties at Gallatin. Stating that he believed his acceptance of the nomination "was the highest service [he] could render the kingdom of God," Kelley asked Bishop J. C. Keener for permission to run; if denied authorization, Kelley asked for a statement of explanation for the refusal. Keener replied ambiguously, telling Kelley that he could not both minister and campaign but apparently leaving the choice to Kelley. The presiding elder, Benjamin F. Haynes, an ardent prohibitionist, counseled Kelley not to give up the nomination, fearing that the antiliquor press would assume from the action that the Methodist church did not favor Prohibition. [62]

Kelley secured a retired minister to fill in at his church and canvassed the state in favor of the Prohibition Party. Although he led the party to its highest level of support ever in Tennessee, Kelley garnered only 11,000 votes statewide, less than 10 percent of successful Farmers Alliance–Democrat John P. Buchanan's tally of 113,000 votes. To add insult to the injury of electoral defeat, Bishop Robert Hargrove, who presided over the Tennessee Conference that year, had Kelley charged with deserting his station and suspended from the ministry for six months, despite the fact that the majority of the members of the Tennessee Conference supported Kelley and his Prohibition cause. Several other tensions were swirling among Tennessee Methodists at the time, but at least some of the reason for Kelley's censure was his open engagement in politics and his break with the Democratic Party. [63]

Tennessee Baptists were similarly stirred by the 1890 political campaign, creating controversy within the denomination when the annual convention put itself on record in favor of "the absolute prohibition of the manufacture and sale of intoxicating drinks." The opposition to alcohol was less controversial than the perception by some of the delegates that the resolution, though not stating so explicitly, was an endorsement of the Prohibition Party and Kelley as its candidate for governor. [64] Beyond any concerns about disloyalty to the Democratic Party, the discussions at the convention and thereafter in the *Nashville Baptist and Reflector* concerned the proper level of political action in pursuit of moral aims. S. E. Jones, a longtime Murfreesboro pastor and a conservative social and theological anchor for Tennessee Baptists, waged verbal war on the convention floor and in the press against Baptist entanglement in politics. The only real cure for intemperance, Jones argued, was not political action but "the constant, persistent, and never ceasing business of preaching repentance toward God and faith toward our Lord Jesus Christ." George Lofton, pastor of Nashville's Central Baptist Church, countered Jones's conservative stance, arguing that "It would be a crime against Christianity and the nineteenth century for a Baptist Convention under the present circumstances to be silent upon the great issue of the age—prohibition."[65]

Jones and Lofton continued their controversy through several issues of the *Baptist and Reflector,* at many times merely talking past each other but nevertheless laying out the parameters for Baptist political involvement that would shape denominational actions for the coming decades. Jones maintained the primacy of individual conversion as the only true purpose for church activity, while Lofton argued that the church had an interest in present social conditions, at least as far as Prohibition was concerned. Both preachers as well as Folk, the paper's Prohibition-promoting editor, criticized Kelley's action of leaving his pastorate for active political office, warning that "his action tended to lower the pulpit in the eyes of the world." But short of entering politics directly, Lofton argued, the church should do everything in its power to fight the saloon: "Passing a resolution in a Baptist Convention, or in a Baptist church, for moral effect against a great moral evil is not dabbling in politics." Instead, Lofton suggested, such actions showed Baptist concern for the "general welfare of humanity and religion."[66]

In the decade and a half that followed, Tennessee Baptist and Methodist newspapers waged an unrelenting war against the saloons while constantly and consciously assuring readers that the effort represented a moral campaign rather than partisan politics. With Tennessee and southern politics in general disrupted by the challenges of third-party politics, the editors feared that attaching the church to any one party would harm its moral voice. A minister was supposed to be "God's messenger to all . . . parties"; if not careful, a minister could find himself "committed to a course of action incompatible with his obligations to the Church of God, and calculated to embarrass and weaken him in the discharge of his sacred functions."[67] Though they attempted to remain nonpartisan, the minister-leaders of Tennessee's Prohibition movement had to adopt political means to achieve their goals. While professing that the *Christian Advocate* had "consistently and uniformly opposed the partisan method of dealing with the liquor problem," Hoss warned legislators that he was watching and intended to publish a record of how each party and member voted on Prohibition issues. Explaining that "the time has passed when mere sentiment has any value" and "what is needed are votes at the ballot box," Hoss, along with the *Nashville Baptist and Reflector*'s Folk and James I. Vance, a prominent Presbyterian minister in Nashville, became the guiding forces and most powerful publicists for the Local Option League (after 1899 affiliated as a state branch of the Anti-Saloon League) in the campaign against alcohol. Conscious of their potential political strength, individual churches urged politicians to heed the calls to abolish saloons. The 1901 Tennessee Baptist Convention resolved that "we, the representatives of the 135,000 white Baptists in Tennessee, . . . hereby record our determination not to vote for any man of any party for any office who is known to be or supposed to be in sympathy with the saloon. *The saloon must go!* Down with the saloon!"[68]

The Prohibition campaigns picked up speed in the new century, and although some Tennessee Evangelicals continued to worry about becoming too involved in politics, the majority of the denominational leaders and many church members strongly favored banishing alcohol through whatever means proved necessary. Responding to one of many criticisms in antiprohibition papers about political preaching, Folk of the *Nashville Baptist and Reflector* wrote, "If it be said that the preacher has no business in politics, we reply: It is the business of the preacher to fight the devil. The devil is in the saloon. The saloon is in politics. And so it becomes the business of the preacher to go into politics." In Folk's recounting of history, preachers had, by proclaiming their desire to avoid politics, allowed saloons to prosper.[69] Marching at the head of the Anti-Saloon League, Tennessee Baptists and Methodists fought back, leading the charge for Prohibition from the pulpit, in the press, and even at the polls.

The campaigns for statewide Prohibition finally succeeded in 1909 when the General Assembly overrode Democratic Governor Malcolm Patterson's veto to pass a measure extending the Four Mile Law to encompass the entire state. As for the lingering pull of Democratic loyalty, Freeman's prediction in the wake of the 1887 referendum defeat proved prescient, for the ultimate statewide Prohibition victory was accomplished through the split of the party. The 1908 shooting death of Edward W. Carmack, vituperative editor of the *Nashville Tennessean* and the recently defeated Prohibition-favoring Democratic gubernatorial candidate, on the streets of Nashville by prominent advisers to the victorious "wet" Governor Patterson galvanized the temperance forces and sundered the Democratic Party.

Reminding readers that "Senator Carmack has died the death of a martyr to the cause of civic righteousness and public sobriety," editor George Winton of the *Nashville Christian Advocate* predicted that "prohibition, the choicest flower in our public life, will spring from his grave and give fragrance and beauty to this fair state of the South."[70] After Patterson not only vetoed the statewide Prohibition laws presented to him by the legislature (which easily overrode the vetoes) but also pardoned Carmack's killer (a political crony of Patterson), the Democratic Party split wide open. With two Democratic factions running candidates for governor, Republican prohibitionist and Baptist layman Benjamin Wade Hooper won election in 1910 with the support of many Evangelicals.[71] The Prohibition battles called Evangelicals out of their churches into the public sphere, forcing them to articulate not just their right but now their duty to act for the preservation of the church and the state.

Prohibition and Public Education

In their crusades against alcohol, Tennessee Baptists and Methodists took a more active role in social and political affairs, awakening to their own political power and responsibility not just to save individual sinners but also to work to eradicate temptations to sin. This active interest in society also played out in evangelical battles over the content and control of public education, but the temperance and Prohibition campaigns were particularly closely linked to education. In spite of educational historian Andrew Holt's erroneous assumptions that "the dominant political issue in the decade 1903-1913 was prohibition" and that "education was not intimately involved in the issue," the two in fact went hand in hand, not just in that decade but at least as far back as 1877. The Four Mile Law, which eventually extended Prohibition across the state, turned the struggle into a "contest between the school and saloon" as Tennesseans were forced to choose which institution their community valued more.[72] Tennesseans also saw education as a means of teaching a whole new generation the lessons of health, sobriety, and morality. Furthermore, Evangelicals rehearsed many of the arguments they would adopt in their struggles to control the public schools in their battles against alcohol. As in their arguments regarding the Bible in public schools, evangelical prohibitionists endorsed "home rule" and "local control" as long as it was expedient but abandoned such arguments in favor of "majority rule" to overcome localism that supported alcohol.

It may have been nothing more than a constitutional or legal accident that the Four Mile Law became the preferred method for driving saloons out of Tennessee, but the measure inextricably linked saloons and schoolhouses. The schoolhouse became a vaccine, clearing out an alcohol-free zone eight miles in diameter. As Fairbanks, the original bill's chief proponent, remarked a quarter century after its passage, "this law has been of wide influence and is said to be the best temperance measure ever put in force, . . . and is an inducement to build and sustain schools."[73] But as the schoolhouse became the tool for removing the saloon, some antiprohibitionists struck back. Citizens of Lebanon quickly erected new schools "in order to prevent the sale of liquor, under what is known as the 'four-mile law' " but complained when four of those schoolhouses "were wantonly fired and destroyed by incendiaries," presumably intent on restoring alcohol to the Middle Tennessee town.[74] After Hooper's 1910 election, D. L. Cougar of Fayetteville sent the new governor a postcard boasting of the "Progress of Education in Lincoln Co., since Prohibition in Tennessee." Carrying an explanation that the buildings pictured were within one-half mile of the town of Mimosa, Tennessee, the postcard contained images of an abandoned distillery, an abandoned one-room schoolhouse, and a brand-new consolidated school building. Congratulating the governor on his support for both education and Prohibition, Cougar wrote on the card, "here is a practical demonstration of the workings of prohibition in the country in Old Lincoln Co."[75]

Thus, the school and the whiskey trade became diametrically opposed, and neither could flourish in the other's presence. But rather than using only the physical existence of the school as a tool, prohibitionists also sought to use the curriculum to inoculate the rising generation against alcohol through lessons on its physical and moral ill effects. As early as 1872, the Washington County schools were "carrying on extensive temperance programs." Middle Tennessee's southern Methodists proclaimed that the "greatest hope for the final overthrow of the saloon and whisky power" was the "education and Christian enlightenment of the people," not just "through the pulpit [and] press" but also through the "schools of our country." West Tennessee Baptists called on state lawmakers to require schools to teach students about the "hygenic [*sic*] effects of alcohol upon the human system." Their entreaties were not in vain, and in 1895 the Tennessee General Assembly passed a law requiring that "physiology and hygiene, with a special reference to the nature of alcoholic drinks and narcotics, and smoking cigarettes, and their effects upon the human system, shall . . . be made a regular course of study for all pupils in all schools supported entirely or in part by public money."[76]

Tennessee Evangelicals saw the public schools as an important training ground for the state's future citizens and church members and thus took a great interest in the content and control of what those schools taught. In 1912, after Prohibition had been extended statewide but before difficulties regarding enforcement in some larger cities had been resolved, Governor Hooper instructed the state superintendent of public instruction, J. W. Brister, to ensure that city school districts were observing the requirement to teach temperance.

The difficulty of adequately enforcing Prohibition and of changing adults' behavior inspired the governor and prohibitionists to turn their attention back to the schools.[77] It is probably not purely coincidental that this renewed interest in school temperance lessons coincided with the increased pressure for and subsequent passage of the Daily Bible Reading Law of 1915 (see chapter 5). In fact, the leadership and strategies of both movements—pro–Bible reading and antidrinking—often overlapped.

Although they would eventually resort to majoritarian arguments in the twentieth century, most nineteenth-century Tennessee Evangelicals advocated "home rule" and "local option" in matters of community control over alcohol. Billing alcohol and liquor interests as outsiders, these religious leaders assumed that most if not all communities would vote to ban alcohol. In the fall of 1885, only a few months after he had reiterated his argument for home rule with regard to the use of the Bible in the public schools, Fitzgerald used the same terms and reasoning as they applied to alcohol: "Local Option in Georgia and the Four-mile law in Tennessee recognize the same sound principle—home rule." Part of the home rule compromise in control of public education had assumed that parents would provide a nurturing environment in the home, supplementing the nonsectarian instruction of the public school and teaching children morality and religion. One of the prohibitionists' chief arguments pointed to the disastrous effects of alcohol on that home life and the breaking down not just of the individual family but also of the church's and state's future hope in that child. If homes were to bear up under the weighty burdens Fitzgerald and other Tennessee Evangelicals assigned in the late nineteenth century, prohibitionists believed that families needed to be protected from the disastrous effects of alcohol.[78]

Evangelical leaders temporarily abandoned the local-control policy in the 1887 campaigns for constitutional Prohibition but continually returned to that argument. After the 1887 defeat, when it became obvious that the majority of the state's voters—a disproportionate number of them city dwellers—opposed Prohibition, Tennessee Evangelicals and antidrink advocates turned back to securing local-option legislation that would result in Prohibition in most parts of the state. After the 1909 changes had extended the Four Mile Law to cover all of Tennessee except for four cities, evangelical prohibitionists again turned to arguments of majority rule. Addressing legislators, Methodist R. N. Price wrote, "Local option is too local and too optional. It recognizes the right of bad citizens to say, by vote, whether an immoral and demoralizing institution shall be set up and maintained in the community." What was needed, he explained, was legislation to allow the "better citizens of the State to banish saloons from the entire territory of the State."[79] Sam Jones had attempted this kind of argument in the 1887 campaign for constitutional Prohibition, saying that in the cause of Prohibition, the religious majority should speak out so that the "*vox populi* was, indeed, *vox dei.*"[80]

Tennessee's evangelical prohibitionists also sought to privilege their voices within any majority. Price and other Evangelicals had definite ideas about who exactly comprised the "better citizens of the state." Methodists and Baptists often reminded their readers that the American "government and the civilization it has produced and fostered was founded, and has been maintained, under the auspices of Christianity, based upon a Christian Bible and a Christian Sabbath."[81] This same Christian nation/majority rule argument would play a prominent role in twentieth-century evangelical efforts to require daily Bible reading and ban the teaching of evolution in Tennessee public schools.

Tennessee Methodists' and Baptists' growing concern about the effects of alcohol on individuals, families, and the larger society demonstrates an interest first in the soul of the individual but also a growing recognition of the interdependence of individuals and society. "Prohibitory laws," the Tennessee Baptist Convention proclaimed, "are for the protection of society or the social system. It is the duty of civil government to protect the innocent and helpless against the vicious." But to get the laws passed and enforced, Evangelicals recognized the need "to strengthen the sense of the personal responsibility of each citizen for every other citizen's well-being and well-doing."[82] Swept into the governor's office on a platform of Prohibition enforcement, Hooper encapsulated these views of the modern interdependent society in his first legislative address of 1911. Arguing that "the individual citizen of Tennessee is a member of a complex social organization, and, as such, sustains relations to millions of individuals," Hooper proclaimed that "the State has a right to restrain him" in "the drinking of any liquor . . . not for the petty purpose of tyrannizing over him, but for the great and righteous purpose of protecting society."[83]

In the late nineteenth century, when Methodists and Baptists clearly constituted the majority of Tennessee's population, they forsook their dissenter heritage to embrace a vision of society more akin to the Anglicanism their British and southern evangelical ancestors had fought to overcome. As Professor George Broadman Eager of the Southern Baptist Theological Seminary suggested at the time, Baptists had come to recognize the new realities of society: "The problem of life used to be the problem of the individual; now it is the problem of society in its organized form. One hundred years ago the family was the little world; now the world is fast becoming one vast family and government is paternal."[84] The duty of the churches in such a new environment would be not only to maintain their relevance for individuals and families but also to spread their influence over and even through the growing and paternal government of the New South. Such an expanded conception of the evangelical churches promised to expand Tennessee Baptists' and Methodists' social vision to ameliorate some unpleasant social conditions stemming from southern industrialization, such as poverty, child labor, and orphanhood. Rarely, if ever, however, could Tennessee Evangelicals progress beyond managing the symptoms to diagnosing the social, racial, economic, and political causes of southern problems. Democratic religious denominations such as Baptists and Methodists remained social captives, unable to move far beyond their base if they hoped to retain and continue to gain membership and support. In fact, evangelical support for prohibitory liquor laws and the resulting social and political tumult associated with passing and enforcing such legislation may have warned white southern religious leaders about the dangers of challenging other social conditions.

Nevertheless, the Evangelicals' involvement in Prohibition campaigns and the resultant backlash forced Methodists and Baptists to justify their involvement in a particular political question and to explain their growing understanding of a social mission for their churches. The explanation was worked out in many forums but perhaps found its best voice in the white southern Methodist Memphis Annual Conference's 1922 temperance report:

> We must make it plain that Christ has outlined the spirit in which all matters pertaining to social life can be adjusted and this spirit must first begin in the home and in the school life. Christ came to create a new earth where righteousness would dwell. His aim was health—whole bodies, whole minds, a complete manhood.
>
> Christ was also the transformer of social conditions, the founder of a divine social order. He proclaimed a new era of justice and kindness in which men should live together. He sought to change society by transforming individuals and creating a society of love. This process works from within, out upon a world. His aim was a world of new men. Along with the saving of our lives we must seek to transform social conditions which destroy men's lives. We must look also into social institutions to detect sources of selfishness. We must keep our eyes upon our schools to see that no erroneous ideas poison the minds of our youth. [85]

Despite maintaining the centrality of the individual conversion and the supremacy of divine authority, the report's authors clearly believed in the church's responsibility to act not just in the world but on it and not just on individuals but on the societies in which they lived.

Such clear articulations about the need to reform society became intricately linked to evangelical efforts to supervise public school education. An important legacy of the late-nineteenth- and early-twentieth-century evangelical moral campaigns lay not just in their provision of a view of the larger society but also in their giving Methodists and Baptists experience in using a coercive paternalist state to impose their religious behavioral standards on a broader culture. If Prohibition, divorce, Sunday-closing, antismoking, and motion picture laws were attempts to curb behavior, it did not take religious leaders long to recognize the importance of controlling the education of Tennessee's youths. Prohibition laws were imperfect restrictions on the behavior of adults. Moral training in the home and school—especially if it supplemented the Bible with lessons on the physical dangers of intemperance—would raise a new generation of Tennesseans to lead both church and state and to recapture the moral supremacy of southern society. But this topic would remain a source of tension within and among evangelical denominations: What was the proper balance between reforming social conditions and converting individuals? The question few Tennesseans paused to ask was whether, in their efforts to enforce religious temperance on the larger society by law, they were settling for an appearance of morality in place of a genuinely converted church, state, and region.

5. Legislating Religion into the Schools

Evangelicals and Public Education, 1900–1925

Writing in the early 1920s, southern Methodist educator Lester Weaver reminded readers of the *Nashville Christian Advocate* of the importance of an educated and religious citizenry. He was, in part, reacting to the recent great European war, arguing that the Allies, with the help of the United States, had won because God was on their side. According to Weaver's analysis, God had frowned on atheistic, warlike, and materialistic Germany while smiling on the morally and religiously pure Americans. But if such divine favor were to continue, Weaver warned, religious Americans would need to redouble their efforts to instill religion and morality in the rising generation. The southern church, he asserted, faced an important choice, either "educating or vacating her place as a controlling influence of society."[1]

Tennessee at the end of World War I was very different than it had been at the end of the Civil War. First, the state was on the winning side, congratulating itself that it had prevailed in a cause that was deserving of God's favor. But despite their recent martial victory, religious Tennesseans were uneasy about the future. In the vanquished Germany, their recent adversary, they saw many similarities to American Progressive-era campaigns for education, efficiency, and scientific culture. The German school system had been the envy of many American educators at the end of the nineteenth century and had even been applauded by some churchmen for spreading literacy and light. Much of the German educational bureaucracy had been copied in the United States as a whole and, to a limited extent, in Tennessee as well.

The problem with German education, many white Tennessee religious leaders argued after the war, was that it was at best only a partial education and at worst the definitive cause of German militarism, atheism, and aggression. German schools were run by the state and banished religious instruction from the primary grades through the much-vaunted universities. The lack of religion in education had left ordinary Germans unable to distinguish right from wrong and incapable of resisting the emperor's aggression. To avoid a similar fate, Weaver and other ministers warned, the United States must ensure that the next generation would be trained in religion and morality. Americans should learn from German mistakes and protect schools and students from materialism and atheism.[2]

Tennessee evangelical leaders praised the faithfulness of the state's citizens while offering jeremiads about the future should the church fail in its duty to preserve society through proper education. In the first decade of the twentieth century, evangelical leaders supported an expansion of public education, pushing for religious teachers for the public schools, faithful parents in the home, growing Sunday school programs, and strong denominational colleges as the sure guarantees of religion in education and a religious society in the years to come. In the campaigns to strengthen the schools, however, religious leaders unintentionally weakened informal sources of education (home and church) by aiding the institutionalization of the public schools and the state. Confronted with an increasingly centralized school bureaucracy and growing evidence of the decline of supplemental sources of religious education, Tennessee evangelical leaders pushed for a more explicit respect for Christianity in the state schools. Disregarding constitutional protections of minority beliefs, outspoken evangelical leaders marched under a banner of a righteous majority fighting to preserve a Christian nation. No longer willing to leave questions about the role of religion in public education to the whims of individual communities, many Tennessee Evangelicals proposed, lobbied for, and eventually enacted laws requiring school to be opened each day with selections from the Bible and forbidding the teaching of evolution in the state schools.

Public Education under the Home Rule Compromise

Tennessee evangelical leaders of the 1860s and 1870s had originally distrusted public education, labeling state-funded institutions "godless schools" and warning parents of the dangers of sending their children out of the home to be educated. By the close of the nineteenth century, however, most state religious leaders not only had curbed their criticism but in fact had become avid supporters of the common-school movement. This religious accommodation of public schooling was possible in general because of the evangelical Protestants' broad endorsement of literacy as a key to an individual's ability to read the Bible, believe, and achieve salvation. But in more specific terms, Tennessee

Evangelicals came to accept public elementary schools through what Methodist editor and public education advocate Oscar P. Fitzgerald termed the home rule principle.[3] Protestant parents and leaders should endorse, aid, and supervise the public elementary schools; under the watchful eyes of religious parents, teachers, and local school directors, the schools would reflect the values and religion of Tennessee's local—presumably Protestant—communities.

Most church leaders agreed that the public schools could not and perhaps should not teach denominationally specific religion, but their nonsectarian instruction could be supplemented by parents in the home, by the church in the Sunday school, and by denominational colleges if children continued their education. But this by no means meant that the public schools were to be atheistic or antireligious. Despite occasional protests, most Tennessee Methodists and Baptists favored the public schools as natural extensions of the churches' educational mission and worked to include religious and sometimes even denominational instruction wherever and whenever it was possible to do so without raising objections from other denominations or non-Protestants. Evangelical leaders secured positions as school administrators, pushed the importance of placing Christian teachers in the public schools, and urged local ministers and school patrons to use every opportunity to spread the Gospel through the state schools.

Preachers and prominent laymen of most denominations secured positions as school officials throughout the state. Often building on their status as some of the more educated members of rural communities or as some of the most interested members of a better-educated public, many Tennessee ministers worked as local school directors, members of county boards of education, and even as the state superintendent of public instruction, the highest administrative position in the state's school system. Such positions were not reserved solely for the traditionally better-educated denominations, although the late nineteenth century had seen a progression of Presbyterian and Episcopal administrators.[4] While disclaiming any desire "to enter into politics at all, or [to cast] any reflection on the other candidates," Baptist editor Edgar E. Folk openly suggested the appointment of Southwestern Baptist University professor and president G. W. Jarman to the state's highest school post in 1891. To Folk's chagrin but probably to Southwestern Baptist's advantage, Jarman did not get the job, although Governor Benton McMillin appointed a Baptist layman, Morgan Fitzpatrick, as state superintendent of schools in 1899.[5] J. W. Brister, a Methodist layman, led the state's public schools in the first decades of the twentieth century, assisting in the statewide campaigns to improve the schools while serving as treasurer of the Methodists' Twentieth Century Educational Fund, raising money and taking an active interest in the Nashville Sunday school movement.[6] More typically, state religious journals noted the appointment of evangelical laymen to head city or county school districts.[7]

Both Baptists and Methodists believed that ensuring that the public schools were properly staffed was even more important than securing jobs for ministers or laymen as school officials. Given the decentralized nature of public schools in the 1890s, Evangelicals recognized that "after everything has been said and done, the truth still remains that the great thing in the school is the teacher himself"; therefore, they needed to concentrate on getting Christian teachers into the schools. State Superintendent James Killebrew agreed with the arguments for Christian teachers, calling in 1873 for instructors who could be nonsectarian yet not irreligious. "The remedy" to fears of secular education, all commentators seemed to agree, lay "in conscientious Christian teachers" who would set a moral example for students and strive to educate both intellect and morality.[8]

Denominational leaders argued that hiring Baptists or Methodists as teachers in the local public schools could help the churches in two ways. First, the presence of well-trained teachers would directly aid in the organization and instruction of the local Sunday schools—a Baptist teacher hired for the weekday school could be a volunteer teacher in the Sunday school. Second, Christian teachers would indirectly further the church's educational mission by inculcating a religious spirit into all public school lessons, thereby planting seeds to be nurtured at home, in church, and in Sunday school.[9]

Some ministers urged an even more direct relationship between Tennessee's churches and public schools. While admitting that the teachers probably should not teach denominationally specific religion, Folk argued that "there is still the need and privilege of religious leaders to lend some support and even direction to . . . the public school system." He noted that a preacher had many opportunities to speak to students during school time: "he may read the Scriptures, make a short address and lead in prayer. He thus can secure a religious contact with the children with propriety."[10] Several rural Baptist ministers reported their success in preaching in the public schools: J. W. Storer from Paris, Tennessee, wrote to the *Nashville Baptist and Reflector* that he had led revival services in the Henry County high school twice a day for a week, speaking for forty-five minutes in the morning and thirty minutes at the end of the school day. He concluded his report by charging his fellow ministers to do likewise: "If any of the brethren over the State can find a High School which will open its doors to a meeting of this kind, by all means make the most of it."[11] Baptists and Methodists utilized any opportunity to inject explicit religious teaching into the public schools, with only occasional dissenting voices from within or outside of the denominations. By the end of the nineteenth century, most Tennessee

Evangelicals had accepted the public elementary school not only as a necessary state intrusion into what they believed should be the province of the church but also as a powerful ally in the churches' mission to evangelize the state, region, and world.

The Unintended Consequences of School Reform

In February 1915, educator Greer Peoples addressed a crowd of fellow Methodists on the relationship between churches and the public schools. Observing that "the public school is with us and is going to stay for generations and centuries to come," Peoples concluded that "therefore it is necessary for us of the Church, who have to deal with people from the cradle to the grave, to interest ourselves in the work of the public school." His was not a new or novel opinion in Methodist or Baptist circles: state religious leaders and prominent laymen had accepted and even endorsed public elementary schools since the 1880s. But the first two decades of the twentieth century saw an increased involvement of Tennessee Evangelicals with the public schools. By the time of Peoples's 1915 address, public elementary schools had been transformed from decentralized, unstable, and possibly transitory to the expected source of primary education for the overwhelming majority of the state's children. The public school was no longer an experiment but would, as Peoples noted, "more and more mould the life of the people."[12]

Tennesseans were actively involved in the southwide educational revival of the early twentieth century and provided several leaders for the regional movement. The Conference for Education in the South, a regional movement that began in Capon Springs, West Virginia, in 1898 and met annually throughout the South (twice in Tennessee) until 1914, provided a clearinghouse for money and information, coordinating efforts in the various states. Comprising regional religious leaders, northern philanthropists, and school and social reform advocates, the conference originated out of a desire to improve black and rural education but quickly shifted its focus to a wider improvement of southern (especially white) public education as a whole. The conference established a bureau of information and research at Knoxville's University of Tennessee and provided funds for the annual Summer School of the South conducted on that campus to train current and prospective teachers in improved pedagogical methods.[13]

Tennessee school reformer and education historian Andrew David Holt refers to the first decade and a half of the twentieth century as the "campaign era" in Tennessee's educational history. Between 1903 and 1913, Holt argues, state and regional school reformers, aided by a generally improved economy and supported by contributions from the Southern Education Board, the executive arm of the annual Conference for Education in the South, aroused public and legislative interest in improving the public schools.[14] University of Tennessee professor and Southern Education Board Information Bureau chief Philander Priestly Claxton coordinated summer and fall educational campaigns throughout the state in an effort to stir up grassroots support for educational reform and to encourage present and prospective government officials to support the public schools. Scheduling educational rallies throughout the state, Claxton and State School Superintendent Seymour Mynders spoke in every Tennessee county at least once during the 1906 campaign. They would cancel classes for the day; invite local political officials and candidates to appear on the platform and explain their views on education; schedule bands, parades, pageants, and barbecue basket dinners; and arrange for special excursion trains and rates. Organizers increased attendance at the rallies by coordinating them with other meetings, such as farmers' institutes or county fairs, rounding out the day by presenting the crowd with a list of resolutions on school issues to be endorsed and forwarded to the next meeting of the state legislature.[15]

Claxton and the state superintendents did not discover the format of the school rallies by accident: similar public convocations had long been a staple of rural southern life. More than one observer noted that the rallies resembled religious revivals. Although this was a campaign for improved education, many members of the intended audience were poorly educated; reform leaders consequently could not depend on newspapers and written campaign materials to convey the message. Claxton, a native Tennessean and future U.S. commissioner of education, believed that rural southerners' experience with religious revivals would prepare them for the school rallies. As he explained in 1908, "the people in the Southern States were raised on camp meetings, and when they go and carry their dinner with them it is an offense to speak a half hour and dismiss them. . . . They have the power to sit and hear it, so that you can appeal to them morning and afternoon and they will remain."[16]

State religious leaders lent voice, pulpit, and press to aid the movement, joining in calls for more and better elementary schools, professionally trained teachers, increased state and local funding, more intelligent spending of school monies, and improved attendance. Rev. J. D. Hammond, editor of the "Education Notes" section of the *Nashville Christian Advocate,* offered his support of Mynders's 1906 school campaign, dubbing it a good idea, encouraging other states to start similar efforts, and urging school reformers to pay particular attention to the plight of Tennessee's rural schools. Middle Tennessee Methodist preacher Jeremiah Cullom took an even more active role in the school campaigns, attending school rallies and even bringing a wagonload of schoolchildren with him to a Williamson County gathering.[17] By the end of his 1906 school campaign, Superintendent Mynders remarked, "Education and public schools have been preached from the pulpit, the bar, the stump; at picnics, barbecues, circuit and county courts, school commencements, county fairs, race tracks and even at a wedding ceremony."[18]

Holt paid little attention to issues of religion in public education, although he did suggest that many private school patrons and teachers opposed the expansion of public schools. Holt dismissed such opposition as "selfish" and as stemming from a desire to protect private colleges from a potential loss of students to a strengthened state school system, but he did not pause to consider any ideological motivations for criticisms of the state university.[19] Some denominational college leaders, including President Millard D. Jeffries of the Baptists' Carson-Newman College, were indeed concerned about the increased funding for the University of Tennessee and the prospects of increased competition with the church schools.[20] Jeffries proved to be the exception; few Tennessee Baptists or Methodists—even those in charge of denominational colleges or proprietors of private preparatory schools—publicly opposed the campaigns to improve public elementary education. In fact, most Methodist and Baptist laymen, ministers, and college officials spoke at one time or another in favor of the public schools, while the denominational journals offered frequent editorial support for the school campaigns.

Editors of the Baptist and Methodist weekly papers generally favored the extension of public elementary education throughout the state. Fitzgerald had been actively involved in public education long before moving to Tennessee to take charge of the *Nashville Christian Advocate.* Under Fitzgerald's leadership, the paper came out forcefully in favor of public elementary schools as long as the state did not transgress the terms of the home rule compromise. Fitzgerald's advocacy was continued by his successors, former college president E. E. Hoss and George B. Winton, a missionary to Mexico and later a professor at Vanderbilt.[21] James R. Graves, the editor of the *Memphis Baptist,* enthusiastically supported Southwestern Baptist University and expanded education in general, while his successor, E. E. Folk, often lent his editorial voice in support of the public school movement. Under Folk's editorship, the *Nashville Baptist and Reflector* publicized the beginning of Mynders's 1903 school campaign, encouraged better attendance, and endorsed many of the aims of the school reformers.[22] Questioned about his use of the denominational press to support public education, Winton explained, "We make no apology for giving all this space to the question of public schools. Concerning education, temperance, and morality, the Methodist Church never needs to define her position or to defend her policy."[23]

Perhaps no Tennessee evangelical leader after Fitzgerald was a more forceful advocate of the public schools than was Rufus Weaver. In addition to his duties as pastor of Nashville's Immanuel Baptist Church from 1908 to 1917, adjunct professor of religious education at Vanderbilt 1913 to 1917, and member of the Sunday School Board of the Southern Baptist Convention from 1909 to 1918, Weaver served as secretary of Christian education for the Tennessee Baptist Convention and was an outspoken supporter of public elementary schools, especially those in rural areas. In the spring of 1917, Weaver authored several full-page articles on public education for the back cover of the *Nashville Baptist and Reflector*. He encouraged his fellow Baptists to take an interest in improving public schools because "the educational problem of this state is a Baptist problem." Reasoning first that "one-half of the people of this state are Baptists in fact or in sentiment" and then that the majority of the denomination were "a country people," Weaver begged his readers to call on their legislators to confront "the educational problem of the Baptists of Tennessee . . . the development of our rural schools."[24] In several other articles, Weaver provided maps of all of Tennessee's counties, detailing the school expenditures and session days in each and surmising that many of the thirty-nine "Baptist counties" (in which between 45 and 93.4 percent of the churched people were Baptists according to the 1906 federal census of religious bodies) were in the bottom rank of both categories.[25] Throughout his time in Tennessee, Weaver urged other Evangelicals to take an active interest in education, acting in denominational and public circles to stir up support for expanded opportunities at all levels. State evangelical leaders recognized that much of the churches' strength lay in the rural sections but that the rural churches were in trouble as country people moved to the cities for jobs and better school opportunities. Improving the rural schools would strengthen the rural churches, the denominations' bulwarks.[26]

In their support for the school reform campaigns, state denominational journals often emphasized one particular component of the reform plan: better teachers. This call offered religious leaders a way to improve the quality of instruction in the public schools while aiding denominational colleges and gaining greater indirect control over the public schools. The school administrators who responded to Mynders's call and met in Nashville in 1903 created a list of eight objectives for the upcoming summer reform campaign, among them proposals for the "higher training of teachers" and the "elimination . . . of nepotism from the public schools."[27] Writers in the *Nashville Christian Advocate* apparently agreed, urging the "best professional training on the part of the teacher" and arguing that poorly qualified teachers should not be able to "step into the classroom because Uncle is on the school board."[28]

In an effort to aid the campaigns for better trained teachers and, not coincidentally, to increase their student bodies, Baptist and Methodist denominational colleges greatly expanded their normal school (teacher-training) courses in the early twentieth century. In its early years, Vanderbilt had offered free tuition as an inducement to students preparing to be teachers, while in the twentieth century, Chancellor James Hampton Kirkland made nearly constant efforts to affiliate the university with the George Peabody College for Teachers, which was located on adjacent property in Nashville.[29] In an article clearly titled "Demand Better Public School Teachers," an anonymous Baptist-college supporter reminded readers and county school officials that "every one of our Baptist colleges now has a department for teacher training."[30] President G. M. Savage advertised the particular advantages of Union University, explaining that the school's teacher-training program was approved by the state and that its students could practice teaching in the Jackson city schools, graduating as experienced teachers and therefore becoming more desirable to school boards.[31] Harry Clark, the educational secretary of the Tennessee Baptist Convention, urged school superintendents in 1921 to hire teachers educated at Baptist colleges, noting that such graduates "have been professionally trained to teach."[32] Tennessee Baptists expected Clark, who had previously been an instructor at the Summer School of the South and the University of Tennessee, to increase state school officials' appreciation of teachers trained in denominational colleges, to turn "the faces of many of our young men and women from our public high schools to our denominational colleges," and to help graduates of church schools "find places of leadership in the educational system of the State."[33]

In addition to their efforts to bolster attendance at denominational colleges by advertising education departments, state religious leaders sought to increase the number of public school teachers trained in church colleges for other reasons as well. As one supporter of a Methodist normal school argued, "the Church alone can furnish a school that can give its students Christian education." In the wake of Vanderbilt's separation from the Methodist church, supporters of the proposed Emory University in Atlanta pointed to its teachers college as a center for "the regeneration of the ideals of our teachers. . . . The only practical thing for us to do if we would redeem ourselves is to build a truly great teachers' college in the South—the greatest in the world."[34] Tennessee Evangelicals argued that Christian teachers trained in denominational colleges would make the best impression on the pupils.[35] If there were doubts about to what extent religious instruction could be conducted in the public schools, state Evangelicals argued, the schools should be at the very least staffed with consecrated Christian teachers who could endorse religion through the force of their examples.

Throughout the campaign era, state religious leaders continued avidly to support efforts to improve and expand public elementary education. School reformers quickly realized that religious bodies could aid in reform campaigns and sought to directly enlist evangelical support. In addition to inviting ministers to participate in local school rallies, reformers took to the religious press and denominational conventions to encourage ministers to take an active interest in the local schools. W. R. Bourne, the state high-school inspector, appeared at Methodist meetings across the state in 1913 and 1914. He made a presentation and then gave the participants prewritten resolutions to pass and include in their minutes. Bourne was well received by the denominational bodies, and the *Nashville Midland Methodist* made several notes of the Methodist layman's commencement sermons and efforts to inculcate morality into public school students. [36] Most state Evangelicals could easily endorse the plans to have ministers more involved in the public schools, believing that the religious leaders could thereby influence students, teachers, and community leaders to guarantee a favorable hearing for religion and morality in the schools.

At the end of the campaign era, former school reform activist and current president of the new East Tennessee Normal School S. G. Gilbreath was invited to speak at Rev. William Gentry's inauguration as president of Carson-Newman College. Gilbreath's address provides a good indication of what state school officials thought of the relationship between the churches and public education. "The work of the public elementary schools," he argued, "should find no duplication in the course of study in any denominational institution." Furthermore, "organized Christianity and denominational institutions are under obligation to give loyal support to the public school." Such support, Gilbreath suggested, could "be given by the co-operation of ministers with public school officials and teachers, by earnest exhortation in the church for regular attendance on the schools, and for the co-operation of parents and teachers, by attendance at teachers' meetings and by active personal interest and work for universal education." [37]

The crusade for improved Tennessee public education had immense success, and the school boosters secured legislation to lengthen the school term, increase state and local funding, set higher standards for teachers, and begin to establish a complete school system stretching from elementary levels to college. State religious leaders had supported the campaigns in general and had been especially vocal in their endorsement of better rural schools and professional standards for teachers. But ironically, in the long term, the school reform efforts so energetically supported by denominational leaders would weaken and eventually destroy the home rule compromise that had originally won their support for public schools. The school campaigns focused on streamlining school bureaucracy, removing district or local school directors, and placing control of schools into a single school board in each county.[38] Passed over the objections of several rural legislators who argued for "local self-government" of schools, the county board bill rationalized the school bureaucracy but at the same time limited the possibility of genuine local control of the schools.[39]

The movement to increase professional standards for teachers, while in part giving churchmen an opportunity to provide professionally and religiously trained teachers for the schools, ultimately weakened the power of local school boards and communities to determine who should teach in the schools. The school law of 1873 had required teachers to obtain certificates from county school superintendents but did not establish any clear standards for teachers. After 1909, teachers could obtain a "permanent license" to teach in any state elementary school after graduating from a state normal school. Furthermore, the 1913 school laws set uniform statewide standards for teacher certification, and "the great variations in standards which existed from county to county ceased," at least in theory.[40] With the addition of standardizing legislation in 1925, the state school superintendent could enforce uniform standards of school administration, including teacher certification, by withholding state funds from noncomplying schools. By emphasizing professional standards based on training, coursework, and experience, teacher-certification laws lessened local communities' ability to adhere to older standards based on more personal judgments of character, religion, and/or morality.

The reformers urged the establishment of a complete system of state schools, extending public education from the elementary schools through the state college. They achieved part of their goal with the 1903 state budget, finally securing some public funding for the University of Tennessee. University appropriations remained tenuous for several following decades, but a precedent had nonetheless been established that would allow the university to better compete with the denominational colleges. State religious leaders such as Weaver raised some objections to the "top-heavy" funding of the Knoxville school, arguing repeatedly that Tennessee should spend more on rural elementary schools for all students before providing higher education for a select few.[41]

A more important achievement of the school reform efforts may have been the creation and funding of middle and high schools by state and county taxation.

After the enactment of an 1899 law, counties slowly established high schools throughout the early twentieth century. By 1916 forty-two of the state's ninety-six counties had high schools, and a 1921 law required the establishment of at least one high school in every county. [42] The growth of high schools represented both a threat and an advantage to denominational academies and colleges: the state schools would compete with the academies for students but would also provide a larger pool of potential students for the denominational colleges. Vanderbilt's Chancellor Kirkland and Presidents H. E. Watters, G. M. Savage, and William Gentry of the Baptist colleges all agreed with Gilbreath's assessment that "with the larger growth of the public schools will come larger prosperity to the denominational college," but they nonetheless feared a temporary decline in enrollment as the public schools siphoned off some of the less prepared students. [43] The establishment of public high schools would have an unanticipated yet critical consequence. State elementary schools concentrated on basic academic skills such as reading, writing, and arithmetic, but the new state-supported high schools would teach biology and other higher academic subjects. Thus, the growth of state education would provide the arena for the controversy over the teaching of evolution. The expansion of the state into high-school and college-preparatory education not only led to direct competition with preexisting academies but also exposed increasing numbers of students (and parents) to potentially controversial subjects such as biology and geology. [44]

Parents, Children, and Compulsory Education

As the capstone to the "campaign era," the comprehensive school law of 1913 marked an important watershed in the history of public education in Tennessee. Finally, after years of abortive efforts and over the objection of some parents and industrialists, school reformers, supported by many state religious leaders, had secured the enactment of a statewide compulsory-attendance law. It was a momentous occasion not because it signaled a sudden legislative or ideological shift but because the measure's wide support indicated how far Tennesseans' conception of the state and their place within it had changed. Ever so gradually, both church and state had radically reconceived the relationships among parents, children, churches, and the state. Few Tennesseans, religious or otherwise, recognized what was happening or the potential long-term ramifications of transforming the state into a surrogate parent for all children. Parents gave their children to the Sunday schools for religious education and to the public schools for intellectual and manual education but only gradually recognized the loss of authority over how children should be trained or what they should learn.

Tennessee's first recorded legislative proposal for compulsory education came in 1885, when Representative William A. Fields, a black schoolteacher from Shelby County (Memphis), introduced a bill in the General Assembly. The measure received little support and died in committee. Beginning in the 1890s, many Tennessee education reformers promoted compulsory-attendance laws, speaking in favor of them at local school rallies and commenting on their necessity in annual school reports, addresses to the Public School Officers' Association, speeches before the General Assembly, and in mass-distributed pamphlets sent to schoolteachers and newspaper editors. [45] Throughout the 1890s, various county school superintendents mentioned attendance problems, and an increasing number of these officials advocated state compulsory-attendance laws in annual reports to the state superintendent of public instruction. [46] From 1898 to 1909, lawmakers introduced compulsory-attendance bills into every session of the General Assembly. If the proposals were not defeated outright, the legislators changed the bills to affect only the county introducing them. [47] With Hooper's support, the school lobby finally managed in 1913 to persuade the legislature to pass a law that required all children ages eight through fourteen to attend school at least eighty days each year. A 1919 law amended the original compulsory-attendance statute, requiring children aged seven through sixteen to attend "the full school term." County school boards were to appoint attendance officers and to fine parents or guardians for children's truancy unless it could be proven that the child was "incorrigible," in which case the board could send the child to the truant (reform) school. [48]

The significance of the compulsory-education bill and the school reformers' new conception of the relationships among the individual, the state, and society is easier to recognize if compared to the patriarchal conception of society that educational reformers sought to supplant. According to Peter W. Bardaglio, the "patriarchal household was . . . the cornerstone" of antebellum white society, encompassing not just wives and children but also slaves as dependent members under the authority of the male head of the house. Antebellum southerners, he argues, held onto a patriarchal conception long after northerners had moved toward a more individualistic conception of society and a more interventionist conception of the state. An 1843 Tennessee Supreme Court case reveals the judicial view of the relationships among patriarch, family, and state in antebellum Tennessee. In the case of *State v. Paine,* the court ruled that it could recognize a man's wife and children only "as the property of the husband and the father, having no will of their own, no rights in contradiction to his power and authority, and only considered *through him* as a portion of the community in which they lived." Such a relationship kept the state at arm's length, not preventing it from acting on the patriarch of the family if it so chose but giving to the male head of the household nearly absolute power under his own roof.[49]

Southern courts were beginning to make inroads into patriarchal homes during the late antebellum period, but the experiences of the Civil War simultaneously increased both the opening of the patriarchal home and opposition to that intervention. The experiences of the Civil War and Reconstruction reinforced the old suspicions of federal intervention, leaving most Tennesseans, as one reformer lamented, "more inclined than ever toward freedom of the individual and less inclined toward governmental interference, either state or national, with individual enterprise."[50] During the 1880s, the "governmental interference" many white Tennesseans feared most concerned public education. Throughout the decade, the U.S. Congress debated the Blair education bill, which proposed federal funding for local schools based on the number of illiterates in each state. The proposed measure touched some raw sectional and racial nerves in Tennessee, especially since the 1880s saw the largest number of blacks in government since their 1867 enfranchisement and federal support for education was widely believed to mean desegregated schooling despite Tennessee constitutional provisions against it. Speaking to a convention of county school superintendents in 1887, Governor Robert L. Taylor explained that he was "not, and never [had been], in favor of that terrible Blair Bill." He explained that he did not want any federal aid for schooling unless it came to the states to be used as they saw fit and did not seek to impose federal civil rights statutes on southern schools.[51]

Collins D. Elliott, a Methodist minister and schoolmaster, was perhaps the most outspoken critic of the developing public schools. His criticisms of nineteenth-century Tennessee school reform efforts were grounded in that older, patriarchal conception of society. Outraged at the supposed invasion of New England schoolmasters and foreign ideas of education and society into Tennessee schools, Elliott offered a blunt, regional distinction: in Tennessee, "the family is the central power, recognizing that the Children belong to the Family, in [Massachusetts] the State is the central power, as if the Children belonged to the State."[52] Elliott was not, however, arguing that the state had no role to play in education; he supported state funding for schools but wanted to maintain family influence and choice in how schools were run.[53]

Progressive-era education reformers rejected arguments such as Elliott's that favored local and familial control of education. In the minds of these reformers, the proper understanding of society was not as the voluntary association of patriarchal families but as an organic community in which illiteracy increased crime and obstructed economic advancement. Underlying all other arguments was an understanding of an interdependent society in which individual actions had far more than individual consequences. Governor Hooper provided perhaps the clearest enunciation of this assumption, explaining in his first legislative address to the General Assembly of 1911 that "the individual citizen of Tennessee is a member of a complex social organization, and, as such, sustains relations to millions of individuals who have the right to demand of him that he so conduct himself as not to injure his brother, whose keeper he is." This is certainly a different conception of society than the antebellum patriarchal society in which family members were, for the most part, subsumed under the head of the household and the state acted only in response to a crime committed. Progressive reformers justified extending state power to preventative actions and criminalizing behaviors that had previously been considered individual prerogatives. Most education reformers shared Hooper's conception of society, although few stated it as explicitly as did educator Samuel E. Hill, who warned, "The illiterates are here. They hang as millstones about our necks, making progress uncertain and slow. Our society cannot move faster than the slowest element in it."[54]

In spite of Elliott's opposition not just to compulsory education but to any extension of public schools or decline of parental authority, most Tennessee religious leaders had, by the early twentieth century, strongly endorsed the campaigns for compulsory education. Just as they had turned from moral suasion to legal prohibition in their battle against alcohol and to the Sunday school to pick up where recreant parents failed in religious education, religious leaders endorsed efforts to compel student attendance at the public schools. "As to compulsory primary education," Winton argued, "it is scarcely a question at all." Such a law "would be no hardship to right-minded parents, and such of our children as have parents too ignorant or too selfish to care for their training need the protection of just such a law."[55] Folk offered a similar endorsement to state Baptists, stating that he was "inclined also to believe in compulsory education. . . . Of course, the compulsion ought to come from the parents, but when it does not, is it not a duty the State owes itself and owes its citizens, after providing education for them, to see that they shall take advantage of it?"[56] Folk urged ministers to use their influence on parents and communities to encourage better school attendance and better compliance with the compulsory-education law.[57]

One of the most frequent arguments used by the supporters of compulsory education was voiced by Claxton in 1907: "Children have rights . . . and the State must protect them in these rights. Chief among them is the right to such education and training as will enable them to . . . become intelligent and self-supporting citizens."[58] The question of just where these children's rights originate highlights a central tenet in the reformers' understanding of the relationships among individual, state, and society. Educational reformers replaced the patriarchal society lionized by Elliott with a system of state patriarchy, viewing education as a right that the child "inherits from the state."[59] The reformers refuted arguments about parental rights, instead placing the welfare of the child and the society over the parent's prerogative.

A 1915 Tennessee Supreme Court case ruling reveals how the court saw the true importance of education for the state and suggests that the Progressives' invocations of the rights of the child were, at least on one level, calculated rhetorical devices. Asked to consider the legality of the compulsory-education law, the court ruled that "the public school system of the State" exists "for the general benefit of all the people of the State, and not primarily, but incidentally, for the benefit of the pupils." Furthermore, the justices declared that "free schooling furnished by the State is not so much a right granted to pupils as a duty imposed upon them for the public good." The court and the school reformers shattered the old patriarchal model, inserting the state's interest and power between and above the parent and the child. Not only must "the State . . . be protected against the dragging down influence of the ignorant," but "a parent who permits a child to grow up in ignorance is committing an offense not only against the child, but against the State."[60]

Tennessee evangelical leaders' support for compulsory elementary education, based as it was on their arguments regarding children's right to an education and parents' inability to withhold that right, raised serious questions about parents' role in education. Religious leaders had grown wary of parents' ability and willingness to provide religious education for their children even as public school reforms had weakened local communities' ability to determine for themselves questions of curriculum or teacher qualification. The "home rule" arrangement had been a serviceable modus vivendi, but the newly reformed and centrally controlled public school system that could compel student attendance provided an even more potent tool for moral and religious education. Because the state had assumed the parental role in the education of children, religious leaders argued, it then had to assume further parental duties such as providing for not just intellectual but also moral training: "Since our government has taken this parental care of the young, she should see to it that education is thorough and strictly moral."[61] If children were not receiving sufficient religious training in the home or the Sunday school, then the church must reach them where it could—in the public school: "the Christian Church must adopt some method of giving the children of our public school[s] a form of religious instruction during the week."[62]

Failure of the Home Rule Compromise

Following on the heels of Superintendent Mynders's successful public school rallies during the summer of 1906, public school supporter, former editor, and now Methodist bishop Oscar Fitzgerald authored a lengthy editorial in the *Nashville Christian Advocate* on "The Old South and the New." Fitzgerald praised the recent educational achievements but worried about their direction: "There has been unquestionable progress in the matter of popular education in the New South as compared with the Old South. The expenditure of money for educational purposes is larger, the percentage of illiteracy is smaller. But the question may be permitted, Has public and private morality exhibited a corresponding ratio of progress? While it is true that ignorance is the hotbed of all that is vile and ruinous to a people, it is as certainly true that mere knowledge is not sufficient to save a nation from destruction. Nobody but an idiot has anything to say against education. But it depends on the kind of education as to whether it is good or evil."[63] Fitzgerald's questions were not new, at least not for the *Advocate*'s pages. While Winton, the paper's editor, generally endorsed the Southern Education Board's plans, he nonetheless asked as early as 1903, "will any place remain for the Church schools" in the grand scheme of education reform? Or, more importantly, would "any provision be made for religious training" of the pupils in the state schools, or shall "religion . . . be neglected" entirely? Winton concluded that "a godless educated population is a very poor exchange for a religious and moral[ly] ignorant one" and warned school officials and his readers that "the South should not be forced upon the horns of any such dilemma."[64]

Despite most Tennessee Evangelicals' vocal support for the school reform campaigns, many state religious leaders became increasingly concerned about the stability of the home rule compromise that had provided a truce regarding questions of religion and public education since the 1880s. Winton and Fitzgerald's concerns about the future growth of the supposedly secular state's control over public education coincided with mounting evidence that parents, Sunday schools, and denominational colleges were not fulfilling their appropriate roles in the religious education of children.

Under the home rule compromise, state religious leaders frequently asserted that the public schools could not operate safely without moral and even Christian teachers in the classrooms. Denominational officials agreed with state school officials that teachers should be of sound moral and religious character.[65] Hoss encouraged "the good people in every community [to] give due attention" to the schools, arguing that "the first thing to be looked after is the character of the teachers." Nothing could "be of more benefit to boys and girls than . . . a sincere and earnest Christian teacher; but what" would happen if the teacher were "a cold-hearted skeptic?"[66] Such comments did not represent baseless criticisms of public school teachers: many people who could do so looked for other work because the pay for teachers was abysmal and the sessions were too short to earn a living, and most teachers used the job as only a temporary stop or stepping stone.[67] Applicants for teaching positions were not always model religious citizens and in some cases owed their jobs and therefore political allegiance to the patronage of local school directors or county school board members. Other teachers, such as John Harell and Edgar E. Puryear, embodied some of the worst fears of religious leaders and school reformers. Both young men applied for a teaching position in Dilton, a small community southeast of Murfreesboro, in the winter of 1896. It is unclear whether the two fought over the school position or the affections of a young lady also applying for the job, but Harell allegedly attacked Puryear, who "instantly drew a revolver and fired at his assailant, sending a ball crushing into his bowels, and inflicting a dangerous wound." As the *Nashville Banner* editorialized the following day, "It is a sign of serious social demoralization when school teachers go about unlawfully lugging pistols in their hip pockets."[68]

The growth of public education to include secondary and high schools further undermined the home rule compromise, restricting definite denominational education to time outside of school or to college. Reiterating arguments for "limiting education by the State to the primary branches," Winton lamented as early as 1903 that "the State has taken upon itself the work of carrying pupils far beyond the simple requisites of citizenship." The problem, he explained, was that children of high-school and college age were highly impressionable: entrusting them to potentially "godless" public schools run by possibly immoral teachers represented a terrible risk.[69]

Part of the motivation behind the Southern Education Board's school campaigns had been a desire to provide public education from elementary school through college. The new precedent of publicly funding the University of Tennessee increased the pressure on denominational colleges: public money altered the balance of state and denominational schools, providing state schools with funding that did not come from either endowments or tuition payments. The generally less equipped denominational colleges had to compete for students and at the same time solicit funds from sponsoring churches. As chapter 3 discusses, this increased competition forced some church colleges to look beyond their denominations for donations. Chancellor Kirkland's efforts to balance Vanderbilt's denominational ties with its voracious appetite for foundation monies eventually led to the school's acrimonious split from the southern Methodist church. The loss of Vanderbilt represented a terrible blow to many Methodists' dreams of a great church university in Tennessee but had an even more powerful ripple effect on Evangelicals statewide. The home rule compromise was predicated on a belief that strong denominational colleges would be the capstone of the state's educational system; the loss of Vanderbilt and the resulting uncertainty about the future of all religious colleges seriously jeopardized an important component of the arrangement.

An even more disturbing development, at least from the point of view of evangelical adherents to the home rule compromise, was the mounting evidence that many parents were failing to teach their children morality and the basics of religion. As one Baptist minister observed at the turn of the century, "the ideal is that in the home there will be family prayers, the Bible will be read and explained, reverence for God will be taught, the religion of Christ will be emphasized above everything else." But he asked rhetorically how many homes approached that standard and answered that many more should.[70] Even Fitzgerald expressed grave concerns about parents fulfilling their duties to educate children in religion and morality. The family, he argued, "should be the nursery of the Church and the palladium of the State" but was instead allowing "millions of children" to grow "up to manhood and womanhood with a disregard of all authority." Because, Fitzgerald asserted, the church was only "the family on a larger scale," any decline in family life and religion would jeopardize the future of the church as well.[71]

In the spring of 1917, the *Nashville Christian Advocate* reprinted an excerpt from an article by an unnamed clergyman who objected to religious education in the public schools and argued that such instruction should remain in the hands of parents and churches. Methodist editor Thomas Ivey's response to the passage succinctly demonstrates the extent to which most Tennessee religious leaders had abandoned the home rule compromise: "Just think of leaving the spiritual and religious element in education to 'the Churches and families' when the Churches reach only a handful of child life [*sic*] and virtually most of the parents who are halfway Christians are leaving the religious instruction of their children to the tender mercies of the secular school!"[72] Rev. W. C. Owen would echo these thoughts five years later, stating clearly his and other Evangelicals' perceptions that the "home is not functioning very effectively in the religious training of children."[73]

Recognizing that too many parents were disregarding their obligations to train their children in religion, denominational leaders urged the founding of Sunday schools throughout the state. Baptist Sunday school advocate J. M. Phillips had practically given up on many parents as early as 1880: "Talk about it as much as we may, preach against it as we should, the fact still remains that if the religious training of the children is left to the homes of the country, thousands of children will grow up without Christian culture." Faced with parental abdication, Phillips argued that it would have to be "the work of the Sunday-school" to "look after their moral training" and "lead them into the light of saving truth."[74] But as Hoss observed, these problems only worsened as parents increasingly relinquished their child-rearing roles to the public schools and the Sunday schools. Some parents, "relieved by the State of the necessity of educating their children, and by the Sunday School and Church of the necessity of giving them a religious training, . . . take things quietly, and seem often to forget even their most elementary duties."[75] As for the future if the religious life of children were neglected, Hoss argued, "the danger [lay] not in the public schools, but in the home."[76] These concerns would only increase in the ensuing decades as modern entertainments multiplied and evidence mounted of the decline of family religion in a rapidly changing society.

A new wave of concern crested after World War I as state and national religious leaders became even more concerned for young people's moral and religious health after witnessing what officials perceived as the German example of the results of godless education. By 1921 a religious commentator would suggest that "the old-time Christian home of Bible study and prayer has all but entirely disappeared" because too many families "find life too strenuous to give religious instruction in the homes."[77] Tennessee Evangelicals both had grown suspicious of parents' success or faithfulness in educating their children religiously and worried that Sunday schools would be insufficient for the task. The problem with leaving religious education to the churches alone, Owen rationalized, was that the "Church is not reaching millions of the children and the youth of this country." If the churches were to pass on their religion to the rising generation and have some hope of Christianizing the future society, they would have to find another means of proselytization.[78]

Protestantism in the Public School

Looking around, early-twentieth-century Tennessee Evangelicals saw a number of signs that society was drifting far from the religious ideal. Efforts to reach the hearts of children and adults, though successful in individual cases, were proving ineffective on a larger societal scale. On the particular issue of alcohol, evangelical moralists shifted from persuasion to coercion, campaigning for and eventually winning prohibitory laws. Prohibition was an effort to change the behavior of adults; would not it be more effective, state religious leaders rationalized, to begin teaching morality and restraint to children in the home and school? But since Evangelicals had already grown dubious about the prospects for true home religion that would reach every child and even about the power of local communities to guarantee a role for religion and morality in the public schools, religious leaders' campaigns began to focus on legislating religion into the public schools. With the new centralized school bureaucracy and compulsory-attendance laws, Evangelicals could spread their beliefs widely, even establishing in the next generation the religious society for which they had long hoped.

Many of the same Tennessee evangelical leaders who had been active supporters of the public school reform campaigns and who had been speaking and preaching on the importance of the public school for the future of society realized that those same public schools could be strong allies of religion and the church's mission to educate the world. With the expansion of the public schools throughout the state and the growing attendance rates, more students were receiving greater portions of their education in the state-funded elementary schools. As school hours increased, parents' and churches' relative time devoted to and influence on the education of children decreased. State Baptists and Methodists gradually realized that, as one of the their number explained, "the school-teacher has fallen heir to the largest share of the minister's former mantel of influence in the community."[79] This new recognition of the power of the public school and its teachers shaped Tennessee Evangelicals' view of the proper relationship between religion and education in the wake of the home rule compromise's demise. Though parents and churches should retain their responsibility for religious education, teachers in the public schools could provide at least a modicum of religious and moral education to all children.

Most Tennessee Baptists and Methodists had accepted and endorsed public schools in the belief that the schools would support, if not actively lead, children's religious and moral development. According to Fitzgerald, Christians did not have to and probably should not force religion into the public schools. Most teachers were religious, most schools began with Bible reading, and nearly all schools were morally safe. But this evangelical complacency vanished in 1903 when U.S. Commissioner of Education William Torrey Harris announced "that religious instruction should be confined to the Church, and that it should be divorced entirely from the public schools." The first part of Harris's opinion supported the old home rule compromise, but his further directive to remove religion from the schools was too much for many Tennessee Evangelicals to stomach. He did receive some support, including a letter from *Nashville Christian Advocate* correspondent David H. Bishop, who argued that forcing nonreligious or sectarian teachers to teach religion could do more harm than good by usurping the proper role of the home and church.[80] Among the Methodists, at least, Bishop's was a lonely voice. W. P. Lovejoy responded by arguing that "If Dr. Harris's contention be followed, if 'religious instruction should be divorced entirely from the public schools,' there is nothing in reason or religion that can justify the existence of a public school. Nothing is or can be education that has not religion for its corner stone."[81] At the very least, Lovejoy and many others argued, the public schools should teach and reinforce morality based on religious principles.

Winton responded unequivocally to Harris's call for the "absolute banishment of religious instruction from our public schools" with a series of articles in the spring of 1903. Although Winton avidly supported public education, he placed the blame for controversy squarely on the shoulders of both Harris and state school boosters. The present "difficulty" concerning the place of religion in public education "ought to have been foreseen and obviated by limiting education by the State to the primary branches," but "the State has taken upon itself the work of carrying pupils far beyond the simple requisites of citizenship." As such, Winton argued, the state must then assume its share of responsibility for the moral and religious education of children.[82]

It is difficult to estimate the extent of religious influence in Tennessee's public schools, but public opinion in the late nineteenth and early twentieth centuries latched onto an important symbolic issue: the place of the Bible in the classroom. Opinions on the Bible's role in the public schools had differed within and among Baptist and Methodist state organizations beginning in the 1870s, but in the first decades of the twentieth century, Evangelicals would approach a nearly unanimous agreement on the necessity of including the Bible in the regular program of Tennessee public schools. Such had not always been the case. In general, nineteenth-century Tennessee Baptists had raised principled objections to requiring the use of the Bible in the public school. Responding to a proposal to petition the state legislature "that the Bible . . . be used as a text-book in the public schools," the 1882 meeting of the Tennessee Baptist Convention, after a lengthy discussion, voted "by a large majority" not to adopt the resolution. In spite of the pleadings from one member that he "had received his first knowledge of the Bible from lessons in a day school" and from another that "the Bible should be taught and explained in all the schools of the land," Tennessee Baptist leaders overwhelmingly endorsed future Mercer University President J. B. Gambrell's opinion that it would "be a departure from established Baptist principles to ask any assistance from the State in the matter of religious instruction." Gambrell's reasoning in part reflected the historic Baptist sensitivity about a union of church and state, a legacy of Baptist protest against the established English church and the Baptists' experience as persecuted dissenters in both England and early America. But Gambrell's rationale further suggested a recognition of the same conditions that had led Fitzgerald to present the home rule compromise: the Bible was already in use in many of the schools and any attempt at legislation would be "impolitic" and would most likely lead "into an ever-lasting muddle."[83]

Folk surveyed Baptist educational leaders in the spring of 1894, presenting their opinions on "Our Public Education System" in the *Nashville Baptist and Reflector.* Many of the respondents seemed to agree with Gambrell's statement that he was "against the Bible's being forced into the public schools." They did not argue that the Bible should not be used, only that it should be there voluntarily, taught by Christian teachers to children whose parents approved.[84] Other respondents, chief among them Wake Forest President Charles Elisha Taylor, argued unequivocally that the "only logical position which I can hold, especially because I am a Baptist, is that prayer and the Bible have no place in schools supported by the State."[85] But President William S. Johnson of Mountain Home College expressed an opinion that more and more Tennessee Baptists would come to endorse in the following decades. Recognizing the state's new relationship to the public schools and to students—Johnson called the state's action a declaration of its intention to assume "parental care of the young"—he argued that the state "should see to it that education is thorough and strictly moral." On this matter, Johnson continued, "I can't refrain from expressing myself in favor of the use of the Bible in the school room." He argued further that taking "the Bible out of the public schools" would be illogical, since the Bible and religion had inspired "the establishment of public schools."[86]

Under the home rule arrangement, most Tennessee Evangelicals had assumed that the Bible would regularly be used in the schools—for morning devotions and as a textbook for reading as well as geography and history—but only if there were no objections to its use. This appears to have been the general rule in rural Tennessee, and the wisdom of not forcing the Bible into the schools seemed even more apparent when some urban Tennesseans petitioned the Nashville and Memphis school boards to require daily Bible reading. The Nashville Board of Education and the City Council debated petitions to have the Bible read and the Lord's Prayer said in the schools every morning, leading to several weeks of acrimonious debate at the beginning of 1896. The motion eventually foundered amid the tumult of the city's nativist politics, with the council splitting evenly on the measure.[87] The bill did not pass, but the practice of Bible reading apparently continued in many city schools.[88] A similar petition in Memphis consumed the city's school board for much of the summer and fall of 1902, with the controversy ending only when the original petitioners withdrew their request, stating that they had "worked only for what [the petitioners] considered the best interest of the children in the public schools."[89]

Unfortunately, secular news sources did not specify who supported the 1896 and 1902 petitions. Governor Bentin McMillin clearly supported the proposals, asking that they be extended across the state in 1902.[90] Neither Baptist nor Methodist state papers explicitly endorsed the efforts, although the publications noted that the petitions had been presented and followed the debates in both cities.[91]

Both secular and religious critics of mandatory school Bible reading generally grounded their objections in a fear of the controversy that would likely ensue, to the detriment of both religion and education. Jordan Stokes, a member of the Nashville Board of Education, demurred on religious grounds, arguing that "religion is a matter of personal choice, and not force. . . . Forcing the teachings of the Bible upon any class of citizens has never and will never do any good for the cause of Christ."[92] The *Memphis Commercial Appeal* editorialized that forcing the Bible into the public schools would ensure "the ultimate destruction of a noble educational system."[93] Other objectors recognized the religious diversity of the two cities and the inevitable controversy of setting one—probably Protestant Christian—standard for all city schools. Stokes reminded the rest of the Board of Education of the schools' responsibility to people of all faiths, arguing that "we collect for school purposes money from every class of citizens, be he Jew, Catholic, Christian or infidel, and I do not think it is compatible with the doctrines of free government, where a man can follow the dictates of his own heart in all matters of worship to take that money and expend any part of it in forcing into our public schools, and teaching therein, a book whose doctrines are opposed, from a religious point, by any citizens from whom we collect taxes." Further, he expressed a tolerance for other interpretations of religion, stating that although he did not agree with Jews, Catholics, or Muslims, it was the duty of the Protestants "to win them to our view, not by force, but by persuasion."[94]

This broad religious toleration, rarely expressed, was nonetheless supported by a general assumption that most schools were at least broadly Protestant institutions and that parents, churches, and local communities would continue to ensure the moral and religious soundness of public school education. In most rural areas, there was little likelihood of any non-Protestant student. But in the following decades, after public school expansion and centralization combined with an increased perception of the failure of parents and churches to provide religious education, Tennessee Evangelicals increasingly presented arguments in favor of Bible reading and in some cases even Bible teaching that were intended to overwhelm potential constitutional or religious objections.

Winton confronted both constitutional and religious objections to Bible reading in the public schools only months after Harris's pronouncement that religion should be completely removed. "Those who contend that no religious instruction whatever can be given in a State institution because of our adherence as a nation to the principle of complete separation between Church and State have the better of the argument," Winton conceded. But, he continued, since the state had gone beyond the original agreement and was attempting to provide a complete system of education for all children, "the State—that is, the public— is now under obligation to be illogical at a further point." Instead of being "intimidated by [the] logic" of the "strict constructionists," Winton argued for daily use of the Bible.

> For though it must be allowed that separation between Church and State is one of our national principles and that a strict allegiance thereto seems to require the banishment of religious instruction from State schools, we are on the other hand confronted with an array of menacing facts. . . . [I]t is time we cut this Gordian knot and throw logic to the dogs. . . . The clamor of the strict constructionists has somewhat deafened others among us, and, intimidated by their logic, we have been consenting to a course of things which both experience and reason pronounce calamitous. We are sacrificing our children on the altar of consistency, and preparing to wreck our country on a syllogism.

Winton suggested that although "we can probably never have religious instruction by enactment," Protestants could build public opinion and "some things can be done by common consent."[95] Surveying the religious and educational scene in the winter of 1914, Ivey, Winton's successor at the *Christian Advocate,* explained that he felt "a sinking of the heart" when he considered the potential obstacle of "the Constitution, whose spirit at least is regarded as opposed to the reading of the Bible and even to the teaching of fundamental religious truth in the public schools." This would not be such a problem, he suggested, if parents, churches, and denominational colleges were fulfilling their obligations. His despair would only grow in the coming weeks as the Tennessee Supreme Court ruled in favor of the Vanderbilt University Board of Trust. Ivey reprinted articles from Tennessee and other states on school and church plans to provide for Bible reading and explicit religious teaching in the public schools.[96]

Evangelical arguments for placing the Bible in the public schools gained new power after 1914, as the outbreak of World War I dramatically increased the supposed stakes of Tennesseans' debates about the proper role of religion in education. The scattered efforts to require daily Bible reading in certain city school systems became irrelevant in 1915 when the Tennessee General Assembly passed a law "regulating the reading of the Holy Bible in the Public Schools of Tennessee." Despite the fact that the bill had been reported "without recommendation" by the House Committee on Education and reported "for rejection" by the companion Senate committee, it passed with relative ease. The only recorded objections came from two urban legislators from Memphis and Shelby County who made arguments similar to those expressed in the earlier debates in Nashville and Memphis. Representative W. M. Stanton said that he voted against the measure "because I do not think religion of any kind should [have] any part in our public schools or institutions. It is not [in] keeping with [the] genius or spirit of institutions or form of government."[97]

The passage of this statewide law went largely unnoticed by the state Methodist papers in the spring of 1915 but elicited a blistering critique from J. W. Gillon, executive secretary of the Tennessee Baptist State Board of Missions. In an article plainly titled "Some Reasons Why I Oppose the Compulsory Use of the Bible in the Public Schools," Gillon presented arguments based not only on an older Baptist church-state sensitivity but also on an expanded interpretation of the U.S. Constitution's First Amendment protections of religion and religious dissent. The measure passed by the Tennessee General Assembly, Gillon argued, was an abuse of majority power at the expense of the rights of "a protesting, respectable minority." Such legislation violated "the spirit of the Constitution of the United States" and the "American doctrine of religious liberty" and threatened the creation of a "State Church." After his constitutional arguments, Gillon turned his criticisms on the churches themselves, suggesting that forced Bible reading was a sign of great spiritual decay; it was an attempt to substitute form for substance: "The very fact that we have come to a period in our history when such legislation can be proposed is an evidence that vital godliness is on the wane and that we are undertaking to put the form of godliness in the place of vital godliness." Not wanting his point to be missed, Gillon warned that such coercive measures as compulsory daily Bible reading in the public schools "will ultimately end in great injury to Christianity itself." For one, compulsory use of the Bible would endanger denominational schools by making the state schools seem Christian: "When we break down, in outward appearance, the line of cleavage between the secular and the religious institution, we inevitably destroy the religious institution without making better the secular."[98] The truthfulness of this statement must have seemed all the more apparent in the wake of Vanderbilt University's acrimonious separation from the southern Methodist church only a year earlier.

Whatever support Gillon's article might have elicited remained mostly out of the pages of the Tennessee Baptist and Methodist journals.[99] Other state religious leaders were by early 1915 turning their attention to the growing European war. Ivey saw the conflict and German aggression in general as a direct result of "godless" German public education and worried about "the almost complete secularization" of American education. He argued that "No European war is needed to teach us that the splendid education which, according to secularists, would bring such richness to our life as a people has failed us."[100] After the *Baptist and Reflector* published an article by W. J. McGlothlin on "The German School System and the Great War," editor Albert R. Bond remarked that "it has provoked more favorable comment among our readers than any article for a long time." Bond summarized McGlothlin's lengthy arguments so that readers would not miss the importance. McGlothlin, he explained "plainly indicates that German kultur was produced through Prussian militarism, disassociated with the religious sanction for deeds, and became inwrought into the national life through the school system of the nation." This, Bond argued, "should be a warning to American life lest we too forget the essential things that ought to be taught in our school system."[101]

Tennessee's evangelical leaders built on this wartime attitude, taking ever more aggressive stances on the necessity of guaranteeing a moral and religious education to children in all schools, private or public, and dismissing as overblown any concerns about a union of church and state. After America entered the war and helped to defeat Germany, southern religious leaders increased their warnings that America could be headed in the same direction. Postwar jeremiads traced the supposedly inevitable decline in public morality to the continued secularization of public education. Methodist Bishop Warren Candler predicted that postwar education would be "missionary work" by which the southern churches should "not only convert the rest of the world, but now the rest of America." The southern churches were particularly suited to this task, he argued, because "the degenerate forms of rationalistic religion have never been able to take root in our section."[102] Rev. Stonewall Anderson, secretary of the Nashville-based Southern Methodist Board of Education, argued in the summer of 1918 that although military victory might come for the Allies, the peace would not end the real war, for "a bloodless war of thought will continue." The war now, Anderson explained, was not to resist Germany but "to resist Germanism" by promoting religious education in America.[103]

During and immediately after the war, most Tennessee evangelical leaders renewed their push for religion in the public schools. Though most religious officials usually balked at efforts on behalf of denominationally specific teachings, nearly all focused once again on the symbolic issue of daily Bible reading in the schools. Ivey clearly stated the plan in a July 1917 editorial: "This great world war, in which our own country has at last become involved, has brought about a most opportune time for restoring religion and the Bible to their former place of fundamental importance in the educational system of this republic."[104] Shortly after the defeat of Germany, Ivey made his argument even more explicit. In case his readers had missed points made by other writers, he reiterated the source of German aggression and defeat: "The awful collapse of Germany was due to the fact that she had allowed her moral foundations to be weakened. She virtually dethroned God and substituted for him ungodly Might." Ivey further cautioned that German "schools made the Bible a thing to be tossed here and there by irreverent critics" and urged Tennesseans to reverse the present American trend toward excluding religion from the schools. "The Bible," Ivey argued, "must be the supreme book" for education, with "a place now in every common school in the land." Finally, he marked the clear departure from concerns about too close an alliance between church and state, writing, "Surely the old fine-spun constitutional objections have been smashed."[105]

Thus, in the wake of the world war, Tennessee Evangelicals again linked religion and education, arguing that both were necessary for the survival of the church and the state. As one Methodist explained, "If this democracy of ours is to survive, if Protestantism is to maintain itself, it is absolutely necessary that our people shall be educated. And it is essential that education must include religion."[106] Winton, Ivey, and most other state evangelical leaders were not ignorant about potential constitutional hindrances to imposing religion on the public schools but nevertheless proposed solutions that either ignored such objections or attempted to overrule them with arguments about majority rule, citizens' rights, or America's history as a Christian nation. In doing so, these Evangelicals countered almost every one of Gillon's arguments line for line, convincing themselves and the state at large that godly form was better than godless form, even if there was no real vital godliness in church or state.

Ivey endorsed "a campaign demanding that the Bible shall be used as a textbook of instruction in the public schools" in the spring of 1916. Although Tennessee had recently passed a law requiring daily Bible reading in the public schools, Ivey argued that even more religious instruction should take place. If anyone raised objections, Ivey countered them by arguing that he and other Christian parents would only be exercising a "citizen's right" to determine what should be taught in the public schools.[107] Although Ivey and other religious and educational leaders' arguments for compulsory education had seemed to downplay or even dismiss the rights claims of parents who withheld their children from school, many times countering these contentions with competing claims about children's right to an education or the state's right to an educated citizenry, evangelical leaders returned to parents' claims regarding their children to bolster arguments about citizens' rights over the legislature and schools. The legislature controlled the schools, but citizens controlled the legislature; therefore, they should be able to determine policy for the schools in the interest of preserving both religion and the state itself.

Tennessee religious leaders attempted to reinforce the distinctions between the United States and Germany by emphasizing that the United States was a "Christian nation." Further, to circumvent constitutional establishment-clause questions, some Evangelicals argued that "No matter how it was framed and amended, we all know that this government was literally founded on the Bible."[108] State religious leaders claimed that "our civilization is based on the Word of God and that we must rely upon its influence over the coming generations to keep the future safe." Baptist educator Harry Clark argued that "From the beginning of our American nation, religion as presented in the Holy Scriptures has given form and character to our national government." Still others argued that the judicial oath, the inscription "In God We Trust," and President George Washington's kissing of the Bible after taking the oath of office proved that the United States was a "Christian nation." They asked: "If our nation stamps on her coins the motto, 'In God We Trust,' why should she not read into young life some information about the God we trust?"[109]

Yet another argument used by Tennessee Evangelicals in favor of requiring Bible reading in the public schools was to redefine constitutional prohibitions of religious establishment as more specific issues of sectarian establishment. Objecting to "the ridiculous assumption that the Bible is a sectarian book," Evangelicals argued that Bible study in public schools should not be objectionable to either the Constitution or other citizens.[110] The problem, Hoss had explained at the turn of the century, was a class of people "unable to see the difference between religion, pure and simple, and sectarianism." He criticized Roman Catholics, Jews, and other "exclusivists who insist that they alone possess the true religion" and demand to teach their own interpretations or none at all.[111] Baptist editor Jesse D. Moore built on the assumptions of the "Christian nation" argument to justify and even require the use of the Bible in the public schools: "the Bible is the property of all Evangelical Christians. If our country be not Evangelically Christian, the Bible would be sectarian and the reading of it would be wrong in principle." But since "our whole national civilization is based on the Bible," Moore argued, it could not be a sectarian book.[112]

Finally, in case their other arguments proved insufficient, Tennessee Evangelicals sought to overcome any further objections by shifting the terms of the debate from protecting minority viewpoints to celebrating majority rule. "If we are democratic in other things, why should we renounce our principles in the management of the public schools?" asked Hoss. He protested that in professions of respect for minority viewpoints, the Protestant majority was allowing "infidels, Jews, and Romanists to dominate and rule out the very basis, not alone of our religion, but of our civilization."[113] Winton downplayed potential constitutional objections by invoking the "higher law of public opinion" to incorporate the Bible and Christian teaching into the public schools, privileging the rights of "the great majority of God-fearing and moral parents" over the "very small minority" of "infidels, atheists, and anarchists" who, "to be perfectly candid, . . . ought to be ignored."[114] Baptist editor Jesse D. Moore similarly dismissed any objections to reading the Bible in the public school, explaining that such daily exercises "would be attended by an offense to none who ought not be offended, and with highly beneficial results to the state and to all its citizens."[115]

W. T. Callaway, pastor of the Baptist Tabernacle in Chattanooga, brought all of the arguments for Bible reading together in a spring 1926 article when he asked rhetorically, "Shall the Bible Be Read in Our Public Schools?" Though he sympathized with arguments in favor of a strict separation of church and state, Callaway professed that he "would dislike very much to meet God at the Judgment, having deprived thousands of His little ones the privilege of hearing His Word read." Callaway then reiterated the Christian-nation argument, stating that the Bible "is the foundation of American civilization, and . . . our main hope for the preservation of this American commonwealth." His version of the majority-rule argument was flavored with a bit more nativism than some earlier arguments, as he suggested that "if we have among us foreigners to whom the reading of the Bible is distasteful, they might find a more congenial clime in their own native hearth." He further ridiculed any objectors, stating, "No one is being 'persecuted' in Tennessee by having the Bible read. . . . Simply because a minority of Jews and Catholics will cry out 'intolerance, intolerance,' is no reason why the reading of the Bible should be withheld from our children."[116]

In addition to these arguments, Callaway sought to preempt any lingering arguments from supporters of the older home rule arrangement: "In this present generation we are seeing the beginning of moral decay and degeneracy in our nation. . . . Surely, then, with the Church only having our children for instruction for about an hour once a week, and the public schools having them most of the remaining time, we should welcome every possible avenue of Bible knowledge that will be the authority and compelling power in their young lives."[117] The home rule compromise had clearly evaporated by this time. Nineteenth-century

Tennessee Evangelicals had recognized religious or constitutional bars to re-quired Bible reading in the public schools of the state and sought to obey or circumvent these restrictions by simply avoiding legislation. In the wake of World War I and perceptions of the declining spirituality of the home and the decreased role of the churches in public affairs, many state religious leaders sought to co-opt the machinery of the state schools to ensure that all Tennessee's children were exposed to the Bible.

6. Evolution and Education

Science and Religion in Church and Public Schools

Understanding the role of white Tennessee Methodists and Baptists in the enactment of the state's 1925 Butler antievolution bill and the resulting *Scopes* trial requires a sensitivity to the law's context on two fronts: not just controversies over the truth, falsehood, and perceived danger of evolutionary theories of human development but, even more important, the long-standing concerns among Tennessee Evangelicals about the content and control of public education. Viewed in isolation, the eleven-day trial in Dayton can be a spectacle, a pitched battle of religious fundamentalism with religious, scientific, and intellectual modernism symbolized in the clash of the two great legal combatants, William Jennings Bryan and Clarence Darrow. Contextualized, the trial appears at the intersection of several intellectual and social patterns: Tennessee Evangelicals' continuing desire to re-create or demonstrate the especially religious nature of the South, some scientists' and theologians' growing militancy regarding their exclusive authority to explain the world, Evangelicals' emerging identification as no longer an isolated and distinct community unto themselves but as a controlling majority of the larger society, and Tennessee Evangelicals' emerging understanding that the public schools were their best hope and means for evangelizing and sanctifying the state.

Many of the same circumstances in the early twentieth century that drove Tennessee Evangelicals to endorse daily Bible reading in the public schools would also alert them to another insidious evil obstructing their creation of a truly religious New South. While much of the impetus for Bible reading and moral instruction in the public schools was occasioned by sins of omission—the failure or inability of parents, churches, and denominational colleges to live up to their duties under the home rule compromise—many Tennessee Evangelicals found the newest dragon to be a sin of commission in the schoolhouse itself. American scientists, theologians, and laypersons had wrestled with theories of evolution and their theological implications since the middle of the nineteenth century, but the early twentieth century—and especially the years following World War I— witnessed a fervent campaign by many Evangelicals to protect schoolchildren from exposure to the supposedly faith-killing theories of biological develop- ment. Having argued for the importance of moral training in the public schools, most Tennessee Evangelicals did not want to see Christianity—the basis not just of that morality but also, in their words, of the American nation—undermined by what many labeled the antireligious theory of evolution.

Although a minority of voices within the churches would continue to endorse the possibility of theistic interpretations of evolution, most early-twentieth- century Tennessee Evangelicals could see evolution only as atheistic and harm- ful to revealed religion. While church papers continued to debate the truth or falsehood of the theory of evolution and its compatibility with revealed religion, the more important battles in both church and state concerned who had the power to determine what would be taught in the Tennessee public schools. After the success of their efforts to sanctify public schools by requiring daily Bible reading, Evangelicals were alarmed that the state high schools and colleges, in- cluding some denominational colleges, were teaching students about evolution. Thus, by the 1920s, most evangelical Tennesseans supported efforts to forbid the teaching of evolution in the schools, believing that children exposed to the theory would be condemned to atheism and that the future state and society could not survive without a widespread belief in an omnipotent God, a divinely created world, and a future life of reward and punishment.

Science, Religion, and Evolution

Writing at the end of July 1925, only weeks after John T. Scopes's conviction under Tennessee's antievolution law, Methodist minister M. M. Black attempted to restore some unity to religious and scientific pursuits in the wake of the public antagonism displayed at the Dayton trial. Expressing a belief in the essential unity of scientific and religious truth that differed little from assertions in the same journal a half century earlier, Black asserted that "the Church no less than science must be a seeker of the truth, nor has she anything to fear from the discovery of truth in any realm." Because there was "no realm over which God does not rule, whether it be material or spiritual," Black explained, there could be "no secular or non-Christian truth. . . . When men discover the so-called laws of nature they are simply discovering the methods by which God works."[1] Such assertions of religioscientific harmony may have seemed somewhat out of place in the intense cultural and political climate of 1925, but they were by no means out of touch with a large number of moderate southern religious writers of the period or of the 1870s. At that time, Methodist educator and naturalist John Darby had written to Bishop Holland McTyeire, offering to serve the proposed Vanderbilt University and explaining what Darby saw as the compatibility of science and religion: "The manifestations of the Deity in creation and Revelation are harmonious and should . . . be alike impressed upon the minds of our young men." Noting his advanced age, Darby explained that he would "like to end my labors in this world . . . teaching the young the wonders their Maker has displayed in fitting up their habitation, and showing the wonderful accordance of the facts and pervading spirits of Nature and Revelation." He went on to explain the importance of church schools including courses in natural history, warning, "It is here that infidelity takes the field and it is here she will make partial triumphs so long as the church leaves it uncultivated ground. It should be the stronghold of the Bible and it will be."[2]

Darby came to teach at Vanderbilt but did not confine his activities to the university, writing several articles for the religious press stressing the same themes of religious and scientific unity. God, Darby explained, "has left on the rocks hieroglyphics that are easily translated, giving the same account of creation as is found in the Bible."[3] Oscar P. Fitzgerald echoed these themes in an 1878 editorial: "Science is of God. The attempt to array it against revelation will fail. Christian scientists already see the harmony between God's two books—the Bible and Nature. The arrogance of materialists on the one hand, and the imbecility of many ignorant volunteer defenders of the truth on the other, may retard the coming of the bridal day, but religion and science will be wedded in a lawful and eternal union. Pending this happy consummation, let speculators be prudent, and let believers be patient."[4] Such paeans were not the exclusive property of southern Methodists: also in 1878, the *Memphis Baptist* carried an essay proclaiming that "all truths must harmonize" and encouraging scientific study of nature "for it is the work of God, and in studying it we study its Creator."[5]

With such professions of harmony between religion and science by Tennessee's two largest denominational journals, what explains the passage of the Butler bill and the accompanying *Scopes* trial and cultural antagonism of the 1920s? The most succinct explanation must engage the question of control of schools and curriculum. The Butler bill did not emerge in a vacuum but was intricately connected to the growing influence and changing supervision of the public schools—it was a reassertion of parental and taxpayer rights to determine what was to be taught in the schools. The growth of high schools throughout the state meant a larger and larger number of Tennessee youth would take courses in advanced subjects such as biology, forcing an ever-growing number of teachers, parents, and religious leaders to deal with social, scientific, and theological questions that could have otherwise been dealt with abstractly, from a distance, or not at all.

In the first decades of the twentieth century, the great mass of southern Evangelicals could not follow the fine theological and scientific arguments espoused by Black and others to reconcile Genesis with the new geological and biological theories. In spite of rosy statements of the unity of scientific and religious truth, even the most liberal Tennessee Methodists and Baptists, when pushed, took their stand on Scripture. While still professing to find unity of truth in his own mind, Black admitted in 1925 that "the general public has become confused" and that "people jump to the conclusion that belief in evolution is synonymous with rejection of God and the Bible and acceptance of the theory that man has descended from the ape."[6] No longer left to abstract theorizing by scientifically conversant religious leaders, the discussions of evolution in the 1920s were very public affairs that sucked the air out of attempts to reconcile "God and the New Knowledge" and replaced the concept of harmony with a rigid polarization over the primacy of science *or* religion—no longer unified truth, whatever that might have been.[7]

Southern thinkers, whether self-identified more as theologians or scientists, had been aware of theories of evolutionary development from at least the 1860s. In spite of assertions by Clement Eaton and W. J. Cash about the essentially unscientific nature of the nineteenth-century South, many southerners were at least conversant in the science of their day, several joined professional scientific societies (some of national scope), and a few even achieved some level of scientific fame.[8] Instead of the anti-intellectual label that settled on the region in the wake of the Butler bill and *Scopes* trial, a brief survey of state Baptist and Methodist newspapers suggests that several religious leaders were aware of and had some limited engagement with emerging knowledge in the fields of geology and biology. Although awareness of the theories of Charles Darwin, T. H. Huxley, and Herbert Spencer does not equal their acceptance, there was no evangelical prohibition on all things scientific in the American South.

Most southern Methodist and Baptist thinkers, like their counterparts throughout the nation in the second half of the nineteenth century, at first opposed Darwinian notions of evolution but gradually softened their stance into a vague advocacy of theistic natural science. Investigations of the natural world, they argued, would only reveal the hand of God and point to the "existence of the *Great Designer*" and creator of that world; thus, science could be another way to study religion. The Evangelicals built on a belief in the unity of truth and emphasized the impossibility of disagreement between a rightly understood observation of the natural world and a rightly understood religion. As Fitzgerald explained, "Between true religion and real science there can be no conflict."[9] Judge John Lea's welcoming address to attendees at the 1877 Nashville meeting of the American Association for the Advancement of Science (AAAS) suggests that theologians did not have exclusive rights to such phrases. Welcoming the visiting scientists, the Tennessee jurist found important symbolism in the meeting of so many men of science in Nashville, the "city of churches": "The mission of science is the ascertainment of truth and that mission, far from conflicting with any principle of religion, strengthens our conviction in the existence of 'a great first cause' which regulates . . . the orderly arrangement of every particle of matter."[10] Such vague professions were generally acceptable to both churchman and scientist alike, but specific endorsements of the potentially conflicting theory of evolution could bring the two into sharp relief.

At that AAAS meeting, the organization's newly elected president, O. C. Marsh, presented a lengthy paper on a series of North American fossils that, he explained, proved the process of vertebrate evolution. Citing the concurrence of fellow evolutionist Thomas Huxley, Marsh explained that he would not and indeed did not need to offer further proof of evolution "since to doubt evolution today is to doubt science, and science is but another name for truth."[11] But the theory of evolution—specifically, a Darwinian version of evolution that posited the creation and transmutation of species through a process of natural selection with no need of divine direction—that caused scientists and theologians in Tennessee and elsewhere the most difficulty in maintaining their professions of unity.

Thomas O. Summers Sr., an English-born Methodist, editor of the *Nashville Christian Advocate,* and professor of theology at Vanderbilt University, provides a good example of a nineteenth-century Tennessee evangelical thinker attempting to reconcile science and religion. Reprinting excerpts from his regular university lectures in the *Advocate,* Summers offered readers a glimpse at theological efforts to accommodate changing scientific evidence about the age of the Earth. Beginning of course with the admonition that he was not attempting a "reconciliation" of Genesis and geology because they were "not in antagonism," Summers argued definitively for God's agency as creator of the universe and all in it but somewhat more tentatively about "the time and manner of the *genesis* of the universe." Summers seemed content to retain Bishop James Ussher's chronology that fixed man's creation "about six thousand years ago" but allowed more latitude for the rest of creation. Ruling out any interpretation of the Mosaic cosmogony relying on natural (that is, nondivine) causes as "a preposterous and gratuitous notion," Summers suggested three possible methods of reconciling the apparent contradictions between Genesis and the age of the Earth suggested by scientific examination of the fossil record. First, the fossils, like Adam and Eve, could have been formed directly and immediately. Second, he proposed a time delay between the first and second verses of Genesis. With such a system, "In the beginning" could stretch back "as many millions of ages as Geology requires for all the phenomena developed by its researches," while the succeeding six demiurgic days of creation still conformed to Ussher's chronology of six thousand years. Summers seemed to most favor this gap theory, but he also presented his students and readers a third possibility of interpreting each of Moses' "days" as not regular, twenty-four-hour days but as lengthy periods that would allow for geological and biological development. [12]

In his efforts to reconcile Moses' account with modern geology, Summers followed many of the arguments presented by his fellow theologians in the late nineteenth century. [13] The early religious opposition that greeted Darwin's theories had the support of the majority of U.S. scientists, who until the mid-1870s disagreed among themselves about the theory's plausibility. As Summers remarked in the wake of the 1877 AAAS meeting, "When doctors disagree, / disciples then are free" to believe or reject scientific theories. [14] Taking their cues from such prominent scientists as Harvard's Louis Agassiz and even Asa Gray, who had helped to publicize Darwinism in America but nonetheless had some reservations about the theory, Summers and other American religious leaders found it easy to reject Darwinian evolution because of the aggressively naturalistic tone of many of evolution's champions before 1875. But, as Jon Roberts, Ronald Numbers, and others point out, after 1875 the majority of American scientists were moving toward an acceptance of some version of evolution, and, therefore, "attacks on the scientific validity of the transmutation hypothesis became more problematic in the face of the mass exodus of scientists to the evolutionists' camp." [15]

Having projected their institution as a bastion of science and religion—in their words, "to vindicate the existence of a perfect harmony between a sound philosophy and a true religion"—the early Vanderbilt University trustees no doubt congratulated themselves on securing the services of a noted churchman and geologist, Alexander Winchell, for the school's faculty. Winchell believed in evolution, but as he demonstrated in an 1877 *Methodist Quarterly* article, his understanding of evolution left plenty of room for God to act in and through the world. Science, Winchell explained, could not reveal " 'the nature of causal efficiency' at the origin of life." Consequently, "the hypothesis of evolution" allowed "the believer in imminent [*sic*] divine power to posit such power in every term of the evolution."[16] Many late-nineteenth-century scientists and theologians moved to accept a theory of evolution that owed some allegiance to Darwinism but stripped it of its most distinctive contribution—the process of random variation and natural selection—and transformed evolution into simply a benevolent and immanent method of creation by which God acted in and on the world.[17]

Despite Summers's and Winchell's pronouncements of unity between Genesis and the new biological and geological theories, evolution was another matter when confronted by Tennessee's rank-and-file Evangelicals. Winchell and his theories of theistic evolution had been well received by Tennessee Methodists generally and by the Vanderbilt leadership specifically, but a new departure, signaled by the 1878 publication of his *Adamites and Preadamites* and his address on "Man in the Light of Geology" at the same year's Vanderbilt commencement, eventually cost him his position in Nashville. Notwithstanding his efforts to craft a thoroughly theistic interpretation of evolution, Winchell pushed his natural science investigations further than his new southern constituency would allow. Winchell's suggestion of "Preadamite" races—earthly humans predating the biblical and historical Adam—tread not just into theology (the Christian plan of salvation posited the origin of sin in Adam's fall and redemption in Christ's atoning death; could such a plan work backwards to Preadamites?) but also into the racial third rail of southern culture by suggesting an older lineage of nonwhites (Preadamites) and therefore possibly challenging white racial superiority (at least as long as superiority was based on age or seniority).[18] Summers was Winchell's chief prosecutor and the chief defender of Vanderbilt University in 1878 when the trustees decided to terminate the prominent scientist's lectureship.[19]

In the wake of his dismissal, Winchell proclaimed himself a martyr to science, argued that his dismissal stemmed from his belief in evolution, and carried on a lengthy self-defense and attack on Vanderbilt in the pages of the *Nashville American*. McTyeire had attempted to protect the university's reputation by asking Winchell to decline a reappointment for the next term just before the incensed scientist delivered the commencement address. Winchell's acceptance of theistic evolution could not have surprised President McTyeire and the Board of Trust: before accepting the Vanderbilt job in 1875, Winchell had published his views in *Sketches of Creation* (1870) and *The Doctrine of Evolution* (1874).[20] In these books, Winchell had professed a belief in theistic evolution and argued that there could be no conflicting truth because "nature is intended as a revelation of God to all intelligences" and because science "prosecuted to its conclusions leads to God."[21] For their part, the university trustees attempted to justify Winchell's dismissal as a cost-saving measure. It seems more apparent that McTyeire was feeling pressure from the school trustees and a number of southern Methodist newspapers, negative publicity about an evolutionist professor that threatened the young university's supply of students and contributions. Defending McTyeire and the board's actions, the *Nashville Christian Advocate* explained that "parents who have sons to be educated prefer the safety of that atmosphere [of orthodoxy] to genteel infidelity." Summers, Winchell's colleague at Vanderbilt and former editor of the *Advocate,* suggested that Winchell's sin lay not in speculating about various "interpretation[s] of the Mosaic cosmogony" but in crossing the line of propriety in a church institution that was charged with training young ministers by bringing those "speculations" out of his private study and into the lecture room, or in Winchell's case, the commencement platform. Such infidelity, Summers explained, "ought not to be announced in the pulpit, or indeed from the Professor's Chair." Fitzgerald suggested that Winchell's announcement of his beliefs in his commencement address was the real sin, explaining that "no brilliant but erratic professor will be allowed to commit the University, though he is free to commit himself, to any side of any question he pleases."[22] In this sense, Winchell's dismissal differed little from the contemporaneous dismissal of Edward Joynes on accusations of too liberal use of alcohol: both represented efforts to protect Vanderbilt's reputation. But the dismissal of Joynes would not receive the same national attention from scientists, who saw Winchell's firing as evidence of a total lack of academic freedom.

In the wake of the Winchell case, Tennessee's Baptist and Methodist newspapers settled back into their patterns of asserting a vaguely abstract agreement of science and religion—both rightly understood—and continued the assault on any but the most assuredly theistic explanations of evolution. If any pattern could be said to exist, the *Memphis Baptist* and its successor, the *Nashville Baptist and Reflector,* tended to see less possibility of any sort of accommodation to evolution than did some writers in the state Methodist newspapers. James R. Graves explained his lack of comment on evolution in the *Baptist* because he believed it to be "a form of error so absurd that it would end by a self-explosion"; therefore, he declined to publicize the theory and engage in unnecessary conflict. Several Methodist authors attacked evolutionary theories as well, but editor George Winton's statement that "from the first we have been of the opinion that there is nothing essentially hostile to Christianity in the evolutionary hypothesis" was more indicative of the *Nashville Christian Advocate*'s turn-of-the-century tone. Both papers continued to assert the possibility of theistic interpretations of nature that maintained God's agency in the special creation of humans and rejected the possibility of evolving new species (as opposed to evolution within a specific species).[23]

As had been the case in the earlier school Bible-reading campaigns, Tennessee Evangelicals' concerns about evolution would take on new importance during and soon after World War I. Editor Thomas Ivey of the *Nashville Christian Advocate* took as his lesson from the years of bloodshed that "the materialistic education of Germany, stripped of Christian ethics and resting on the ethics of the jungle, . . . was responsible for the war and its horrible methods." A chief part of that materialism was said to be rationalistic German science; Ivey and other commentators often listed acceptance of Darwinism as a prime example of German atheism (despite the fact that Darwin was British).[24] Tennessee's Methodists and Baptists became increasingly concerned during the 1910s about the possible encroachment of such atheism in their part of the country. Nashville Baptist pastor and denominational leader George A. Lofton pessimistically warned the Tennessee Baptist Convention in 1910 about the dangers of "Higher Criticism, Evolution and other forms of infidelity that [had] captured the schools of the North, and [were] creeping slowly into Southern schools."[25]

Thus, part of Tennessee Evangelicals' move to reject all theories of evolution was an effort to more clearly distinguish themselves from the national and even worldwide shift toward rationalism and materialism they saw reflected in the recent war. In his account of American Protestant intellectuals' encounter with Darwinism, Roberts suggests that the minority of thinkers who adopted an uncompromising defense of the Bible and remained unwilling to concede any ground to evolutionary science drew such rigid lines as a means of maintaining their status as "outsiders" to a larger American culture.[26] This suggestive idea takes on a new significance when applied to southern Evangelicals, who had been, especially in their Prohibition and public school campaigns, working to extend their beliefs and morals to the larger southern society. The Evangelicals' distinction as outsiders, therefore, was meant for all of the South, not just evangelical Protestant members of specific churches. Denominational leaders wanted to preserve the entire South as distinct from the rest of the nation.

Having already identified the public school as the means through which to shape the rising generation, most Tennessee Evangelicals could be persuaded to support the efforts to ban the teaching of evolution from state as well as denominational schools. Bishop Warren Candler would boast about the Butler bill and *Scopes* trial in the fall of 1925, rejoicing that the trial had attracted "attention . . . to the fact that evangelical Christianity is the dominant type of religion in the South," a region that alone could "maintain unimpaired the faith of historic Christianity, the pure faith of our fathers and the best hope of our posterity." Noting that "the great revival of 1800" had begun in the South, Candler asserted that the "Southern Churches are abundantly able to defend successfully 'the faith once for all delivered to the saints'" and would remain "the stronghold of evangelical Christianity in the United States."[27] To do so, Candler and many other southern religious leaders seemed to suggest, the South would have to remain outside of the increasingly secular national culture.

In spite of their professions of the unity of religious and scientific knowledge, only a small number of early-twentieth-century Tennessee Evangelicals seemed willing to reexamine their theological interpretations in light of new scientific revelations, choosing instead to criticize or dismiss scientists for meddling in philosophy or jumping to erroneous conclusions. In the first quarter of the twentieth century and especially in the wake of World War I, the arguments of the minority of theistic evolutionists in Tennessee would be overwhelmed by the more general perception that "evolution is synonymous with rejection of God and the Bible and acceptance of the theory that man has descended from the ape."[28] When evidence suggested that evolution was being taught in state colleges and public schools, most Tennessee Baptists and Methodists lost what little patience they had for efforts to harmonize scientific and religious theories of natural history. Believing that current theories of evolution—especially those taught in the public schools—were materialistic rather than theistic, the great majority of Tennessee Methodists and Baptists moved to protect their children from learning about such "science falsely so-called" and to assert control over the state's educational system.

Antievolution Campaigns and Public Education

Having taken to the pulpit and press in their campaigns to require and justify the use of the Bible in Tennessee public schools, state evangelical leaders were pre-disposed to join in and, to a certain extent, lead the national campaigns against the teaching of evolution. As perhaps the most visible markers of a national conservative social and theological resurgence in several mainline Protestant churches, the antievolution campaigns of the post–World War I decade really began in the Northeast and Midwest but had their biggest success in the South in the 1920s.[29] Various historians have credited the regional success of such to a lack of industrialization, the poor quality of scientific education, or the overwhelm-ingly conservative nature of southern theology.[30] Despite the presence of some high-profile believers in various forms of theistic evolution, most evangelical

Tennesseans in the first quarter of the twentieth century knew only enough about the scientific theories of evolution to fear the potential ramifications of undercutting biblical literalism. That was sufficient; the antievolution campaign and subsequent *Scopes* trial had far less to do with scientific understanding than with the same battles religious Tennesseans had been fighting since the 1870s over the direction of southern society and the control of public schools.

The process of formalizing education in public elementary schools with compulsory-attendance policies that had led Tennessee Evangelicals to argue for a positive requirement of daily Bible readings eventually led them also to pursue negative legislation banning the teaching of evolution. Opposition to evolution was the more visible of the two fundamentalist crusades of the post–World War I era, the other being a campaign against the perceived liberalism in theology and social policy in mainline Protestant denominations. Tennessee Protestants had only a small number of recognizable theological or social liberals in their ranks and thus were less concerned with them than with fortifying buttresses against liberals in other parts of the country. Highbrow theological discussions rarely incite popular protest, much less popular understanding. But because Tennessee Evangelicals had so recently mobilized to Christianize the public schools, the group provided especially ripe prospects for the fundamentalists' antievolution campaign. By 1915, Tennessee Evangelicals had in essence sanctified the public school. The same arguments of majority rule, citizen's rights, and the Christian nation that had been effective in justifying daily Bible reading were quickly employed and equally successful in the campaigns to ban the teaching of evolution in Tennessee schools.

Some Tennessee Evangelicals had expressed concerns about evolution and especially its presence in public and denominational schools from the beginning of the twentieth century. Methodist L. H. Brown urged his fellow Evangelicals "to cease mincing matters with the scientists" and rally church "members and all Christians [to] line up with all their strength and stand forth for the rectitude and truth of the Bible." Further, he implored, "The Christian Churches should at once take such measures as they can," including any efforts "to stop their colleges and universities from teaching the [evolution] theory to the youth of the nation."[31] Despite Brown's call to action, neither Tennessee's Methodists nor its Baptists took notice until after World War I, when three important issues combined to inflame passions and inspire the successful extension of the antievolution campaign. The first of these issues was the fear that parents were failing in their duties to properly educate their children in religion and that Germany's lack of religious education had caused the recent war, as discussed in chapter 5. Second, the much publicized allegations by a former student that evolution was being taught in one of the state's Baptist universities made Tennessee Evangelicals fear that even their own colleges were unsafe. The third and perhaps most important element was the ascent of William Jennings Bryan, a hero to most religious and Democratic white Tennesseans, to the leadership of the national antievolution campaigns and his and others' well-timed visits to the state to further fan the flames.

In spite of Vanderbilt University's history of having dismissed a professor in the 1870s for his efforts to explain "Man in the Light of Geology," *Nashville Christian Advocate* editor George Winton argued in the summer of 1908 that "theology and science go well together, and church schools have some advantages in both." The former missionary and fervent supporter of Vanderbilt suggested some of the advantages of a church school over a state institution were that "the professor who teaches in the church college the theories of [Charles] Lyell and Darwin is not suspected of heresy on that account. In fact, he is above suspicion. He is a teacher of up-to-date science, but he is also a Christian."[32] In spite of Winton's perhaps generous view of the situation, allegations in 1921 that Dr. C. W. Davis, a young professor of agriculture and biology at the Baptists' Union University, had been teaching about evolution set Tennessee Baptists on a statewide search for heresies that were supposedly driving students away from the faith of their parents. The charges were first levied by a disgruntled former student but gained strength when Selsus E. Tull, the pastor of Jackson's First Baptist Church and a member of the university's Board of Trustees, continued to press for an investigation within the school and by the Tennessee Baptist Convention. The faculty, students, and president of the university supported Davis, and, after he signed a statement affirming his faith in "the Bible as the fully inspired and infallible word of God" and his acceptance of "the articles of faith and practice as generally held by Baptists," Davis was allowed to stay.[33]

Davis's predicament offers a good example of how, despite the repeated professions of both Baptists and Methodists of the essential unity of religious and scientific truth, the air was getting exceptionally thin for advocates of theistic evolution in postwar Tennessee. After interviewing Davis, his students, and the university president, the investigating committee appointed by the Tennessee Baptist Convention concluded that the professor was "a thorough believer in the Personal God as the Creator of all things" and "in the Bible as the authoritative Word of God." The committee reported that the controversy had arisen from Davis's unwise use of the term *evolution* so "as to leave his position in doubt in the minds of some" but concluded that there was nothing heretical and "that his teachings are now free from the use of such terms as might lead to doubt as to his position."[34] The committee's report, its acceptance by the state convention's executive board, and endorsement by the editor of the *Baptist and Reflector* may have reflected a limited acceptance of the possibility of theistic evolution among some Tennessee Baptist leaders. But Tull, who had first publicized the charges against Davis and would not be satisfied with the results of the investigation, pointedly asked, "WHAT SORT OF EVOLUTION IS NOT CONTRARY TO THE BIBLE?" Writing before the results of the investigation were made public, Tull proclaimed his belief that *"any sort of Evolution,* when carried to its logical conclusions and effects, is 'contrary' to the Bible, and is a dangerous element to be propagated in the classrooms of any Baptist College."[35]

The mere allegations of evolution at Union brought a firestorm of criticism from Tennessee Baptists, prompting *Nashville Baptist and Reflector* editor Jesse D. Moore to caution authors to "be considerate of each other" in their exchanges.[36] The previous controversies over the control of Vanderbilt University had already alerted Tennessee Evangelicals to the importance of supervising the teachers and curricula of their colleges, but the Davis affair renewed the calls for vigilance. Baptist commentator T. A. J. Beasley warned his coreligionists to supervise the colleges and "promptly dismiss any teacher who teaches any science so-called which contradicts the Bible." In like fashion, Methodist George W. Read suggested that Christians needed to be vigilant and "demand that nothing shall be taught in the Church school that undermines the very foundations of our religion."[37]

Although some conservative Evangelicals in Tennessee and elsewhere had expressed concern about the teaching of evolution, it took the leadership of Bryan, a Presbyterian layman and former politician, to focus a variety of vague fears into a nationwide campaign for religiously "safe" schools. As George Marsden suggests, Bryan's leadership "ensured wide press coverage, which of course always invited further simpli[fi]cations of the issue."[38] Besides earning the favor of Tennessee's Democrats and farmers, Bryan had long been noticed and for the most part praised by the state's religious press. As early as 1897, E. E. Hoss expressed his "admiration for [Bryan's] character and . . . honest patriotism."[39] Like numerous other Evangelicals, Bryan's faith had been stirred during and soon after the war, believing as he did that Germans' atheism, materialism, and acceptance of Darwinism had led to their military aggression. But what most galvanized Bryan's attention was a study by Bryn Mawr psychologist James H. Leuba that showed religious belief among youths declining with each year of education they received. Bryan first turned to a biblical metaphor, inquiring, "What shall it profit a man if he shall gain all the learning of the schools and lose his faith in God?" Bryan, who had remained in the public eye by traveling on the lecture circuit after resigning as Woodrow Wilson's secretary of state, added two new antievolution speeches to his repertoire and aptly titled them "The Menace of Darwinism" and "The Bible and Its Enemies."[40]

In his earliest antievolution speeches, Bryan echoed many of the themes that had driven the Bible-reading campaigns of the previous decade, but he offered little more than a rehashed version of the home rule compromise as a solution: he encouraged parents and local communities to be vigilant about their schools and teachers. Kentucky Baptists had a more specific plan, which Bryan latched onto and championed until his death in 1925. At their annual meeting in late 1921, the Kentucky Baptist State Board of Missions debated and passed a resolution imploring the legislature to prohibit the teaching of evolution in the state public schools. With Bryan's endorsement, the antievolution bill came within one vote of passing in 1922 despite the courageous and vigorous opposition from University of Kentucky President Frank L. McVey. Tennessee Baptists and Methodists paid attention to the debates in the Bluegrass State and noted the bill's defeat. Baptist editor Jesse D. Moore expressed some concern about the legislation, admitting his dismay "that the lines have been drawn at the point of legislation. Kentucky schools now have state license to teach Darwinianism." Moore seemed to be hearkening back to the days of the home rule compromise, fearing that legislative battles, especially unsuccessful ones like that in Kentucky, would weaken the movement.[41]

In the summer of 1922, O. L. Hailey, a prominent Tennessee Baptist minister and former co-owner of the *Nashville Baptist and Reflector,* published an article in the state Baptist paper effectively drawing the battle lines in Tennessee. Choosing a title that spoke volumes, Hailey posed a rhetorical question in bold type: "Church or State, Who Shall Define the Education of Our Children? Shall the State Teach Evolution?" Hailey, like so many earlier Tennessee Evangelicals, recognized the importance of education to both church and state and sought to justify the prototypical Christian's concern about his child's soul: "Since [the] Christian must look to the word of God, and in that word finds that he will reap what he sows, he knows he must guard the education of youth for the future." Questions about evolution may have been new, Hailey admitted, but the bigger issue of "who shall decide the sort of education that shall be aimed at?" was "a question as old as Christianity." Hailey's criticisms were no doubt aimed at the teaching of evolution in denominational schools, especially Union University. But Hailey also warned that evolutionary teaching was more widespread: "more and more the doctrine of evolution is taking possession of our schools and we are growing a generation of infidels and skeptics."[42]

Hailey's article apparently expressed the concerns of many Tennessee Baptists, rehashing the arguments of the Bible-reading campaigns and setting the agenda for the antievolution campaigns that would eventually lead to Dayton in 1925. He did find some opposition within the denomination, much of it from defenders of Union University. E. E. Northern, a former Union professor and apparently a believer in some form of theistic evolution, addressed an "Open Letter to Dr. O. L. Hailey" professing the desire, like Hailey, to combat "materialism wherever we find it." But, Northern warned, Hailey might have been simplifying the issue too much in his campaign against evolution. Northern asked Hailey for more specific definitions of *Christianity, evolution,* and *materialism* and further implored Hailey to name names: "From your article the only fair inference is that all professors in all state schools are teaching the dreadful things you and I are fighting. . . . Now evidently you did not intend to make such a broad charge as this."[43] Hailey and Northern exchanged several letters in the paper, and Hailey's second letter set the framework for the campaigns of the next three years within the church and the legislature.

As for Northern's questions about where evolution was being taught, Hailey warned that it was everywhere, as could easily be determined by "examining almost any text-book on science which is taught in our schools above the grammar grades." Hailey was building on T. A. J. Beasley's May 1921 argument that "The Southern Baptists should have a text-book committee composed of competent men who are sound to the core on the doctrines of the Bible, and whose business it should be to supervise the selection of text-books for our schools." Though not a party to the Hailey-Northern exchange, Ivey would certainly have agreed with Hailey's arguments. A few years earlier, in the midst of the campaigns to require Bible reading in the public schools, Ivey had stated unequivocally his belief that "while the enemies of our Christian religion are laboring so assiduously to prevent the teaching of the Bible in public schools, it would be well for us all to see that no atheistical books are being used."[44]

Hailey's second justification, which had been pressed into service in the Bible-reading campaigns and would continue to be prominent even after the *Scopes* trial, concerned majority rule. Hailey again elided constitutional prohibitions of an establishment of religion by making control of the schools (and thus enforcement of religiously based curricula) subject only to the will of the majority. As Hailey explained, "Evangelical Christians, . . . who constitute the majority of the citizens of the United States, have a right to object, and do object to the teaching of anything in the schools which are supported by the state, which is contrary to the doctrines taught in the Bible." The majority of parents and taxpayers, as Bryan also argued, should control teachers and curricula. Campaigning against evolution in West Virginia, Bryan told the state legislature, "The hand that writes the pay check rules the school."[45] Methodist

A. M. Mann argued that antievolution laws represented a legitimate instance of the legislature acting on the "sacred rights of parents and guardians over their children and their charges."[46]

Hailey and other Tennessee leaders of the antievolution campaign also restated their earlier arguments that America was a Christian nation and that the public schools were responsible for upholding that heritage. Consequently, any teachings that might undercut that heritage could and should be barred from the schools. As Alfred F. Smith explained to Tennessee's Methodists, "American education must be Christian if we are to preserve our Christian inheritance." Moore went even further, explaining that the country was not only Christian but "Evangelically Christian"; therefore, not only should the Bible be read daily in the public schools, but also "legislation among us can, and should take account of certain phases of Christian doctrine and practice. It must do that or else it would sanction irreligion and would be opposed to Christianity."[47] Methodists, Baptists, and Bryan argued that because the majority of America's (or at least Tennessee's) citizens were evangelical Protestants, they could properly pass legislation that reflected that belief and preserve what they considered to be the nation's Christian foundations.

In addition to these arguments recycled from the Bible-reading campaigns, Bryan added another theme that moved from majoritarianism toward a populist embrace of the elusive concept of fairness. In an argument that seemed more suited to the rest of the country than to a Tennessee that had so recently required daily Bible reading, Bryan proclaimed that if Christians "cannot teach the views of the majority in the schools supported by taxation, then a few people cannot teach at public expense their scientific interpretation that attacks every vital principle of Christianity."[48] Bryan's argument played well among Tennessee Evangelicals because they did not believe that they were teaching Christianity or at least any objectionable form of Christianity. As they had so often proclaimed, daily Bible reading, prayers, and devotions were acceptable because they were nonsectarian activities. Hailey went along with arguments that Bible reading was nonsectarian and attacked the teaching of evolution in public schools as the teaching of a form of religion—scientific sectarianism, as it were. As he explained in 1922, "The Christian portion of the commonwealth has accepted their part of the agreement, and refuse to teach in the public schools, any particular doctrine which impinges upon the rights of their fellow citizens who hold to a different view from them. But the State has violated that compact, and is doing so every day. By parity of reasoning, those who are estopped from teaching Christianity, out of regard for their neighbors, are also estopped from teaching anti-Christianity upon the same ground."[49] Such arguments were staples of Hailey's and Bryan's arsenal and were repeated even after the *Scopes* trial, when the *Watchman Examiner* erroneously reported that "Tennessee, like many other States, has a law prohibiting the teaching of the Bible in the public schools." If that were true, the paper explained, "is it fair that the Bible shall be attacked where the Bible cannot be taught and defended?"[50]

Bryan's national antievolution campaigns and Hailey's efforts in Tennessee led to the introduction of antievolution measures in six states in 1923.[51] Hervey Whitfield, a Tennessee state senator from Montgomery and Robertson counties, introduced an act "to make it unlawful to teach or permit to be taught in any institution of learning, supported by public taxation, atheism, agnosticism, Darwinism, or any other hypothesis that links man in blood relationship to any other form of life." After an attempt to table the measure, it was referred to the Senate Education Committee, which rejected the bill.[52] Although the Senate passed a resolution inviting Bryan to address a joint session of the General Assembly in favor of the measure, the House did not concur. There appears to have been little organized support for or against the measures; Nashville's secular newspapers seemed most concerned that such a bill would lead to lengthy and acrimonious debate that would divert attention from more important legislation.[53] Moore expressed some misgivings about the concept of legislating against teaching evolution, explaining in the *Nashville Baptist and Reflector,* "It is not for us to say whether some other approach to a solution of the problems would be better; but since the bill has been introduced, the alternatives are: whether we shall favor the measure or oppose it." After rehashing most of the arguments, Moore stated that Baptists should support the law and not give evolutionists and modernists strength by allowing them to defeat it.[54]

The lack of organized support doomed the 1923 bill. In an editorial printed at the beginning of the 1923 legislative session, Moore listed three pieces of "important legislation" that Baptists hoped to secure from the Sixty-third General Assembly. The list, which included better enforcement of Prohibition and Sunday-observance (blue) laws and the restriction of divorce to "Scriptural grounds," omitted any mention of antievolution legislation despite Kentucky's much-publicized efforts a year earlier.[55] The antievolution bill was not introduced until mid-March, well into the legislative session, further suggesting a lack of preparation or support. Finally, the bill may have been defeated because of its wording. In linking the prohibition of teaching Darwinism with atheism and agnosticism and further in explaining evolution as only a "hypothesis that links man in blood relationship to any other form of life," the 1923 bill lacked the important biblical authority that the successful 1925 law would cite.[56]

Despite the inglorious fate of the 1923 bills, Tennessee's antievolutionists launched a full-scale campaign to pass a similar measure at the next legislative session two years later. As one supporter explained in a letter to the *Nashville Banner,* the antievolution cause was not lost: "like the prohibition question—it is coming. . . . God is not dead, and the Christian people of this state will not stand supinely by and see the Bible trampled under foot while they are forced to pay the bills."[57] Bryan and other national fundamentalists, including William Bell Riley, T. T. Martin, John Roach Straton, and J. Frank Norris, toured the state, while superevangelist Billy Sunday held revivals in the state both in 1923 and during the 1925 legislative session. The most direct offensive came from Bryan's rendition of his "Is the Bible True?" speech before a crowd of supporters in Nashville's Ryman Auditorium in January 1924. Not just a gathering of religious fanatics, the audience included a former governor as well as current governor Austin Peay, a prominent Baptist layman. Peay was obviously swayed by Bryan's speech; the governor's special message to the legislature on signing the Butler antievolution bill borrowed largely from Bryan's themes. Smith applauded Bryan's speeches in the *Nashville Christian Advocate,* noting how he "eloquently defended the Scriptures against evolution and . . . rightly advocated the protection of our children against those who would disturb their belief in the supernatural and the miraculous." Bryan supporters and antievolution advocates, led by Nashville attorney W. B. Marr, distributed copies of the speech in an effort to stir up opinion in advance of the 1924 state elections. Evolution opponents also sent copies of the text to the newly elected legislators before the opening of the 1925 session.[58]

As a result of the efforts of Bryan, Sunday, Marr, and others, two different legislators introduced antievolution bills in the 1925 General Assembly. John Washington Butler, a farmer, former teacher, Primitive Baptist, and occasional newspaper essayist from Macon County, submitted House Bill 185, "An Act Prohibiting the Teaching of the Evolution Theory in All the Universities, Normals and All Other Public Schools of Tennessee, Which Are Supported in Whole or in Part by the Public School Funds of the State, and to Provide Penalties for the Violations Thereof." Butler was a second-term legislator who had long been interested in education and rural life in his native Upper Cumberland region. Like many other Tennesseans, Butler mourned the loss of local control over such matters as teacher qualifications, textbook adoption, and curriculum. Like Bryan, Butler latched onto the symbolic though meaningful issue of evolution, which Butler feared undermined a proper education in Christian citizenship.[59] Butler's bill quickly passed the House with only five dissenting votes and then went to the upper chamber, which had already rejected a similar bill. Butler's bill looked sure to suffer the same fate until Speaker of the Senate Lew D. Hill of Sparta announced his support and delayed consideration of the bill until after the legislative recess, allowing antievolution forces to mount a campaign to sway votes. The tactics apparently worked: when the Senate reconvened, the education committee reported in favor of the bill, and, after a spirited debate, the Senate passed the measure by a vote of twenty-four to six.[60]

The *Nashville Baptist and Reflector* praised the Butler bill and the General Assembly for passing it, stating, "We are convinced that the Legislature is not only within its powers but also within its duty in this matter." Moore rehashed several of the campaign's themes, arguing forcefully that "While the state cannot teach religion, it is clearly not the duty of the state to teach irreligion." The legislation passed more quietly beyond the notice of the Methodist papers, although one correspondent expressed approval of the measure in June: "My hat's off to the Tennessee Legislature for having enough Christian courage to take an initial step in a heroic effort to drive out this would-be usurper in the field of American education."[61]

During the legislative recess, supporters and opponents of the measure mobilized letter-writing campaigns to legislators, the governor, and local newspapers. Opponents variously argued that evolution was not necessarily irreligious, that an antievolution statute would violate the constitutional protections of freedom of religion and separation of church and state, and that such a law violated academic and intellectual freedom. Vanderbilt Professor Edwin Mims drafted a petition and solicited the signatures of prominent ministers, educators, and politicians in the state. He earnestly sought the support of University of Tennessee President Harcourt Morgan: Mims was reluctant to lead the opposition because "Vanderbilt is of course already branded as heretic, modernist, etc.," and "we have held back because we thought we might hurt the cause." Morgan did not support the petition, sheepishly explaining the university's position to Mims and the governor: "The subject of Evolution so intricately involves religious beliefs, concerning which the University has no disposition to dictate, that the University declines to engage in the controversy."[62]

Opposition to the bill from religious quarters showed both the persistence of belief among some state Protestants in the possibility of theistic forms of evolution and the quickly evaporating room for holding or expressing such opinions. Methodist Black restated his belief in some form of the day-age theory of creation and reiterated the old mantra that "the Church no less than science must be a seeker of the truth, nor has she anything to fear from the discovery of truth in any realm." Some prominent Nashville religious figures protested the bill. In addition to members of usually suspect liberal denominations such as the Episcopalians, many prominent Methodists, Baptists, Presbyterians, and members of the Disciples of Christ and Church of Christ, including Dr. John L. Hill of the Baptist Sunday School Board and Dr. Stonewall Anderson of the southern Methodist Board of Education, signed a petition. Dr. Richard L. Owenby of Columbia's First Methodist Church criticized the House vote, explaining in a sermon that the representatives "were making monkeys of themselves at the rate of 71 to 5" and that "the missing link . . . might be found near Capitol Hill."[63] Some other Methodist laymen and ministers criticized the bill and the logic of taxpayers' rights. In a defense of scientific expertise and intellectual freedom, Methodist Rev. Rembert G. Smith suggested that it was "as sensible for a man to tell the doctor what sort of medicine to give his sick child on the ground that he was going to pay the bill as for the State absolutely to dictate to the teacher what he shall teach."[64]

Other religious writers strongly supported the proposed law and criticized their brethren for opposing it. A fellow Methodist strongly rebuked Smith in the *Christian Advocate,* reinforcing support for the bill with a repetition of the postwar fears and explaining that evolution was "on a par with Bolshevism, anarchy, and even atheism" and therefore had to be opposed by any honest American. The Baptist Pastors Council of Nashville, claiming to speak for "ten thousand laymen of twenty local churches," supported the bill and called on Peay to sign it.[65] The opposition of some of the denominational leaders and urban pastors, when contrasted with the overwhelming legislative support (in a rural-dominated General Assembly with a majority of Methodists among its members), provides a reminder of the divided opinion of some state Evangelicals about the theory of evolution and the growing urban and rural tensions within Tennessee's Methodist and Baptist denominational structures.[66] The months leading up to and following the *Scopes* trial also reveal the power of arguments for the control of the public schools as even some of the most vocal defenders of theistic evolution eventually conceded state power to regulate education.

Both the Baptist and Methodist newspapers expressed some misgivings about the legislation, especially after the onslaught of correspondence and public statements for and against the measures. *Baptist and Reflector* editor O. E. Bryan, after announcing that the bill had passed and giving it a halfhearted endorsement, warned that neither "Culture" nor "Legislation" could "save a people; if so, Rome would not have fallen. She surpassed the world in legislation. Rome fell because of the absence of character." As southern Evangelicals had so often done before when faced with social conflict, Bryan returned to the oldest evangelical theme: What was most needed, he argued, was the "regeneration of the individual." His Methodist counterpart, Smith, faced with a denomination far more divided over the evolution issue, similarly called for a social and theological big-tent policy for the church: "The Church has in it people of many shades of opinion upon all possible questions. If one group should throw out all others who do not agree with them, they would not only damage the body of Christ, but would also manifest such a spirit of intolerance as Christ could not approve."[67]

In the days following the Butler bill's passage by the Tennessee Senate, concerned citizens showered Peay with letters and personal entreaties for and against the bill. Peay had built his gubernatorial campaigns on promises of government reform, new highways, and better education for the Volunteer State, and he would win election to three consecutive terms (most Tennessee governors only served two).[68] Opponents of the bill looked at his progressive record and outspoken support for the University of Tennessee and public education in general and believed that he would veto the bill. Supporters of the antievolution measure took heart in his southern Baptist background, frequent recourse to populist and majoritarian themes, and his conspicuous presence at William Jennings Bryan's 1924 Ryman Auditorium fulmination against the teaching of evolution. Peay's political biographer, Joseph Tant Macpherson, has described the governor as a "latter-day agrarian" in businessman's clothing who "conceived of his particular mission as the rescuer of Tennessee's numerical majority, the farmers." At his second inaugural, in 1925, Peay praised the people of Tennessee who voted for him, reminding himself and his opponents that "Sovereignty is theirs in this country." Pastor W. M. Wood of Nashville's Edgefield Baptist Church, identifying himself as a "friend and supporter" of the governor, implored him "to sign the present bill and help us in Tennessee who are making a desperate fight against the inroads of Materialism to protect our children and make our public schools safe places for the next generation." Rhea County School Superintendent Walter White wrote to Peay on official Board of Education letterhead, stating, "I am of the opinion that this is the greatest step Tennessee has taken since the saloon was abolished. You deserve the thanks of all honest people."[69] Opponents from a variety of religious, educational, and occupational grounds urged Peay to "veto the fanatical measure," arguing that "Ignorance is rank enough around here now. Conditions will change for the worse when the State's Scientific, progressive men and women go elsewhere to invest their services."[70]

With all of the correspondence he received both for and against the Butler bill, Governor Peay surely recognized that whatever his decision, he would be criticized. Various contemporaries and later historians have criticized Peay's religious reactionism and intellectual shortcomings or attempted to absolve him from criticism by explaining that his signature was politically expedient, necessary to ensure the passage of his massive General Education Bill and

expanded appropriation for the University of Tennessee.[71] The governor had
to have noticed the large majorities in both houses of the General Assembly that
had supported the bill and would presumably override a veto. Furthermore, he
announced that the bill was a symbolic "protest" and that "nobody believes that
it is going to be an active statute." In the absence of significant surviving private
correspondence, it is difficult to determine with certainty Peay's real motives
for signing the bill, but he did take the unusual step of writing an explanation to
accompany his signature. Besides displaying his at best naive if not dishonest
statement that he could "find nothing of consequence in the books now being
taught in our schools with which this bill will interfere in the slightest manner"
and that "it will not put our teachers in any jeopardy," Peay's language clearly
shows that he was not only paying attention to Bryan's 1924 Ryman address
but apparently taking notes as well. Taking pages from Bryan, Peay explained
that "comments on the Bible are forbidden; hence any theory which disputes
the integrity of the Bible is forbidden also." In addition, Peay echoed Bryan's
populist theme of majority rule over the schools: "the people have the right and
must have the right to regulate what is taught in their schools."[72]

Peay's justifications for the measure echoed both Bryan and the decade-old
Baptist and Methodist arguments in favor of Bible reading, even to the point
of using the existence of the 1915 Bible-reading law to justify the antievolution
measure. Since the state constitution "recognized God," a state law required
daily reading of "His holy word," and the Bible "teaches that man was created
by God in His own image," Peay supported a ban on teaching evolution, which,
he explained, "is at utter variance with the Bible story of man's creation."[73]
Arguing first that the Bible-reading statute was constitutional because it was
nonsectarian, Peay further justified the antievolution statute because it did "not
require any particular theory or interpretation of the Bible regarding man's
creation to be taught in the public schools." As for the establishment clause in
Tennessee's constitution, Peay explained that the Butler bill could not infringe
on freedom of thought or religion because a teacher "has the undoubted right
to believe and think on the subject without restraint from any human authority,
but the constitution does not accord to the teacher the right to teach in our
schools in matter whatever he may choose." Teachers, explained Peay, Bryan,
and the antievolution advocates, were employees of the state and in their official
capacity could be restrained from teaching evolution even if they believed it to
be true.[74]

Peay's ultimate justification for the bill, which strayed from his usual reserved
and analytical language toward a more emotional theme, is perhaps the most
revealing about his and others' support for the measure. The governor explained

that the Butler bill was "a distinct protest against an irreligious tendency to exalt so called science, and deny the Bible in some schools and quarters—a tendency fundamentally wrong and fatally mischievous in its effects on our children, our institutions and our country." Furthermore, the bill represented a reaction to the "deep and wide-spread belief that something is shaking the fundamentals of the country, both in religion and morals" and that "an abandonment of the old fashioned faith and belief in the Bible, is our trouble in large degree." Peay's signing of the antievolution bill elicited a firestorm of protest from some critics within and outside the state but nonetheless garnered the support of many members of disparate denominations. As Baptist editor John D. Freeman reported from Dayton in the summer of 1925, "Baptists, Methodists, Congregationalists, Presbyterians, Disciples of Christ, Adventists, and Catholics have joined hands for once in a concerted effort to defend the Lord Jesus Christ against unlicensed propagation of the doctrine of brute ancestry and denial of supernatural religion."[75]

The antievolution campaign united conservative Christians and fundamentalists precisely because it was a symbolic protest. The unsuccessful 1923 antievolution bill attempted to specify on scientific terms what was to be prohibited (a "hypothesis that links man in blood relationship to any other form of life"), while the Butler bill specifically prohibited "any theory that denies the story of the Divine creation of man as taught in the Bible, and teach[es] instead that man has descended from a lower order of animals." Both bills discussed humans' relation to other creatures, but the Butler bill specified divine authority for human creation. There may have been some confusion or debate about humans' relationship to other animals, but believers of many different creeds could line up behind "the story of the Divine creation of man as taught in the Bible," especially if nothing too specific was said about that story. In other words, biblical authority was a powerful slogan; as long as no one attempted to parse out exactly what was meant or how to interpret the Bible, Christians of many stripes could support the bill.[76]

One way to uncover the symbolic importance of the Butler bill is to compare its fate with that of a similar but unsuccessful bill also submitted to the 1925 General Assembly. House Bill 252, "An Act to Make It Unlawful to Employ Atheists as Teachers in Public Schools of the State of Tennessee," though recommended for passage by the House Education Committee, was opposed by the judicial committee and eventually tabled after several attempts at amendment. The bill, which would have required a teacher to believe "in the existance [*sic*] of God and the deity of His Son Jesus Christ," incited protests to the governor and legislative attempts to amend in favor of a denomination "which teaches the Divinity of God, alone." Members of the General Assembly, like the rest of the state, were overwhelmingly Protestant, but even they quibbled over the theological questions of God or Christ's "divinity" or "deity."[77] The bill was too specific to be a slogan and therefore was defeated forty-one to thirty-three in the House.[78]

In his message accompanying the signed bill, Peay stated his hope that "probably, the law will never be applied."[79] He did not count on the combination of circumstances that eventually led to Dayton: a nascent American Civil Liberties Union anxious for justice if not just attention, enterprising boosters seeking to put Dayton on the map, and an aging Populist leader eager to defend his principle of Christian majority rule. After the publicity surrounding the passage of the Butler bill, the American Civil Liberties Union advertised its willingness to fund the defense of a case to test the new law. A group of Dayton citizens, perhaps more out of a desire for notoriety than out of any deep support or opposition to the law, persuaded Rhea County High School teacher John Scopes to be charged with the crime of teaching evolution.[80] For eleven days in July 1925, the whole world seemed to converge on the small East Tennessee town of Dayton—fundamentalists and modernists, newspapermen and WGN-Chicago radio reporters with microphones, William Jennings Bryan and Clarence Darrow, among others.

Much of the attention at the trial and subsequently has focused on the issue of evolution, characterizing the trial as a confrontation of religion and science. But if Bryan and the state's other attorneys had had their way, the trial would have avoided any lengthy discussion of evolution. In their correspondence before the trial, Bryan and Prosecutor S. K. Hicks discussed their strategy and attempted to anticipate defense arguments. Expecting that "quite a number of noted scientists and Modernists will attend the trial and give testimony in behalf of the defendant['s]" claim that "the theory of evolution does not conflict with the story of the Divine Creation of man as taught by the Bible," Hicks asked Bryan to suggest a number of "prominent" "able men and Fundamentalists" who could testify "that the theory of evolution does conflict with the Bible."[81] Although Bryan had often spoken strongly that evolution was not true, he warned Hicks away from such a strategy: "While I am perfectly willing to go into the question of evolution, I am not sure that it is involved. The *right* of the *people* speaking through the legislature, to control the schools which they *create* and *support* is the real issue as I see it. If not the people, who?"[82] Bryan repeated the same argument he had been making since his entry into the antievolution campaigns; it was the same argument he had used during his Populist days when he first stormed out of Nebraska onto the national stage in the 1890s.

O. E. Bryan, the acting editor of the *Nashville Baptist and Reflector,* picked up on William Jennings Bryan's argument, explaining to state Baptists that the upcoming trial was not about evolution but rather about the powers of a legislative majority in a democracy:

> Tennessee has a right to pass laws to prohibit the teaching of Anarchy in her tax-supported schools. She has a right to prevent the teaching of infidelity in her schools. She has a right to pass a law compelling the reading of the Bible in her schools. . . . Let every preacher and layman keep before the public the fact that the thing on trial is not a doctrine, not a scientific hypothesis, but a fundamental principle of Democracy. If Tennessee has no right to pass a law preventing the teaching of Darwinian Evolution in its public schools, then it has no right to pass any law regulating its public school system. If the recently enacted Anti-evolution law is unconstitutional, then every law in the state that sets forth what shall and what shall not be taught in the public schools is unconstitutional. The court of Dayton ought to rule out of order every speech, every effort to bring before the juries discussions of the doctrine of evolution per se, and compel the attorneys to stick to the one relevant point, namely Did or did not the defendant-teacher violate the law?[83]

The trial judge seemed to agree, disallowing expert testimony on evolution before the jury at the trial. The defense attorneys prepared briefs of the testimony to be entered into the record for appeal, proved (perhaps erroneously) that Scopes had taught evolution, and then asked for a guilty verdict. After the shortest of deliberations, the jury returned a unanimous guilty verdict and Judge John T. Raulston fined Scopes $100.[84]

Methodist minister M. M. Black, writing a vain protest in July 1925 that there was still room for a theistic version of evolution, argued that "while the testimony of science is that higher forms of life have developed from lower forms, yet God is needed at every step of the process." Strongly denouncing some materialistic interpretations of natural history and the evolution of life on earth, Black nonetheless reminded readers that both scientific and religious truth came from the same source and thus could not contradict each other. "Science without religion" may be "a curse to society and a frightful menace to civilization," he conceded, but he cautioned that "on the other hand, religion without science becomes fanatical and bigoted and dogmatic and engages in wars and persecutions of the most relentless type." Yet in spite of his concerns for the long-term compatibility of science and religion, Black saw in Germany the perfect example of why science and religion needed each other: because Germany during the past thirty years had "divorced culture and religion, her science became the ally of death and destruction of the most diabolical character. Science untamed by the gospel is the greatest destroyer known to man." In such a climate, Black admitted that he could support the Tennessee antievolution law and the majoritarian principles of state governance that buttressed Butler's bill and Bryan's prosecution. Regardless of Black's long-term aspirations for the free association and long-term reconciliation of science and religion, he "venture[d] to express the opinion that a State has the right to forbid any form of teaching or instruction in its schools and colleges which the majority of its citizens regard as hurtful to morals and the Christian religion."[85] Black and most Tennessee Evangelicals thus bowed to the demagogic majority.

The trial was over and the prosecution had won the legal contest. If the case really only concerned whether Scopes had taught evolution, eight court days was far too long to reach a verdict. Defense counsel Darrow had wanted the trial to vindicate evolution, a goal shared by many of the national press correspondents who crowded into Dayton in July 1925. Because of the monumental confrontation between Darrow and Bryan on the last day of the trial—Bryan's "expert" testimony in which Darrow forced Bryan to admit to the possibility of differing interpretations of the Bible—the contemporary press and many later historians have labeled the trial a stunning defeat for the antievolution movement. Such an interpretation has been substantially reinforced by the popularity of the *Inherit the Wind* stage play and film, with its stunning dramatic focus on Bryan and Darrow's confrontation and fictive depiction of Darrow explaining to Scopes that he had won the case in the all-important court of public opinion.[86] Bryan did not aid his historical case much by dying five days after the trial, supposedly a "broken" man. H. L. Mencken, who had covered the trial with ruthless invective, at first from Dayton and then, when threatened by the local townspeople, wisely from afar, taunted the antievolution advocates, suggesting that God might have "aimed at Darrow" but "missed, and hit Bryan instead."[87]

Bryan did not die a broken man, and the antievolution campaign did not end in Dayton with the *Scopes* trial or Bryan's death. If anything, his supposed defeat at the hands of Darrow only reinforced fundamentalists' and many other Tennesseans' understanding of the harm that came from disbelief in divine creation and therefore the necessity of controlling the public school curriculum. George Fort Milton, a New South liberal, editor of the *Chattanooga News,* and outspoken opponent of the Butler bill, rallied to Bryan's defense in the wake of the trial and agreed to publish the Great Commoner's undelivered closing address. In the days immediately following the trial, Bryan revised his address, gave portions of it to crowds in Jasper, Winchester, and Cowan in southeastern

Tennessee, read the publisher's proof, and led Sunday morning prayers at Dayton's southern Methodist church before dying in his sleep that afternoon.[88] Both the Baptist and Methodist state papers lamented Bryan's passing and carried resolutions by various religious and secular gatherings, professing, as the McMinn County Baptist Association did, that they could "join the vast majority of East Tennessee Baptists, and we think, Southern Baptists, in indorsing whole-heartedly the law which forbids the teaching of the Theory of Evolution in the Schools maintained by the tax payers of Tennessee."[89]

Bryan's death may have deprived the antievolution campaign of a clearly recognized head, but the movement continued, now with the memory of a martyred leader to drive it onward.[90] Mississippi passed similar antievolution legislation in 1926, more than a dozen states debated statutes in 1927, and Arkansas passed an antievolution law in 1928.[91] Bryan's arguments for the movement lived on: in the state's brief for Scopes's appellate trial, the prosecution banked heavily on the same themes of majority rule and taxpayer control of the schools through the legislature. The state presented a brief from Bryan's son, defending the statute, much as his father had, as a Christian majority's effort to "protect the children of the state in the public schools in their common belief."[92] A majority of the state supreme court agreed with Bryan's logic, upholding the constitutionality of the statute but overturning the conviction on a technicality and thus preventing an appeal to the U.S. Supreme Court. The Butler antievolution law would remain on the books until 1967.[93]

Tennessee Methodists, who were more divided over the propriety of the antievolution legislation than their Baptist counterparts, had nonetheless come to favor the bill out of their continued belief in the necessity of religion for education. Thomas O. Summers Sr. had argued in 1872 that "there can be no education without religion," and his editorial successor, Alfred Smith, echoed the same theme in 1925: "Since education in the South has always been dominantly Christian, it is proper and to be expected that care should be exercised to keep it so, especially by the Church, which is the chief agency of educational protection." Though worried about the repercussions of "questionable enactments for the control of teaching," Smith nevertheless argued that the "State itself knows that it cannot continue to exist without the imperatives of God."[94] Both Baptists and Methodists believed they had a divine calling to educate present and future generations, hoping to shape society into the model religious South they had apotheosized since the late antebellum era. Even in the wake of the *Scopes* trial, the two denominations continued to assert that both religion and education—properly the functions of the church, even if performed in state-funded schools—were necessary to the survival of church and state alike.

Science "falsely so-called" was the immediate cause of the current controversy, but the real enemy was a perceived secularism of the public schools and the larger southern and American society. Most Baptists and Methodists remained convinced of the necessity of controlling the public schools so that they would be, in effect, handmaidens to the churches in creating and sustaining a Christian society.

7. Before and after Scopes

Social Christianity, Formal Education, and the Scopes Legacy

In the spring of 1921, the *Nashville Christian Advocate* presented a special thematic issue on education. Although the paper was most concerned with boosting the educational endeavors of the Methodist Episcopal Church, South, several of the articles nonetheless reveal the immense importance Tennessee Evangelicals placed on education in its many forms as a natural extension of their religious mission. Dr. W. J. Young began one essay by proclaiming that "the mission of the Church is the salvation of the world." Although the exact meaning of "the world" is unclear—does he mean *the world* as in all of the people in the world or did he mean *the world* as in present conditions and society—his expansive view of the Christian mission soon becomes evident. "We are coming to see that this salvation is a much broader work than we at one time supposed and looks to the development and use of every ransomed power of our common humanity. In this work and purpose education has a prominent part." Young then recorded his belief that the future leaders of the world would be an educated class and that if the church wanted to maintain and expand its influence in the world, it would need not just educated members but also a say in the process of education. Such observations led Young to conclude that the "Church, then, has two important tasks before it—to develop its own schools, emphasizing more loyally and definitely the religious side, and to put itself in such relation to the secular schools as to be able to exert its influence for service of a denominational, though certainly not of a sectarian, sort, so that it may keep itself supplied with workers in its chief task of saving the world." According to Young and many of his contemporaries, southern Christians' mission to save the world required an active engagement in both state and denominational education.[1]

Part of Young's and other Tennessee Evangelicals' interest in education clearly emanated out of a desire to replicate and possibly enlarge individual denominations. But there was also a second desire, to reform and improve the surrounding society, not simply to convert isolated individuals within that society. Members of the Tennessee Baptist Convention had reached a similar conclusion at least as early as 1883, when they encouraged the "Baptists of Tennessee [to] take a bold stand in favor of Public education" and endorsed state-funded public schools as capable of accomplishing far more than a few scattered denominational institutions could on their own. "Where Public Schools are fostered and made efficient," the convention resolved, "the people are intelligent, society is desirable, crimes are less frequent, Sunday Schools flourish, Churches are prosperous, and denominational Schools" prosper.[2] Not only would "public education" aid the denominational colleges, but expanded education in all its forms would also make for a more intelligent, law-abiding, and generally "desirable" population. Twenty years later, an association of East Tennessee Baptists asked rhetorically if it were not the church's mission "to help in the betterment of the social conditions of the country?" and called on fellow Evangelicals to lend moral, physical, and financial support to both denominational and public schools as a means of improving the church as well as the society.[3]

This examination of the foundation, growth, and disagreements regarding the content and control of Tennessee schooling offers insight into some important cultural contests of the New South period. The growth of educational institutions can only form part of the story. What is more important and more interesting for historians is how debates about the process, content, and control of education—based consciously or unconsciously on a forward-looking attempt to shape the future of society through children—illuminate larger cultural issues.[4] I argue that Tennessee Baptists' and Methodists' changing relationship to public education—from opposition to accommodation to efforts at control—reveals southern white Evangelicalism's growing social consciousness and mission. There were obviously limits to democratic religious groups' ability to sit in judgment of the society in which they were enmeshed, as their meager and often problematic endorsements of or provisions for the education of women and black Tennesseans too often revealed. But agitation for expanded public education (even for blacks and women) also signified a hope for progress, not merely in an industrial or material measurement but also in matters spiritual. As Methodist educator Stonewall Anderson warned in 1926, "general education with the element of religious education left out" was "incomplete, unsound, and may be dangerous because its products are unsound, defective, and dangerous";

however, "religious education integrated with a sound general education" was the key to individual and social salvation.[5] Expanded public education, especially when infused with religious imagery and spread by Christian teachers, would fuel the growth of the church, aid the establishment of a truly religious New South superior to the materialism of the rest of America and the world, and form the nucleus of a new evangelical reformation.

Evangelical interest in religion as a proper subject and basis for education predated the rise of public schooling in Tennessee. Most antebellum education occurred in the home or the church and continued in religiously affiliated academies, if at all. Depending on a family's circumstances, education in reading, writing, and arithmetic may have paled in comparison to other necessary lessons—what, when, and where to plant or how to construct a corn crib could be equally important. So, too, could parents consider necessary education in more social concerns, such as the racial and honor codes of southern community life or, even more importantly, instruction in religion and how to strive for eternal life. Antebellum families played a crucial role in determining what kind of education was necessary, proper, and possible. Postbellum Tennessee families would remain essential to the educational process, but the creation and gradual growth of a statewide system of public education eventually transformed the cultural landscape and moved education from a personal to a political process.

Formalizing the process of education into tax-supported public schools offered promises and pitfalls for parents and churches in postbellum Tennessee. While providing opportunities for math and language literacy (and thus, supposedly, access to economic, social, and spiritual growth) for many children who would otherwise depend on what could be gleaned from their often undereducated parents, formalized education also subtly undermined parental authority. With the establishment of a special place and time for "education," children came gradually to recognize at least two alternate sources of authority or knowledge: parent and schoolteacher. This distinction was by no means absolute or immediate; many teachers' diaries are full of accounts of parents and even students asserting control.[6] Parents still wielded powerful influence on the curriculum and choice of teachers, but a wedge had nevertheless entered between parents and the direct control of and responsibility for their children's education. With schools lasting for such brief periods and not penetrating into much of rural Tennessee until well after the end of Reconstruction, parents retained a great deal of responsibility for children's education in the home as well as by influencing the newly emerging, communally responsive public schools.

In the minds of many nineteenth-century Tennesseans, education—even if formalized into public schools—would remain intricately related to the same concerns that had driven previous processes of informal education. While growing into formal institutions attended by more and more Tennessee children, the public schools assumed responsibilities previously reserved for parents and churches. John M. Fleming, an early state school superintendent, reported in 1874 that the public schools were not "merely civil organizations, subject only to political government." Education, even if delegated to the new schools, remained "too close to the family circle not to be subject in a great degree to social laws and influences."[7] But what would happen as the systems of public education grew in availability and influence through the end of the nineteenth and into the twentieth centuries? How would the "family circle" continue to influence children's education? One aspect of this education—training in morality and religion—would reappear frequently in the debates regarding the Bible's place in the public schools. What had been treated as a local issue, subject to Oscar Fitzgerald's home rule compromise, became a legal affair after Progressive-era school reforms both removed the discretionary power of local school officials and provided an attractive mechanism for religious leaders eager to spread biblical familiarity and morality more widely among Tennessee schoolchildren.

Not only was there a decline in the direct family influence on education, but there was also a similar sense of deterioration among state religious leaders and a perception that their influence on children's education was likewise waning. Tennessee Methodist W. W. Richeson noted that "the school-teacher has fallen heir to the largest share of the minister's former mantel of influence in the community." W. T. Callaway, a Chattanooga Baptist minister, in turn used time as a measure of educational influence, noting that "the Church only" had the "children for instruction for about an hour once a week and the public schools [had] them most of the remaining time."[8] By the first decades of the twentieth century, parents' or religious leaders' control of children's education had become much more indirect. Elementary schools existed in nearly every community, and high schools were sprouting all over the state. County boards of education replaced district school directors and had to choose books from a list of state-approved texts and hire teachers with certificates from state-approved programs. While education was spreading and becoming more accessible, control of education was threatening to become more centralized and, in many cases, less accessible to individual parents or local community leaders.

Education, whether in the home or the public schools, nonetheless remained important to various groups as the way to shape society's future. Industrialists, landlords, blacks, whites, men, women, and religious leaders might have had differing goals for education, but all likely could have agreed with Fitzgerald's 1880 assessment that "Those who educate the present generation of children in these United States will hold the reins of power when they are grown." As public schools grew, as more and more children attended, their potential power—and consequently the stakes of control—also continued to grow. Fitzgerald had warned his fellow Methodists in 1880, "If we turn over the education of our children to others, we renounce our hold upon the future"; this theme was echoed in 1916 by Elizabeth Denty Abernethy, a Pulaski schoolteacher, who cautioned that "the future of the land we love depends upon what we make of our public school system."[9]

The growing size and importance of the formalized system of public education meant that these competing interests and visions for education increasingly had to turn to the legislature for control of education. Progressive, centralizing, and bureaucratizing reforms to the nineteenth-century public education system undermined Fitzgerald's home rule compromise by lessening the local community's discretion. At the same time, the reforms potentially offered religious leaders, or whoever else could seize the chance, more power over formalized public education by securing legislation to further their ends. State religious leaders recognized the school bureaucracy's new power to shape the future generation's minds, but, as Baptist educator Rufus Weaver explained, Evangelicals and parents would have in the future "to enter . . . into politics to preserve the rights of the little child." And most Tennessee Evangelicals believed that these rights included access to religious instruction and, later, protection from the supposedly irreligious instruction of evolution in the public schools.[10]

Southern education historian John Hardin Best suggests one way to track this process of formalization of education within the schools themselves: by examining the use (or lack of use) and selection criteria for textbooks. When asked by historian James Silver why there were few if any southern-specific textbooks in the antebellum period, Best suggested that the late antebellum and postwar emergence of textbooks could indicate not just regional identity formation but also increasingly formalized education. Antebellum education, he suggested, did not require separate textbooks because it was such an uninstitutionalized cultural process. Informal sources of education—specifically parents, churches, and community leaders—supplemented the texts; instructors were expected to put their "correct" interpretation on the histories and philosophies of the texts. The postbellum formalization and expansion of public education, combined with the obviously lingering sectional tensions, created a new market for regionally acceptable textbooks.[11] Unsure of how the history of the Civil War was being portrayed, the United Confederate Veterans in the 1890s launched a campaign aimed at "securing a true and reliable history of the late civil war" to be taught in state schools. Likewise, the Tennessee State Teachers Association at its 1902 annual meeting encouraged members to teach using texts and literature written by southern authors. [12]

This concern over school texts may have been most pronounced in the South but was in fact indicative of a larger effort by parents and politicians to curtail educators' autonomy. Walter Lippmann, lecturing at the University of Virginia not too long after the *Scopes* trial, interestingly connected the Butler bill and Dayton trial with a contemporary battle in the Chicago public schools over history textbooks that some residents and politicians considered insufficiently patriotic or even antipatriotic. "In fact," he noted, there is "hardly an organization in America which has not set up a committee to investigate the schools and rewrite the textbooks. Apparently every organization feels itself eminently qualified to teach the teachers how to conduct the schools." The result, Lippmann warned, would be endlessly fractious debates about textbooks and school control as well as the emergence of "dangerously prudent" and "second-rate" teachers when "first-rate" teachers refused "to submit to the democratic inquisition" exemplified by the Dayton and Chicago spectacles. [13]

The southern concern regarding textbooks increased in the early twentieth century as state religious leaders encouraged parents to examine the texts used in public and church schools. The Tennessee Baptist Convention created a commission to examine the books in the denomination's schools, while the editor of the *Nashville Christian Advocate* encouraged parents to examine carefully for religious soundness the books assigned in Methodist colleges and the state's public schools. [14] After Dr. C. W. Davis, a young agriculture professor at the Baptists' Union University, had weathered several accusations that he was teaching atheistic evolution to his students, school president H. E. Watters explained his belief in Davis's innocence and announced that the professor was "engaged in writing a textbook on biology that will be absolutely free of any objectionable statements or teachings." Watters further explained that Davis's book was needed because there was "no such book in print that [was] both scholarly and teachable"; Baptist schools had consequently been forced "to use objectionable texts." [15] Revelations in 1925 that John Scopes had taught evolution from the state-approved biology book, George W. Hunter's *Civic Biology,* unleashed a new round of criticism and oversight. In reality, Scopes admitted that he was not sure he had actually taught evolution; he finally concluded that because he had taught from the book and because the book covered evolution, he must have violated the law. Porter Claxton, the son of Tennessee Progressive-era school reformer P. P. Claxton, wrote to his father just days after Governor Austin

Peay signed the Butler antievolution law, detailing a plan to "make a million" by writing "a science book without evolution in it. It will be the only one of its kind on the market, and Tennessee will be forced to adopt it."[16] No longer did teachers appear to be considered capable of putting their own interpretation on those "objectionable" parts of common national textbooks. Now the books had to be as morally and religiously safe as the nineteenth-century teachers had been.

The antievolution campaigns and preceding Bible-reading legislation suggest that while the formalization of education into state public schools provided greatly increased opportunities for people to receive at least some sort of education, expanded education also had several unfortunate if unintended consequences. For one, the change removed from many parents a sense of direct responsibility for children's training. Education, many parents came to believe, was what occurred during set hours and in another place, the schoolroom. Second, by endowing schools with so much weighty responsibility for teaching youth and shaping the future, society set up educational institutions as a location for seemingly insoluble and interminable conflict. Instead of concentrating on local solutions, would-be reformers reinforced parental alienation by working to change education from the legislature down. Witnessing the failure of their temperance and Prohibition campaigns to change the hearts or behavior of adults, Tennessee Evangelicals of the early twentieth century refocused their attention on teaching religion and morality to the public schools' captive and impressionable children.

Formalizing education went beyond establishing public schools as training grounds in reading, writing, and arithmetic; the schools soon took on other responsibilities as well. Horace Mann, the influential nineteenth-century Massachusetts school superintendent, understood that the public school's mission was to teach lessons in nonsectarian religion, morality, and civility. While many early-twentieth-century Tennessee religious leaders approved of the expansion of public schooling as a means for providing at least a minimum level of moral and religious training, some others feared that parents would grow dependent on the schools and become negligent in training their children. Noting the danger of the public school "supplanting the home and its sacred duty" to look after "the moral training of the child," a 1914 essay in the *Nashville Midland Methodist* warned readers of the serious consequences to children, families, and the state. It is interesting to note just what kind of moral education had elicited such an editorial, however. Tennessee Methodists and Baptists had supported efforts to require public schools to teach lessons on health and hygiene, especially as they related to the harmful effects of alcohol and smoking, and these efforts bore fruit in an 1895 state law requiring such classes. But the Methodist editor's notice of an article in the *Ladies Home Journal* advocating the introduction of lessons on "sex hygiene" led to his criticism of schools for trying to do too much and of parents for abdicating their moral responsibility.[17] Sex and health education continues to provide a cogent example of the lingering effects of placing such previously private issues into a centralized public education system; questions about whether schools should teach abstinence or disease prevention continue to plague not just parents but teachers, school administrators, legislators, and courts in the twenty-first century.

The clearest effect of the formalization of public education and politicization of moral questions that had previously been settled on familial and local community levels is the antievolution efforts of the 1920s. Indeed, if one is searching for continuing legacies or resonating issues from that period, the issue of evolution in public schools looms large. Though both the title and the organization of chapters put discussion of the *Scopes* trial at the end of this book and thus suggest an ending point to the controversy, such a placement is unintentionally misleading. Many of the same tensions and arguments that drove the enactment of the Butler bill and set the stage for the trial in Dayton refuse to go away even eighty years later.

Edward J. Larson, Ronald L. Numbers, Larry A. Witham, and others have provided compelling accounts of the continuing struggles regarding the teaching of evolution in U.S. public schools. These scholars correctly point to some of the changing beliefs and tactics within the creationist camps, including the near monopoly Young Earth Creationists—believers in a biblically literal, six twenty-four-hour-day creation only a few thousand years ago—have had on the post-1960s movement and the shift from absolute opposition to teaching evolution to endorsements of "creation science" and "intelligent design" and campaigns to require equal time for alternative explanations to be presented in the schools.[18] At the same time, a survey of recent antievolution campaigns forces one almost to agree with the *Little Rock Arkansas Democrat-Gazette*'s editorial observation that "the problem—well, one of the problems—with these evolution trials is that they don't seem to have evolved at all."[19] The editorial comments resulted from Arkansas state representative Jim Holt's introduction of House Bill 2548, which would have banned the use of textbooks that presented evolution as anything other than an unproven theory. The bill, which passed committee but not the full House in March 2001, utilized many of the stock resources of antievolutionists in both 1925 and today by attempting to discredit evolution as "only a theory" and a "fraudulent" one at that.[20] Trading on popular misconceptions of the meaning of a scientific "theory," modern creationists continue to search for any small scientific disagreement about the particulars of evolution and elevate them to the status of crippling indictments of the "scientific guess" of evolution to predict that the whole evolutionary house of cards is about to fall down. While denying that his purpose was to insert creationism into the school curriculum or to single out the theory of evolution exclusively, Holt nonetheless brought along a "visiting expert" to testify on flaws in evolutionary theory. The witness was even from Florida, William Jennings Bryan's retirement home before his fatal trip to Dayton as a prosecutor and perversely the defense's "expert" witness on the Bible.

Beyond similarities in tactics and other coincidences, contemporary discussions of evolution and public education seemingly cannot avoid references to Tennessee's famous 1925 trial. In its editorial on the proposed Arkansas house legislation, The *Arkansas Democrat-Gazette* explicitly referenced the infamous "Monkey trial" in its title and much of the article while only briefly mentioning Arkansas's role in the antievolution saga. Indeed, Arkansas's 1927 antievolution law made it all the way to the U.S. Supreme Court (although not until 1968), which found the measure unconstitutional.[21] References to the *Scopes* trial are perhaps more appropriate for Tennessee, whose legislature has gone out of its way to keep the connection fresh in the public mind. Even before the summer 2000 festivities in Dayton to commemorate the seventy-fifth anniversary of the trial, the Tennessee state Senate only narrowly defeated (by a vote of twenty to thirteen) a law that would have empowered school boards to dismiss teachers for presenting evolution as a fact instead of an unprovable theory. Dubbed "Scopes II" or "Son of Scopes" by opponents, the legislation ensured an onslaught of national media attention, much legislative and religious posturing, and of course, plenty of short clips and longer showings of *Inherit the Wind* on television and even a Broadway revival of the stage production.[22]

Despite all of the continuing media attention and hand-wringing about the continued "warfare" between science and religion, the issues in Tennessee, Arkansas, Louisiana, and elsewhere still boil down to a basic question of who controls the public schools. U.S. Supreme Court rulings in *Epperson* (1968) and *Edwards* (1987) suggest that the high court remains the final arbiter, at least as far as state antievolution laws raise First Amendment questions about the establishment of religion. But the creationist movement is turning in a different direction, evolving backward, as it were, by returning to the strategy, championed by Fitzgerald in the 1880s, of allowing Bible reading in the public schools. Fitzgerald's home rule compromise evaded constitutional questions by avoiding top-down legislation and letting "each community . . . settle the question for itself."[23] In a similar manner, many of the most recent antievolution efforts have returned to the strategy of demanding "local control" of schools.

Agitation over the Kansas state school board's 1999 decision to remove evolution from the listing of science standards required to be taught in public schools fits this mold. According to Larson and Witham, "the state Board of Education members who rejected evolution were also trying to strike a blow for local control and against national education standards." Although part of a larger trend of opposition to the push for national educational standards begun by the George H. W. Bush administration and copied by many state school boards, the new cries for local control can often seem, as in Fitzgerald's hands, an expedient rhetorical and political tool.[24] The formalization, bureaucratization, and standardization of education that began in the Progressive era gave various groups desiring to shape the education of the next generation a more centralized target for changing all state schools. The school reforms of the early twentieth century no less than those at the end of the millennium set up state school boards and curricula as lightning rods of controversy between populist pleas and the authority of scientific and education experts. When nineteenth-century local-control arguments were found to work against Evangelical Protestants—as in the larger and more ethnically and religiously diverse cities such as Memphis, which rejected city school Bible-reading plans and repeatedly voted against Prohibition—these religiously motivated reformers turned instead to invocations of "majority rule." John Washington Butler embodied this contradiction, promising his rural Tennessee constituents that he was fighting for their local values but arguing for majority rule in his 1925 antievolution bill that enforced those local values on the state as a whole.

Modern-day creationists, defending the rights of public school teachers to challenge the evolutionary synthesis with either scientific or thinly veiled religious objections, have adopted the inverse strategy of their fundamentalist ancestors of the 1920s. In this new millennium, when antievolutionists now consider themselves an embattled minority, they reject William Jennings Bryan's majoritarianism and find themselves instead championing the words (if not always the ideas) of Scopes's defenders. Clarence Darrow pled for freedom to challenge religious laws in Dayton; modern antievolutionists (mostly in the guise of the "intelligent design" movement) try to point to Darrow's defense of intellectual dissent and warnings that the stifling of scientific disagreement had the country "marching backward to the glorious ages of the sixteenth century, when bigots lighted fagots to burn the men who dared to bring any intelligence and enlightenment and culture to the human mind." Modern antievolutionists might even more powerfully concur with the arguments of Scopes's other prominent defense attorney, Dudley Field Malone, and his plea to give "the next generation all the facts, all the available data, all the theories. . . . For God's sake," begged Malone, "let the children have their minds kept open—close no doors to their knowledge; shut no door from them."[25]

Evolutionists and antievolutionists alike can leverage their arguments by appealing to the public school as the incubator of the future society. With so much at stake, the argument shows no sign of soon waning.

Notes

Chapter 1. Laying Foundations: Constructing a Christian Civilization in the New South

1. [James R. Graves], "Laying Foundations," *MB*, January 25, 1879, 742. Graves was probably the author of nearly every piece of writing in the paper that was not copied from another paper. I have placed the name of the paper editor in brackets when citing unsigned editorial matter that is likely the work of a particular editor.

2. Ibid.

3. Ibid.

4. Dannelly, "Development," 1.

5. "Education," Central Baptist Association Minutes, 1907, 10, University Archives, Emma Watters Summar Library, Union University, Jackson.

6. The most succinct account of the revivals and the resulting evangelical mindset is Boles, *The Great Revival: Origins of the Southern Evangelical Mind,* which was reprinted in 1996 with the new subtitle *Beginnings of the Bible Belt.* More recently, Heyrman, *Southern Cross,* has looked even earlier than Boles for the origins of southern religious distinctiveness, tracing the intersection of northeastern Evangelicalism with southern culture in the eighteenth and early nineteenth centuries. The "distinctiveness" of southern Evangelicalism, as perceived by both historic southerners and modern historians, will be important to this study and merit closer attention later in this chapter. The best bibliographical guides to the question can be found in two essays: Boles, "Discovery," esp. 512–38; Sparks, "Religion."

7. The best national view of American fundamentalism is Marsden, *Fundamentalism.* Though sensitive to the theological and social elements of fundamentalism, Marsden's otherwise excellent book, in its effort to situate fundamentalism as a reaction to theological liberalism, concentrates on controversies within northern denominations and seems to dismiss the South as already and always fundamentalist, just waiting for the label to be invented. In his phrasing, "there was a strong anti-modernist impulse in Southern religion well before modernism became a distinct movement in America." Consequently, "when in the twentieth century fundamentalism became a distinct entity, Southerners with a long history of revivalist conservatism eventually flocked to the movement" (103). On the same page, Marsden erroneously refers to the "vitriolic *Western Recorder* of Tennessee," which was published in Louisville, Kentucky. Glass, *Strangers,* looks more closely than Marsden could at the regional situation, suggesting both that the South had fundamentalists throughout the period and that they did not comprise an unquestionable majority of the southern population. I do not argue that the South did not prove remarkably receptive to fundamentalism in the 1920s, but I do contend that the level of diversity was greater than Marsden's dismissal suggests. Future research in southern and particularly Tennessee religion should concentrate on liberal Evangelicals such as Nashville's James I. Vance, Will Alexander, and James McCulloch and their creation of a pocket of religious liberalism in the "City of Churches" as well as on the growing gaps between Baptist and Methodist denominational leaders and their rural constituency in Tennessee and throughout the South.

8. Statistics cited in Moran, *Scopes Trial,* 2; Mencken, "Sahara," 136–37.

9. Tennessee Baptist and Methodist churches claimed three-fourths of the state's church members in 1890 and 1916. White Tennessee members of Southern Baptist Convention and Methodist Episcopal Church, South–affiliated churches comprised 44 percent of the state's population of church members in 1916 (U.S. Bureau of the Census, 46–47; U.S. Bureau of the Census, *Religious Bodies: 1916,* 309–11).

10. The *Nashville Christian Advocate* was published in Nashville throughout the period of study, and although in the twentieth century it increasingly took on a southwide constituency and focus, its editorial offices and much of its content remained focused on Tennessee. The *Advocate* will be supplemented where possible with extant copies of the *Nashville Midland Methodist,* which attempted to fill the *Advocate*'s place as a state paper. The *Baptist and Reflector* moved to Nashville in 1889 as the combination of the *Memphis Baptist* (previously the *Memphis Tennessee Baptist,* edited first by R. B. C. Howell and later by Graves) and the *Chattanooga Baptist Reflector.* Usually owned by the editors, the paper continued to absorb other local Tennessee Baptist newspapers throughout the early twentieth century until the Tennessee Baptist Convention bought the paper in 1921.

11. Kousser, "Progressivism." There has been too little examination of how black Americans responded to theories of evolution, even outside of the public school context. There are, thankfully, some exceptions, notably Eric D. Anderson, "Black Responses to Darwinism, 1859–1915," in Numbers and Stenhouse, eds., *Disseminating Darwinism,* 247–66; and two promising new articles by Jeffrey Moran: "Scopes Trial" and "Reading Race." Both Anderson and Moran look at national black reactions to Darwinism and the *Scopes* trial; neither offers much light on Tennessee black Evangelicals' role in or response to the antievolution movement.

12. Hill, *Southern Churches,* 73. While by no means rejecting Hill's pioneering and enduring work outright, *Before Scopes* is meant to be in an extended historiographical engagement with Hill's and others' emphasis on the individual—almost to the exclusion of societal—focus of southern white Evangelicalism. A new generation of scholars— Keith Harper, Paul Harvey, and Beth Barton Schweiger, among others—has nibbled at the edges of Hill's central theme, with Wayne Flynt taking perhaps the biggest bite, but these authors have mostly been unable to show if or how southern advocates of what Harper terms "social Christianity" moved beyond organized charity or whether they were any more than what Boles describes as "clerical radicals" "on the very fringes of southern Protestantism" ("Discovery," 541). Eighmy provides a persuasive investigation of southern Baptists' social concerns, emphasizing both their interests in and limitations on social reform efforts. The relatively democratic structure of southern Evangelicalism left the churches largely subject to other social conditions but not powerless. Instead of focusing on isolated incidents or reforms or a southern incarnation of the Social Gospel with its attendant liberal theology, *Before Scopes* recognizes the limitations of Tennessee Evangelicals on some questions of race, economics, and political culture yet argues that religious ideas and language contributed to these Evangelicals' efforts to organize society, particularly through the creation and control of systems of education.

See Harper, *Quality;* Harvey, *Redeeming;* Schweiger, *Gospel;* Flynt, "Southern Protestantism"; Eighmy, *Churches.*

13. [OPF], "Authority," *NCA,* January 28, 1882, 1.

14. Bailyn, *Education,* 14; Best, "Education," 11.

15. Rufus Weaver, "The Obligation of Southern Baptists to Improve the Rural Elementary School and the Method Which Ought to Be Employed to Secure This Result," *NBR,* January 31, 1918, 1, 4.

16. [OPF], *NCA,* March 5, 1881, 8.

Chapter 2. Reading, Writing, and Religion: Evangelicals and the Creation of Public Education

1. OPF, "Welcome Address," in Frank M. Smith, *Proceedings,* 5.

2. Elliott, *Eagle Wing,* 15. Elliott apparently gave this address several times between the 1860s and the 1890s; he introduces this published version as the "second edition," "printed for the benefit of the members of this present General Assembly." A similar, undated, handwritten version as well as a printed version from 1880 are found in Collins D. Elliott Papers, 1810–1899, microfilm acc. 802, TSLA.

3. Norton, *Religion,* 16.

4. Ibid., 18–40. On the social and theological underpinnings of the revival movement in the South, see Boles, *Great Revival: Origins.*

5. For a broad summary of this trend throughout the South, see Boles, "Evangelical Protestantism." In a more recent approach, Heyrman emphasizes the dialectic relationship of Evangelicalism and southern society in the late eighteenth and early nineteenth centuries, writing, "Southern whites came to speak the language of Canaan as evangelicals learned to speak with a southern accent" (*Southern Cross,* 27).

6. Wardin, *Tennessee Baptists,* 156. There is some debate about the utility of judging church strength by federal census measurements of "accommodations." Wardin counts Baptist association records around 1850 and finds more than 850 churches with only 54,000 members (*Tennessee Baptists,* 150). Since various denominations had widely varying standards for membership (among evangelical Protestants, church membership usually did not equal church attendance), one must take such statistics with caution. Baptists and Methodists had greatly outpaced the pioneer Presbyterians by this time. Presbyterians in the same census had only 363 churches, with seats for 135,517, although the Presbyterians were wealthier, possessing $367,081 in property (Wardin, *Tennessee Baptists,* 156).

7. Ash, *Middle Tennessee Society,* 32.

8. Boles, *Religion,* 142–43. For a fuller description of the individual focus of southern evangelical Christianity, see Boles, *Great Revival: Origins,* 165–74.

9. Howell quoted in Wardin, *Tennessee Baptists,* 82–83; John Abernathy Smith, *Cross and Flame,* 73, 85–93. West Tennessee also quickly migrated into the proslavery camp, but mountainous East Tennessee remained far more divided on the issue of slavery throughout the antebellum period.

10. Snay, *Gospel,* highlights antebellum southern Evangelicals' transition from defending to sanctifying slavery as sectional pressures and criticisms led these Evangelicals to identify more closely with their society. Faust, " 'God Will Not Be Mocked': Confederate Nationalism and Slavery Reform," in Faust, *Creation,* 58–81, emphasizes how the close identification of the church and the Confederacy could cut both ways, suggesting that as the war fortunes of the South soured, some religious leaders were willing to attribute their misfortune to God's displeasure with their insufficient fulfillment of their duties to their slaves and to their God. Owen corrects some of the "lumping" tendencies in descriptions of southern Evangelicals by distinguishing Georgia Methodists' "neutral attitude toward slavery" (*Sacred Flame,* 64); see also Owen's expansion of this theme in " 'To Keep the Way Open.' "

11. Faust, *Creation,* 27.

12. Elliott quoted in ibid., 26. Elliott was the Episcopal bishop of Georgia as well as one of the leaders of a movement to establish an Episcopal university in Tennessee before the Civil War. The college was officially founded before the war, but classes did not begin in Sewanee at the University of the South until 1868. Elliott briefly served as chancellor of the university, though his sudden death in December 1866 came before the university opened (Fairbanks, *History,* 62–81).

13. The "guilt" thesis most closely associated with Beringer et al., *Why the South Lost,* has a long historiographical pedigree. Though most succinctly and effectively rebutted in Foster, "Guilt," the debate has continued in Faust, " 'God Will Not be Mocked,' " and Genovese, *Consuming Fire,* among other sources. Drawing many of his examples from Tennessee and Georgia, Stowell, *Rebuilding Zion,* 33–48, answers the guilt hypothesis by suggesting that white southerners' religious beliefs, though denominationally disrupted, increased during and after the war.

14. Shattuck, " 'Appomattox,' " 4. Daly has suggested that the Confederate defeat's chief effect on regional theology was a growing skepticism about "easy formulas of antebellum moral progress and all good deeds being rewarded on earth." In their place, Daly argues, southern believers adopted an "apocalyptic and prophetic religion" (*When Slavery Was Called Freedom,* 152). The southern Christians represented in this study were ultimately concerned about eventual and otherworldly rewards and punishments but could not escape from long-held covenant beliefs in a God who punished and rewarded his chosen people on Earth.

15. Berger, *Sacred Canopy,* 56. The ultimate test for religion or for any legitimator of the social order is its ability to sustain the socially held *nomos* in the face of aberrant, marginal, or ecstatic experiences or situations. Anomic phenomena such as "evil, suffering, and, above all, death . . . must not only be lived through, they must also be explained—to wit, explained in terms of the nomos established in the society in question" (*Sacred Canopy,* 53). Theodicy, therefore, is the religious legitimization, on any level of theoretical sophistication, of the *nomos* and explanation for these phenomena. Berger explains that there is an implicit theodicy in the social order, even prior to any religious legitimations. In fact, the *nomos* requires a surrender of the self to a larger reality, providing comfort and legitimization in return, a process that Berger terms

"masochistic liberation." Key to understanding Berger's explanation of theodicy is his claim that humans, as biologically created social creatures, "cannot accept aloneness and . . . cannot accept meaninglessness." In such a conception, theodicy must provide meaning even more than it must provide relief from suffering (*Sacred Canopy*, 56).

16. Wilson, *Baptized*, 10–11.

17. Elliott quoted in Wilson, *Baptized*, 77.

18. Memphis Annual Conference Minutes, 1865, Report of Committee on Missions, quoted in Stowell, *Rebuilding Zion*, 85.

19. Stowell, *Rebuilding Zion*, 81. On broader trends of black outmigration from southern white-led churches, see also William E. Montgomery, *Under;* Harvey, *Redeeming*, 45–74; for an investigation of the process in a southern urban setting, see Israel, "From Biracial to Segregated Churches."

20. Wardin, *Tennessee Baptists*, 229–30.

21. West Tennessee Baptist Association, 1866, and Central Baptist Association, 1865, both quoted in Stowell, *Rebuilding Zion*, 118. For an engaging account of Sunday schools as a component of denominational institution building in the South, see McMillen, *To Raise Up*.

22. West Tennessee Baptist Association, 1866, quoted in Stowell, *Rebuilding Zion*, 118.

23. Stowell, *Rebuilding Zion*, 114. Wilson examines another Tennessee denominational college, the Episcopalians' University of the South in Sewanee, as an institutional embodiment of "Lost Cause Education." Wilson is more interested in the prosouthern and Lost Cause apologetics at Sewanee and Virginia's Washington College (later renamed Washington and Lee after the death of school president Robert E. Lee) than in the schools' theological and social importance to the denominations themselves (*Baptized*, 139–60).

24. Elizabeth Denty Abernethy, "The Future of the South," *NCA*, September 29, 1916, 22–23; See also J. M. Hawley, "Southern Ideals of Education," *NCA*, June 30, 1911, 11–12.

25. Fred A. Bailey, "Caste and the Classroom," 42.

26. Tyack, "Tribe," 4.

27. Whitaker, "Public School System," 20, 26.

28. Most histories of education in Tennessee have been written by the early generation of school reformers or their students. The two best examples of this genre are Robert Hiram White, *Development*, and Holt, *Struggle*. As a result, these works have assumed the common school and the centralized state bureaucracy as a triumph for a state school system. They have seen formal education in schools as the goal and have tended to denigrate opponents as ignorant or otherwise politically motivated. Only with the social history revolution of the 1960s did educational history begin to break such shackles, but this phenomenon has been slow to filter into state studies, especially in the South. Probably the best effort to reevaluate southern educational history in its broad cultural context is Leloudis, *Schooling*, which focuses on the North Carolina

educational reformers of the late nineteenth and early twentieth centuries but is in many ways applicable to Tennessee and other southern states. Two Tennessee researchers who have made significant advances in situating public education and reform within the society and culture of the New South are Hoffschwelle, *Rebuilding*, and Keith, *Country People*.

29. Robert Hiram White, *Development*; Utley, "Early Academies"; see also Sizer, *Age*.

30. Wardin, *Tennessee Baptists*, 170–74; E. Alvin Gerhardt Jr., "Samuel Doak," in West, *Tennessee Encyclopedia*, 252; John Abernathy Smith, *Cross and Flame*, 77. Midstate Methodists also attempted to found a larger college in Nashville in the late antebellum period: they gained a charter for the Central University in 1858 but never began classes (John Abernathy Smith, *Cross and Flame*, 132). For more on this failed college and its revival in the 1870s as Vanderbilt University, see chapter 3.

31. John Abernathy Smith, *Cross and Flame*, 136–37; Windrow, "Collins D. Elliott." The Nashville College for Young Ladies, although not specifically designated as a Methodist school, had an exchange program with Vanderbilt in the 1880s and attracted a large number of Methodist girls, as evidenced by Principal G. W. Price's 1889 report to his board of trustees: "the moral and religious tone of the college has been good. A very large percentage of our pupils is composed of professing Christians, the larger portion of them Methodist" (Minutes of the Board of Trustees, 1881–1900, Nashville College for Young Ladies, location I-A-4, acc. 164, box 2, TSLA).

32. Fred A. Bailey, "Caste and the Classroom," 44.

33. Whitaker, "Public School System," 7–8. In Tennessee as elsewhere, tax burdens were related to property assessments; because slaves counted as taxable property, large slaveholders did not want to be taxed for educational services for other people's children.

34. Fred A. Bailey, "Caste and the Classroom," 42.

35. Ibid., 47–48.

36. *Acts of Tennessee*, 1815, chapter 49, quoted in Robert Hiram White, *Development*, 26.

37. Whitaker, "Public School System," 11–12, 21–24. Funds distributed in 1839 amounted to $0.56 for every white child age 6–16 in the state, with the figure rising to $0.75 by 1859; however, as a committee of the legislature remarked, the financial resources of the struggling schools had been "time after time plundered by a thousand hands" (Robert Hiram White, *Development*, 49, 75).

38. Robert Hiram White, *Development*, 77, 79–80.

39. Ibid., 82–83.

40. Robert Hiram White, *Development*, 104–6. The legislature even investigated former State Superintendent of Public Instruction John Eaton, criticizing him for incurring needless expenses in producing his 1869 annual report.

41. Ibid., 117.

42. J. B. Killebrew, "Second Annual Report (January 22, 1873)," 22, Tennessee State Teachers Association Proceedings, TSLA. The same meeting of the Tennessee State

Teachers Association that endorsed the call for a return to state education funding had several ministers as participants, including C. D. Elliott, W. Shelton, D. Rutledge, H. S. Bennett, R. A. Mason, J. Braden, R. D. Black, and T. T. Eaton. Eaton had been principal of the Baptists' Union University in Murfreesboro and would sit on the board of the new Southwestern Baptist University. Elliott was a constant activist in public education but was often at odds with his fellow educators on the extent to which state organization and control of schools was desirable.

43. *Tennessee School Report*, 1885, p. 17, 1875, p. 20, quoted in Holt, *Struggle*, 8.

44. Holt, *Struggle*, 11. In that year, the state paid $157,245.98 to the counties for schools (*Tennessee School Report*, 1899, 23, quoted in Holt, *Struggle*, 11). The large state debt was a divisive issue in Tennessee politics throughout the 1870s and 1880s, as competing political interests battled over whether to repudiate it, repay it in part, or pay in full to protect the state's credit. The issue split the Democratic Party, ushering in Republican Governor Alvin Hawkins in 1880. No matter what side politicians took in the state debt controversy, most knew it was at best impolitic to suggest any great increase in the state tax burden, even for public education. For more on the state debt controversy and its effect on state politics, see Jones, *Tennessee;* Hart, *Redeemers*.

45. Eaton quoted in McAfee, *Religion*, 88.

46. McAfee, *Religion*, 105–22. McAfee suggests that the outspoken support for Sumner's campaign for integrated public education—support that came largely through an 1874 convention in Nashville led by black Tennessee Republican Edward Shaw, who worked to defeat any Republican not pledged to integration—was largely to blame for the loss of black voting power in the state (141–67). For a more nuanced account of the rise and fall of black political power in Tennessee, see Cartwright, *Triumph*. The Blair Education Bill, first proposed by a New Hampshire senator in 1883 and resubmitted for several terms thereafter, proposed to appropriate $15 million plus lesser amounts for the following nine years to states in proportion to their illiteracy rate. The proposal became quite a divisive issue in Tennessee politics. Bourbons opposed the bill because it was a Republican measure, because it contradicted their limited-construction theory of the constitution, and because it would give Republicans an excuse to continue high protective tariffs. New South Democrats supported the bill as a means to improve education in the state while potentially lowering state taxes. Populists tended to favor the bill as well, hoping to improve education without raising taxes; see Hart, *Redeemers*, 92–94. Kiger notes rural newspaper editors' divided opinions on the Blair bill in "Social Thought," 142. The real problem with the agitation over the Blair bill, remarked progressive educational reformer Andrew Holt, was that the continued possibility of federal funding kept agitation centered on the merits of federal aid and kept education supporters from raising money within Tennessee for the state schools (*Struggle*, 17).

47. John M. Fleming, *Tennessee School Report*, 1874, cited in Robert Hiram White, *Development*, 123–24.

48. W. G. F. Cunnyngham, "Thoughts on Education," *NCA*, April 5, 1873, 6.

49. G. R. Shields, "Education: Its Duty to the State," *Southwestern School Journal* 6

(October 1900): 11–12; General Association of Baptists of East Tennessee, Proceedings, 1876, 9, microfilm publication 420, SBHLA.

50. Trousdale, "Plea," 2.

51. Collins D. Elliott, "Blair Bill" (speech), n.d., n.p., reel 1, Elliott Papers.

52. Trousdale, "Plea," 2. In his exploration of Republicans, Catholics, nativism, and the public school in the 1870s, McAfee reaches a similar conclusion about the importance of the public school and about children as the battleground on which social, political, and religious groups fought their campaigns. As McAfee explains, "A common concern for the children of America defined the debate—not as ends in themselves but as the malleable clay of a future national culture" (*Religion,* 7). Southern Evangelicals of the late nineteenth century still believed that their mission as a redeemer nation included maintaining their version of Christianity so that at some point it could further reform the national culture. Southern Evangelicals could not join in the religiously cloaked school campaigns of the national Republican Party in the 1870s—despite their anti-Catholic appeal—because Sumner's presence seemed always to promise racially integrated schooling.

53. *NCA,* July 17, 1880, 8; OPF, *NCA,* May 17, 1879, 1; see also TBCM, 1888, 33.

54. Trousdale, "Plea," 4–6; G. R. Shields, "Education: Its Duty to the State," *Southwestern School Journal* 6 (October 1900): 11–12; Charles W. Dabney, "As Is Education So Is Production," *Southwestern School Journal* 5 [7?] (January 1901): 19–21. Dabney served as the president of the University of Tennessee, was a founder of the Summer School of the South, served as research director for the Southern Education Bureau, and was a longtime campaigner for improved public schools in Tennessee and the rest of the South.

55. E. S. Joynes, "Education after the War," *Southern Literary Messenger,* August 1863, 487–88; Elliott, *Eagle Wing,* 15–16; Ulric, "Southern Culture," *NCA,* December 4, 1875, 3. Born in Ohio, Elliott moved south at an early age and never gave up his belief in a distinctive and correct southern culture. On the occasion of his funeral, the *Nashville American* reported, "For the past fifteen years Dr. Elliott had in one corner of his room an old Confederate flag, in which, by his own direction, his body will be wrapped in his coffin. Thus in his death he will typify his devotion to the 'Lost Cause' by being shrouded in the emblem of the Confederate States." Even in death, Elliott emphasized his faith in his adopted South, an idealized vision that he had fought hard to keep alive in the minds and institutions of the New South ("Dr. C. D. Elliott Passes Away," *Nashville American,* July 29, 1899, reel 1, Elliott Papers).

Much has been written on the Lost Cause disapproval of the industrial aims of the New South movement. Prominent southern clergymen lined up both to support efforts to rebuild the region and to warn that by adopting the industrial aims of the northern victors, the South threatened to lose its supposed moral and religious superiority. Rev. John C. Calhoun Newton warned his fellow Methodists in *The New South and the Methodist Episcopal Church, South* to resist the "tide of grovelling mammonism" he saw infecting the region (quoted in Shattuck, " 'Appomattox,' " 13). Nashville Presbyterian minister James H. McNeilly remained, until his death in 1922, a constant voice of praise of the Old South and voiced nothing but opprobrium for "the whole race of sneering, money-seeking, materialistic apostles of the 'new' South" (quoted in Wilson, *Baptized,* 95). Wilson, *Baptized,* 95–96, has suggested a generational explanation for southern ministerial opposition to New South industrialism, arguing that older ministers who lived through the war and were active defenders of the South during the antebellum period were not likely to embrace the industrial innovations, while younger ministers, though still willing to attack excessive materialism, were at least open to the utility of wealth and of new business methods in spreading the Gospel and enlarging the churches.

56. Holland McTyeire, "A Plea for Denominational Education," *NCA,* December 7, 1872, 6. Tennessee Methodists freely and often applied the "godless" label to schools during the late nineteenth century; see, for example, Collins D. Elliott, "A Fraud on the People: The Closing Scene in the Senate Chamber on the Normal School Bill" (newspaper clipping), reel 1, Elliott Papers; *NCA,* May 11, 1878, 4–5, March 3, 1883, 1, June 6, 1889, 1, February 8, 1890, 3, August 5, 1897, 8.

57. E. S. Smith, "Methodist Schools: Their Advantages over Secular Schools," *NCA,* November 2, 1872, 6; E. S. Smith, "Denominational Education," *NCA,* October 12, 1872, 7. Farish, *Circuit Rider,* 243, argues that different Methodist annual conferences attempted to create district high schools (which would include elementary schools) in each presiding elder district of the Holston Conference, which included eastern Tennessee as well as parts of Virginia and North Carolina. Few schools were created; very few have left any record of their brief existence.

58. On the Cincinnati Bible War's place in Reconstruction politics and the role of nativism, see McAfee, *Religion,* 28–54. For Tennessee religious journals' coverage of Bible-reading cases in other places as well as their attribution of such controversies to a Catholic conspiracy, see B. R. Womack, "The Bible Question," *MB,* November 20, 1875, 3–4; T. L. Fulbright, "The Bible in the Schools," *NBR,* June 26, 1890, 7; [OPF], "Vigilance Not Intoleration," *NCA,* February 11, 1888, 1; [OPF], "The Spectator," *NCA,* June 6, 1889, 1; [EEH], "Around the World," *NCA,* December 21, 1893, 2; [EEH], "Around the World," *NCA,* June 28, 1894, 2. Tennessee religious leaders would become increasingly interested in the place of the Bible in public schoolrooms at the end of the nineteenth century, eventually seeking a state law requiring school to open each day with a Bible reading.

59. Robert Hiram White, *Development,* 120; Tennessee *House Journal,* 1873, 354. The amendment was offered by Democratic Representative Pat J. Mulvihill, an Irish-born Memphis lawyer and Confederate veteran who represented Shelby County. Mulvihill thus begins the list of Shelby County representatives who opposed religious legislation for Tennessee's schools (McBride and Robison, *Biographical Directory,* 649).

60. William Witcher, "Educate Head and Heart," *NCA,* January 17, 1880, 7.

61. "A Live Issue," *MB,* November 13, 1875, 470; see also Professor [Alexander] Winchell, "Religious Essentials in Education," *MB,* March 22, 1879, 74; W. G. F. Cun-

nyngham, "Thoughts on Education II," *NCA,* April 12, 1873, 6; [OPF], *NCA,* March 3, 1883, 1, October 13, 1883, 8; TBCM, 1888, 33.

62. Robert Louis Dabney, quoted in Charles William Dabney, *Universal Education,* 1:156–57. Dabney, a Presbyterian minister and prolific defender of the Lost Cause, conducted a long and acrimonious debate with Virginia School Superintendent William Henry Ruffner in the 1860s. Many of Dabney's complaints about the public schools came not just from his abhorrence of education devoid of religion—a point on which he won wide support from Tennessee Evangelicals—but also from his rather aristocratic bias against popular education. Though several Tennessee religious leaders were similarly inclined to defend the church academies and colleges from the encroachments of public high schools and colleges, most of these leaders recognized that increased common-school education would actually raise the number of students qualified to enter the church schools.

63. W. P. Harrison, "Illiteracy in the South," *NCA,* January 13, 1883, 4. Harrison concluded by citing statistics showing that the growth of public education in England coincided with an increase in crime.

64. J. Wofford Tucker, "Money from the Federal Government for Schools," *NCA,* May 19, 1883, 12; [OPF], *NCA,* March 1, 1879, 8.

65. Elliott, *Family-Craft,* 24; Elliott, *Eagle Wing,* 13. *Family-Craft* was released in response to an address by U.S. Commissioner of Education John Eaton at the 1880 Centennial Celebration of the founding of Nashville.

66. [TOS], "New Publications," *NCA,* November 2, 1872, 9; [TOS], "Church Education," *NCA,* November 30, 1872, 8; Robert Paine et al., "Address of the Bishops to the General Conference," *NCA,* May 11, 1878, 4–5.

67. Trousdale, "Plea," 8; [OPF], *NCA,* June 4, 1887, 8, May 21, 1881, 8; Wharton S. Jones, "President's Address," in *Proceedings of the Seventh and Eighth Annual Sessions,* 25. Similarly, many school systems called for screening teachers for morality but made them pledge to avoid sectarian teaching. The Nashville Board of Education, reconstituted after the Civil War, required the city's superintendent and principals to sign a statement attesting that "I will during my incumbency devote my Exclusive time and attention to the duties of my office and abstain Entirely from all public participation in partisan politics. I will also discountenance in Assistant teachers, and discourage in the general conduct of the Schools Everything calculated to impress a political Sectional or Sectarian bias on the minds of pupils." Similarly, the board's 1879 rules for teachers ordered that "No teacher shall introduce into the schools sectarian views in religion . . . under penalty of removal" (Nashville Board of Education Minutes, July 5, 1866, August 11, 1879, p. 250, J. Emerick Nagy Collection Addition, microfilm acc. 1136, reel 17, box 25, folder 1, TSLA). Similarly, the Jackson city school regulations stated, "No teacher will be permitted to introduce into school any sectarian views as regards religion, or partisan or sectional views as regards politics" (J. C. Brooks, *First Annual Report,* 29; reports are in the Tennessee Room of the Jackson-Madison County Library, Jackson).

68. Collins D. Elliott, "Blair Bill" (speech), n.d., n.p., reel 1, Elliott Papers; Atticus G. Haygood, "General Government Aid to Education in the States," *NCA*, September 15, 1883, 16. Fitzgerald editorialized, "Whatever differences of opinion may exist as to the proposition to appropriate money from the national treasury in aid of education in the several States, there will be general agreement on one point, namely: that if such appropriation shall be made, the money should be disbursed by State authority" (*NCA*, January 20, 1883, 8).

69. [OPF], "National Aid to Education," *NCA*, September 29, 1883, 8.

70. Elliott, *Family-Craft*, 2; Elliott, *Eagle Wing*, 12, 8; *NCA*, July 1, 1882, 1.

71. "Address of the Bishops to the General Convention," *NCA*, May 16, 1874, 2–3.

72. Sears in *Proceedings, Peabody Education Fund*, 1874, 2:408, quoted in Holt, *Struggle*, 19. Holt details several of the "forces retarding educational growth" (*Struggle*, 3–30), including economic disorganization (the large state debt crisis), politics, apathy, and general public mistrust of the government, but does not list church or religious opposition.

73. T. L. Fulbright, "The Bible in the Schools," *NBR*, June 26, 1890, 7.

74. J. C. Brooks, *First Annual Report*, 7.

75. "Address of the Bishops to the General Convention," *NCA*, May 16, 1874, 2–3.

76. Holston Baptist Association Minutes, 1886, 11, SBHLA.

77. Wilbur F. Tillett, "Our Greatest Educational Need," *NCA*, May 9, 1889, 14.

78. "New Publications," *NCA*, November 2, 1872, 9.

79. Summers gradually increased the number of notices he printed regarding public school activities, but he remained adamant that public education had to remain morally and religiously safe and that the state had no business with any more than elementary schools; see [TOS], "Compulsory Education," *NCA*, December 14, 1872, 8; [TOS], "Religious Education," *NCA*, February 15, 1873, 7; [TOS], "The Bible in the Schools," *NCA*, October 30, 1875, 9; [TOS], "Teachers in Council," *NCA*, May 6, 1876, 9; [TOS], "A Teachers' Institute in M'Minnville," *NCA*, July 15, 1876, 6; [TOS], "Tennessee Public Schools," *NCA*, April 20, 1878, 1.

80. [TOS], "The Rev. Dr. Fitzgerald," *NCA*, June 1, 1878, 8.

81. [OPF], "Education," *NCA*, February 4, 1882, 1.

82. Ibid.

83. Holland McTyeire, "Letter from Bishop McTyeire," *NCA*, February 7, 1885, 7; see also "Report on Denominational Education," TBCM, 1887, 24.

84. [OPF], "A Warning Note on Education," *NCA*, November 17, 1883, 8. For Fitzgerald's similar complaints about the free tuition controversy in North Carolina, see [OPF], "Let them Speak Out," *NCA*, March 14, 1885, 8–9; [OPF], "The Primer or the Classics?" *NCA*, March 21, 1885, 8.

85. Holland McTyeire, "Letter from Bishop McTyeire," *NCA*, February 7, 1885, 7; [OPF], "A Warning Note on Education," *NCA*, November 17, 1883, 8. Some Jackson citizens protested public education that sought to teach children higher branches such as Latin and Greek: "Let the people pay for the fancy education, not the public. Some

citizens think it is as much the job of the community to educate a man's children as it is to vote a tax to clothe them" (J. C. Brooks, *First Annual Report,* 3).

86. [OPF], *NCA,* September 11, 1880, 1.

87. Southwestern Board Minutes, June 1, 1881, 1:124; Corkran, *Sumner County Educator,* 2.

88. Holston Baptist Association Minutes, 1886, 11.

89. [OPF], "A Vital Question Now before Us," *NCA,* March 9, 1889, 1; Wilbur F. Tillett, "Our Greatest Educational Need," *NCA,* May 9, 1889, 14; TBCM, 1890, 29; "Denominational Education," *NBR,* September 8, 1904, 2; G. M. Savage, "Our Educational System," *NBR,* November 27, 1890, 1; W. P. Maury, "Dr. Savage and Preparatory Schools," *NBR,* January 29, 1891, 2; J. K. P. Wallace, "Christian Education," *NBR,* February 1, 1900, 2; G. M. Savage, "The University Academy," *NBR,* August 31, 1899, 5; C. C. Crittenden, "The Academy in Southern Education," *NBR,* April 8, 1897, 2; C. T. Carpenter, "Andersonville Institute," *NBR,* July 31, 1902, 5.

90. *NCA,* December 4, 1880, 8. Tennessee Baptists asked rhetorically, "Shall we who believe we hold the truth as taught by Christ and the apostles let others take control of the education of our children?" (TBCM, 1886, 15).

91. Atticus G. Haygood, "One Thing That Is Certain," *NCA,* March 26, 1887, 2.

92. W. G. F. Cunnyngham, "Thoughts on Education," *NCA,* April 5, 1873, 6. For more on the denominational colleges and teaching of science and religion, see chapters 3 and 6.

93. Ulric, "Southern Culture," *NCA,* December 4, 1875, 3.

94. [OPF], "Our Christian Schools," *NCA,* June 23, 1883, 1.

95. Southwestern Board Minutes, June 1, 1876, 1:38–39.

96. [OPF], "Education," *NCA,* February 4, 1882, 1.

97. Ibid.; [OPF], *NCA,* August 6, 1881, 1.

98. [OPF], "Education," *NCA,* February 4, 1882, 1; W. M. Leftwich, "Religion and Public Education," *NCA,* February 22, 1890, 2.

99. W. G. F. Cunnyngham, "Thoughts on Education II," *NCA,* April 12, 1873, 6.

100. Corkran, *Sumner County Educator,* 5.

101. J. M. Phillips, "A Great Work," *MB,* February 14, 1880, 553; W. A. Montgomery, "The Sunday-School the Conservator of Our Free Institutions," *MB,* November 6, 1880, 337–38.

102. TBCM, 1890, 31; [OPF], "Do This Also," *NCA,* March 12, 1881, 8; *NCA,* April 23, 1881, 1; "The Education of Women," *NCA,* November 1, 1884, 1.

103. [EEH], *NCA,* April 8, 1897, 1.

104. [EEH], "Religion vs. the Public School," *NCA,* November 11, 1897, 8.

105. Proverbs 10:14. Unless otherwise noted, all of the quotations in this section are from J. B. Hawthorne, "Lay Up Knowledge," *NBR,* October 13, 1898, 3–4.

106. Hawthorne was a former Confederate officer, minister to congregations on both sides of the Mason-Dixon line, and "for many years . . . the acknowledged orator of the Southern Baptist Convention." He came to First Baptist in Nashville in 1896 at

age fifty-nine and retired because of poor health in 1899 (May, *First Baptist Church,* 166).

107. Kousser, "Post-Reconstruction Suffrage Restrictions"; Cartwright, *Triumph;* Doyle, *Nashville,* 121–42; Paul E. Isaac, *Prohibition,* 73–80, 116–28. In response, Nashvillians elected William McCarthy, an avowed anti-Catholic and Prohibitionist running on the ticket of the American Protective Association, as mayor in 1895. McCarthy's power was short lived, however, as the city's Irish banded together to support Richard Houston Dudley's successful 1897 mayoral candidacy (Doyle, *Nashville,* 102–3).

108. "Report on the Religious Training of Children," General Association of Baptists of East Tennessee, Proceedings, 1883, 25.

109. Hill, *Southern Churches,* 77.

110. W. G. F. Cunnyngham, "Thoughts on Education," *NCA,* April 5, 1873, 6.

111. TBCM, 1899, 12.

112. [OPF], "The Spectator," *NCA,* June 6, 1889, 1.

Chapter 3. Educating Ministers and Citizens: Denominational Colleges and Universities, 1870–1925

1. Big Hatchie Baptist Association Proceedings, 1878, 13, microfilm publication 836, SBHLA. E. Brooks Holifield, *Gentlemen,* 4, has described the upwardly mobile social aspirations of antebellum southern urban clergymen who were responding to these same pressures decades before the Big Hatchie Baptists recorded their thoughts. Beth Barton Schweiger, *Gospel,* has mined quantitative and narrative records of Virginia clergy throughout the nineteenth century, detailing their rising levels of education and efforts to raise standards not just within the clergy but in the surrounding society.

2. H. E. Watters, "A New Era in the History of Union University," *NBR,* July 4, 1918, 2.

3. Tillett, *Methodism,* 18. On the war's disruption of church colleges, see also Farish, *Circuit Rider,* 255–62; Dannelly, "Development," 164–65.

4. Tillett, *Methodism,* 18.

5. Conkin, *Gone,* 16.

6. W. G. Inman, "The History of Union University," *NBR,* July 30, 1891, 2, quoted in Richard Hiram Ward, "Development," 11.

7. As Ward notes, the school was chartered in 1842 but did not open until 1848 ("Development," 12–24, 188).

8. TBCM, 1874.

9. General Association of Baptists of East Tennessee, Minutes, 1873, 15–16.

10. Big Hatchie Baptist Association Proceedings, 1878, 13, microfilm publication 836, SBHLA.

11. G. F. Pierce, "Letter from Bishop Pierce," *NCA,* May 18, 1872, 5. Cherry, *Hurrying,* 20–22, describes the Pierce-McTyeire debate in the context of many denominations' efforts to establish university divinity schools; Cherry points to the irony, given the

denomination's initial suspicion of a learned ministry, of the large number of Methodist schools of divinity.

12. Holland M'Tyeire, "Origin and Plan of Theological Education among the British Methodists," *NCA*, January 13, 1872, 10.

13. Holland McTyeire, "Remarks on Bishop Pierce's Third Letter," *NCA*, May 4, 1872, 4.

14. D. C. Kelley, "Ministerial Education—Theological Schools," *NCA*, June 20, 1867, 1. Landon C. Garland, who would become the first chancellor of Vanderbilt, answered Kelley, arguing for the necessity of a trained ministry to meet the growing secular education of the day ("An Educated Ministry," *NCA*, October–November 1869 [six articles]).

15. D. C. Kelley, "Central University," *NCA*, May 18, 1872, 5.

16. See, for example, the report to the 1895 meeting of the Board of Education, at which Kelley estimated that Vanderbilt had given more than ten thousand dollars over the past twenty years (Tennessee Conference, Methodist Episcopal Church, South, Board of Education Minutes, Commission on Archives and History, Tennessee Conference, United Methodist Church, Nashville). Beginning in 1895 and continuing through 1914, reports on education to the Tennessee Annual Conference cite the amounts contributed by the schools for the education of ministers or their children.

17. Tillett estimated that Vanderbilt trained 950 or 1,000 ministers during its nearly forty-year connection with the southern Methodist Church (1875–1914) (Tillett to Paul N. Garber, August 22, 1931, Wilbur Fiske Tillett Papers, box 1, file 3, VUSC).

18. Rufus W. Weaver, "Union University Religious Work," *NBR*, December 6, 1917, 16.

19. "Report on Reorganization of the Biblical Department," Vanderbilt Board Minutes, May 26, 1885, 2:421. Kelley gave some explanation of the controversies of the early Biblical Department in an 1890 article in a Nashville literary magazine. Kelley asserted that Rev. Thomas O. Summers Sr., the dean of the department, though highly intelligent, was self-educated and thought all preachers could profit from his learned lectures. The truth, Kelley believed, was that ministerial students needed a literary and academic course before they could receive a theological education. Changing the system was apparently a great struggle, with change coming, he asserted, only after the press started reporting on the number of ministers who could not pass the examinations of the annual conferences; the Board of Trust consequently appointed the committee on reorganization (Kelley, "Story of Vanderbilt University," *Round Table*, May 3, 1890, photocopy in RG 101, box 29, file "Divinity School—Students," VUSC).

20. "Report on Reorganization of the Biblical Department," Vanderbilt Board Minutes, May 26, 1885, 2:422.

21. Southwestern Board Minutes, June 2, 1880, 1:12.

22. See, for example, D. C. Kelley, "Some Church Problems of To-day," *NCA*, July 27, 1899, 4.

23. "Ministerial Education," *NCA*, March 21, 1885, 6. Noting that times had changed, the unnamed author argues that ministers still need a divine call but that the church

could be better served by delaying the minister's immediate entry into the field of labor to allow for educational preparation. The author goes further than Kelley probably would in suggesting that some level of theological training be required for full ordination. Although the author might still allow the licensing of exhorters or local preachers, he argues that Methodism must keep up with the changing society: "An uneducated ministry cannot possibly do the work in the coming century which it was easily possible for them to do in the past. If, then, Methodism would hold its own in the coming century, and grow in the future as it has in the past, it must advance with the times, and meet the demand of the times for an increasingly well-trained and educated ministry."

24. [EEH], "A Great Gift—and Its Suggestions," *NCA*, September 13, 1900, 1; see also Vanderbilt Board Minutes, August 22, 1872, 1:11.

25. [James R. Graves], "The Southwestern Baptist University," *MB*, May 25, 1878, 405.

26. Big Hatchie Baptist Association Proceedings, 1879, 6. Tennessee Methodists similarly endorsed denomination-specific education; see especially [OPF], "A Vital Question Now before Us," *NCA*, March 9, 1889, 1.

27. George W. Griffin, "The Influence of a Learned Ministry," *MB*, February 5, 1878, 146–47.

28. "Our Educational Work," *MB*, February 8, 1879, 774.

29. Report on education, Central Baptist Association Minutes, 1884, 9; *Vanderbilt University Register*, 1875, 9, VUSC.

30. [OPF], "A Warning Note on Education," *NCA*, November 17, 1883, 8; [OPF], "A Vicious and Oppressive Policy," *NCA*, June 4, 1887, 1.

31. [EEH], "The Main Object in View," *NCA*, April 19, 1900, 8; [OPF], "A Vicious and Oppressive Policy," *NCA*, June 4, 1887, 1; Holland N. McTyeire, "A Plea for Denominational Education," *NCA*, December 7, 1872, 6; [OPF], *NCA*, March 1, 1879, 8; see also further examples in the *NCA*, May 21, 1881, March 3, June 16, 23, 1883, June 4, 1887, June 6, 1889.

32. Jones, *Tennessee*.

33. *Knoxville Sentinel*, June 7, 1892, quoted in James Riley Montgomery, Folmsbee, and Greene, *To Foster Knowledge*, 376–77.

34. [EEH], "The Main Object in View," *NCA*, April 19, 1900, 8.

35. [James R. Graves], "Our State University," *MB*, December 6, 1879, 408.

36. Leloudis, *Schooling*, 117–41; Gobbel, *Church-State Relationships*, 132–71.

37. McTyeire, the first president of the board of Vanderbilt, wrote to his relative, Frank Vanderbilt, while McTyeire was visiting the German university at Heidelberg, confidently predicting that "Vanderbilt University, before it is half so old, will have done greater work, I dare believe and be more famous for its work" than the august German school (August 25, 1881, John James Tigert IV Papers, box 1, folder 8, VUSC).

38. Garland reported on this problem to the Board of Trust in 1876, noting the poor level of preparation of most of the students and suggesting that "if we had stood firmly by our rules, we should have rejected fully two thirds of those that presented

themselves for matriculation." As a result, they formed "sub-collegiate classes" but this "introduced a large element of a boyish character into the University, which invariably tends to the deterioration of manners and scholarship" (Vanderbilt Board Minutes, June 17, 1876, 1:66–67). For references to a similar situation in Jackson, see Southwestern Board Minutes, June 2, 1880, 1:111.

39. Interestingly, even Vanderbilt University's earliest catalogs list Commodore Vanderbilt as the school's founder, making no mention of the role of the Methodist Episcopal Church, South; see, for example, Vanderbilt University, *Semi-Annual Announcement* [1876?], VUSC.

40. Notes for speech at opening exercises of Vanderbilt University [October 1875], Landon C. Garland Papers (unprocessed), box 1, file 9, VUSC. Garland's handwriting is hard to read, but a summary of parts of this address was reprinted in "Synopsis of Addresses on the Inauguration of Vanderbilt University," *NCA,* October 16, 1875, 9.

41. Vanderbilt Board Minutes, June 1890, 2:5.

42. Garland to McTyeire, February 2, 1874, Tigert Papers, box 2, folder 10. As Conkin comments on Vanderbilt's early faculty, despite efforts to balance academic respectability and moral and theological soundness, the "university's opening profile" was nonetheless one "of age, order, stability, and propriety" (*Gone,* 53).

43. Southwestern Board Minutes, June 2, 1880, 1:111. The Board of Trust of Carson-Newman College, another Baptist school in East Tennessee, ordered its faculty to spend at least one month of each summer in the field canvassing for the school (S. E. Jones, "My Trip to Middle Tennessee," *NBR,* August 1, 1901, 4).

44. Ibid., 122. The issue of faculty salary would remain a seemingly insurmountable problem as long as Southwestern Baptist/Union operated with only a small endowment, a large debt, and limited annual contributions from Tennessee Baptists. The board minutes reveal frequent references to the shortfall in income and the necessity of either reducing faculty salary or borrowing funds to pay instructors. In a 1927 effort to secure accreditation for the school with the Southern Association of Colleges and Schools, President H. E. Watters suggested that since "they were not being paid a full salary they were really donating so much to Christian Education and he would like to follow this plan if they would be pleased with it—that is—list them at full salary, debiting their accounts each month with that amount, and crediting with the amount above which they had been receiving and listing it as a gift to Christian Education." Union University Board of Trust Minutes, May 16, 1927, 3:47–48, quoted in Ward, *History,* 89.

45. George W. Griffin, "To the Churches of the Big Hatchie Association," *MB,* January 5, 1878, 85; George W. Griffin, "To the Baptists of the State—Will You Hear the Voice of History?" *MB,* January 19, 1878, 115–16; George W. Griffin, "The Influence of a Learned Ministry," *MB,* February 5, 1878, 146–47.

46. Southwestern Board Minutes, June 5, 1878, 1:88, July 2, 1879, 1:99, July 3, 1879, 1:105.

47. Conkin, *Gone,* 52; see also Conkin's account of Joynes's dismissal, which Conkin puts in the context of McTyeire's tightening grip on the university (*Gone,* 59–60).

48. McTyeire to Joynes, June 3, 1878, Tigert Papers, box 1, file 7.

49. Vanderbilt Board Minutes, June 22, 1877, 1:123.

50. Ibid. The board expressed some doubt about whether Joynes had violated his pledge and voted to keep its resolutions regarding the cause of their disfavor with Joynes a secret, "unless necessary to vindicate the action of the Board."

51. McTyeire to Joynes, June 3, 1878, Tigert Papers, box 1, file 7. The controversial nature of Joynes's dismissal was soon lost amid the larger national agitation that accompanied another dismissal from Vanderbilt, that of naturalist Alexander Winchell. Winchell's case resembled Joynes's in that the decision to dismiss was largely an effort to avoid alienating the majority of southern Methodist patrons of Vanderbilt University. The *Nashville Christian Advocate* ("A Right Judgment," August 10, 1878, 8), edited by Vanderbilt supporter Fitzgerald, approvingly copied articles from southern newspapers supporting the dismissal of Winchell, including the following from the *South Carolina Christian Neighbor:* "The determination of the powers that rule in Vanderbilt to keep only the right kind of teachers is a certain security of the confidence of the people far and near. Adherence to this conservative line of management will doubtless secure that increasing prosperity and usefulness which the institution already enjoys, and which is still more clear in the probabilities of the future." Because Winchell's dismissal also involved his interpretation of evolution and most specifically his theories of Preadamite humans, the matter is better discussed in the context of Tennessee Evangelicals and evolution; see chapter 6.

52. James Riley Montgomery, Folmsbee, and Greene, *To Foster Knowledge,* 94–96, 108.

53. Vanderbilt Board Minutes, June 18, 1877, 1:108; Union Board Minutes, July 2, 1874, 1:5.

54. Garland to McTyeire, February 2, 1874, Tigert Papers, box 2, file 10.

55. Concerning a faculty appointment, Garland wrote to McTyeire, "We have non-Methodistic element enough in our Faculty to silence the cry of sectarianism—and if we are again to go outside for a man, I had rather have a moral and discreet man" (August 26, 1887, Tigert Papers, box 2, folder 13). At the same time, some Methodists were concerned about having any non-Methodists in the church schools. A writer identifying himself only by the pen name "Methodist" complained, "We humbly submit that (1) If the Methodist Church, with all her boasted talent, cannot furnish teachers for her own schools, it is time to turn her children over to the State or other Churches to be educated. (2) If a Methodist has not sufficient zeal to attend the services of the Methodist Church and assist in her work he is not fit to teach in her schools" ("Church Schools," *NCA,* January 28, 1882, 7).

56. Union Board Minutes, June 4, 1878, 1:83. Jarman noted that Gore had testimonials from among others, Hopkins President Daniel C. Gilman, Rev. Dr. J. L. M. Curry of Richmond, and Rev. Dr. Nathaniel Lupton of Vanderbilt.

57. [EEH], "Association of Colleges and Preparatory Schools of the Southern States," *NCA,* December 3, 1896, 3; J. H. Kirkland, "Vanderbilt University and Prepara-

tory Classes," *NCA,* November 26, 1896, 3; Farish, *Circuit Rider,* 277–78; Conkin, *Gone,* 109–10.

58. Vanderbilt Board Minutes, May 1882, 1:286.

59. James H. Kirkland, "Inaugural Address," [1894], James Hampton Kirkland Papers (personal), box 18, file 9, VUSC. In an address before the Southern Education Association meeting in Memphis in 1899, Kirkland presented a paper on "The Duty of the State towards Higher Education" in which he called for state regulation of colleges and universities to safeguard the value of diplomas. In his address, Kirkland eschewed any idea of antagonism between church and state schools, arguing that both to some extent had been founded by the state and that the state certainly received the benefit from both; consequently, the state had an interest in seeing that firm standards for graduation were established (Kirkland Papers [personal], box 17, file 59).

60. Southwestern Board Minutes, June 1, 1881, 1:124. Southwestern Baptist had from its inception a very close relationship with the Jackson public schools, even contracting with the city's public schools to provide classroom space and teachers for the male students. The arrangement made Southwestern a natural place for city school graduates to continue their studies, provided student teaching opportunities for the college's students, and netted $1,620 in the first half of 1876 for the financially strapped college (Southwestern Board Minutes, June 1, 1876, 1:38–39).

61. Vanderbilt Board Minutes, May 3, 1875, 1:45, September 30, 1874, 1:40.

62. Southwestern Board Minutes, June 4, 1878, 1:86. The previous year, the executive committee had praised the faculty's efforts while complaining that it was nearly impossible to ask teachers to "make bricks without straw" and urging the board to purchase books and scientific apparatus (May 30, 1877, 1:52).

63. Plautus Iberus Lipsey, "Memories of His Early Life (1865–1888)," Plautus Iberus Lipsey Diary, Diaries and Memoirs Collection II-H-4, acc. no. 1888, box 5, TSLA.

64. Southwestern Board Minutes, July 2, 1879, 1:97. Southwestern's board members brought some problems on themselves: for example, they decided to fire the school's first president, William Shelton, but "In order that he might not be thrown entirely out of employment he was made financial agent of the University." George Jarman reported to trustee Thomas T. Eaton, who had missed the meeting, that "to the astonishment of all [Shelton] has accepted it. I admire Dr. S. as noble Christian brother, but it cannot be denied that he has proved a failure in every thing he has ever attempted in connection with a school" (Jarman to Eaton, June 5, 1876, Thomas T. Eaton Papers, microfilm publication 1057, reel 2, SBHLA). At the same meeting in which he was appointed agent, Shelton had resisted his dismissal and had even threatened to open a rival Jackson school to draw off patronage. He was nonetheless offered the post of financial agent, and not surprisingly, his efforts resulted in financial loss rather than gain for the university. The ordeal of getting Shelton to turn over pledges to the school and the school to come up with the money to pay his salary consumed much of the board's time for the following few years. See Southwestern Board Minutes, June 1, 1876, 1:40, 42–43; May 31, 1877, 1:65; June 4, 1878, 1:80; July 2, 1879, 1:97.

65. These conditions were relieved to some extent when Carson-Newman and Southwestern Baptist decided to split the state in 1894, no longer competing with each other for support. This agreement avoided antagonism but did not supply more money. Union's rivalry with Hall-Moody lasted much longer, leading to a 1917 agreement to stop duplicating programs, though the pact appears to have been ignored or violated from the beginning and was formally annulled in 1919 (Union Board Minutes, August 8, 1917, 2:330, April 1, 1919, 2:350–53; see also Ward, *History,* 74–86).

66. Southwestern Board Minutes, June 1, 1881, 1:124; [EEH], "John Smith, President of Blow-Hard College," *NCA,* April 27, 1893, 1.

67. See, for example, [EEH], *NCA,* June 30, 1892.

68. John P. Mott, quoted in George T. Mellen, "*Christian Advocate* vs. State Schools," *NCA,* August 11, 1892, 13; see also Charles Galloway, "Dedication Address at Millsaps College," *NCA,* August 17, 1893, 3; [EEH], "Why Should We Have Denominational Schools?" *NCA,* September 2, 1897, 1.

69. [EEH], "Why Should We Have Denominational Schools?" *NCA,* September 2, 1897, 1; Rev. W. B. Murrah, "Wherefore the Denominational College?" *NCA,* August 16, 1894, 2.

70. J. W. Conger, "What May the College Do in the Religious Training of Students?" *NBR,* December 24, 1908, 3–4; see also S. E. Jones, "Denominational Education," *NBR,* August 4, 1904, 2–3.

71. S. E. Jones, "Denominational Education," *NBR,* August 9, 1906, 3.

72. [EEH], "Religion in the Colleges," *NCA,* March 1, 1894, 1.

73. EEH, "Vanderbilt University," *NCA,* September 19, 1895, 1. Hoss's editorial did not pass unnoticed by the board, which adopted a resolution at a meeting of its executive committee on September 24, 1895, expressing "great regret" at the editorial, which, they asserted, was "apparently written in the interest of Vanderbilt University, but calculated at the same time to do the University great damage." They concluded by instructing Bishop Robert K. Hargrove to "respectfully invite the Editor of the Advocate to furnish the proof of the imputations in the hope that we may be able to show him that the same are not well founded" (Vanderbilt Board Minutes, September 24, 1895, 4:47; see also [EEH], "Our Denominational Schools," *NCA,* October 1, 1896, 1).

74. [EEH], "A Question of Propriety," *NCA,* May 6, 1897, 1. Critics of the university commonly raised such complaints; see, for example, H. H. Hamill to W. F. Tillett, May 25, 1912, Tillett Papers, box 1, file 9. Under Hoss's control, the *Nashville Christian Advocate* regularly criticized the school, bringing student (mis)behavior (dancing, attending the theater, and playing football, for example) before the church readership constantly as proof of the school's atmosphere. Hoss easily emerges from nearly every account of the Vanderbilt crisis as at worst a conniving, anti-intellectual, and manipulative politician, but he was, nonetheless the mouthpiece of a significant portion of the church membership. Conkin takes great efforts to humanize Hoss, "the one most easily identified antihero" in most accounts of the Bishops' Suit (*Gone,* 158–59). While suggesting Hoss was correct in his interpretation of the situation, Burtchaell describes Hoss as "a strident,

impassioned, and unattractive antagonist, who defined the issues in so anti-intellectual a way that he strengthened Kirkland's credibility among those who sought an institution of rigorous learning. . . : Hoss was the very incarnation of that to which an ambitious company of scholars would not wish to be accountable" (*Dying*, 848).

75. James H. Kirkland, "Twenty-five Years of University Work," *NCA*, November 1, 1900, 5.

76. J. H. Kirkland, "Methodists and Non-Methodists in the Academic Faculty," manuscript of brief in response to the complaint of the bishops, RG 300, Chancellor's Office Papers, box 103, file 55, VUSC.

77. Vanderbilt Board Minutes, 1904, 5:196.

78. Conkin, *Gone,* 154–55; Massengale, "Collegiate Education," 526.

79. Kirkland to John J. Vertrees, October 14, 1911, Kirkland Papers, box 1, file 5.

80. Massengale, "Collegiate Education," 492–514.

81. Vanderbilt Board Minutes, June 1901, 5:53.

82. Wilbur F. Tillett, "Why Should the Biblical Department of Vanderbilt University Share in Our Twentieth Century Thank Offering?" *North Carolina Christian Advocate,* March 7, 1900, 6, Tillett Papers, box 2, file 50.

83. Vanderbilt Board Minutes, June 1901, 5:53. In 1914 briefs to the Tennessee Supreme Court, attorneys for the university argued that the twenty-five thousand dollars spent by the Methodist Episcopal Church, South, on the trial was greater than the sum of church contributions to the school in its first twenty-five years of existence (Conkin, *Gone,* 181).

84. Kirkland to Daniel C. Gilman, October 31, 1904, Kirkland Papers (personal), box 1, file 1.

85. Both Massengale and Conkin recognize that the controversies over the Vanderbilt charter were far more complicated than a battle between the church and the school but rather involved several competing church factions and revealed growing rifts in the social and theological unity of the southern Methodist church; see Massengale, "Collegiate Education," 526; Conkin, *Gone,* 150.

86. Vanderbilt Board Minutes, June 20, 1905, 5:252–57. The chronology and issues of the legal struggles are too complicated to cover in great detail here. The best summary of the events and issues can be found in Conkin, *Gone,* 147–222.

87. Conkin, *Gone,* 158.

88. Much of the commission's report was published in the *Nashville Christian Advocate,* where ordinary church members could attempt to wade through the many pages of this quasi-legal "decision" regarding the school's status; see "Report of the Vanderbilt Commission," *NCA,* December 14, 1906, 1, 6–13, 16.

89. Vanderbilt Board Minutes, June 13, 1914, 5:183; see also Conkin, *Gone,* 174. The majority trustees attempted to keep up with Hoss's skillful propaganda and had an able spokesman in the early years of the controversy in the much revered Bishop Hendrix, the president of the board and a strong supporter of Kirkland's vision of the grand university.

90. [Thomas Ivey], "The Church Loses Vanderbilt," *NCA*, March 27, 1914, 4; [Thomas Ivey], "The Opportunity of Southern Methodism," *NCA*, April 17, 1914, 3–4.

91. S. F. Jewell, "Our Relation to Vanderbilt," *Nashville Midland Methodist*, May 6, 1914, Tillett Papers, box 2, file 65.

92. Wilbur F. Tillett, "The Rights and Duties of the Church in Vanderbilt University," *NCA*, April 17, 1914, 12–13, 24–25.

93. Blackwell to Tillett, April 21, 1914, Tillett Papers, box 1, file 6. Tillett's papers contain numerous other letters of support for his argument, but church papers aired few of his allies' views. At the same time, the chancellor's office received and filed scores of angry letters from Methodists who felt "defrauded" by the actions of the board and the ruling of the court (Chancellor's Office Papers, box 106, file 4).

94. Rufus W. Weaver, "The Vanderbilt Decision and Baptist Schools," *NBR*, April 17, 1914, 9.

95. P. T. Hale, who led a successful revival at Southwestern Baptist in 1896, was elected president of the school in 1904 ([Edgar E. Folk], "Revivals in Colleges," *NBR*, March 19, 1896, 8).

96. A. P. Bourland, "The University Question," *NBR*, February 6, 1890, 2; see also Ward, "Development," 61.

97. Union Board Minutes, April 20, 1912, 2:199–200.

98. On Landmarkism generally, see James E. Tull, "Landmark Movement," in Hill, *Encyclopedia*, 399–401; on Landmarkism's disruptions of the Tennessee Baptist Convention, see Wardin, *Tennessee Baptists*, 176–90, 377–91.

99. H. E. Watters, "What Has Become of It?" *NBR*, January 13, 1910, 2.

100. James H. Kirkland, "Twenty-five Years of University Work," *NCA*, November 1, 1900, 5; Professor W. S. Woodward, "Why Denominational Education for Baptists?" *NBR*, January 18, 1917, 2; see also A. T. Robertson, "An Educational Revival in the South," *NBR*, January 2, 1919, 2.

101. P. T. Hale, "S. W. B. Paragraphs," *NBR*, March 1, 1906, 3.

102. TBCM, 1911, 18. While writing the charter for Tennessee College for Women, a Baptist school in Murfreesboro, the committee engaged the assistance of John Bell Keeble, one of the lawyers who had been involved in the early stages of the Vanderbilt Commission. With Keeble's assistance, "a committee of the commission watched over its preparation and incorporated into it every possible safeguard to secure the perpetuity of the institution as a Baptist school under the control of this Convention. . . . All of the Trustees, according to the By-Laws, must be Baptists" (TBCM, 1906, 10).

103. Rufus Weaver, "The Legal Status of the Baptist Schools," *NBR*, January 11, 1917, 16; see also TBCM, 1912, 44–46. For a more detailed account of the efforts to secure denominational control over the Baptist schools, see Ward, "Development," 93–118.

104. *NCA*, July 9, 1915, 30; W. A. Candler, "Our Educational Work Is Now Missionary Work Also," *NCA*, August 13, 1915, 12.

105. Rufus Weaver, "The Great World War and Our Baptist Colleges," *NBR*, August 2, 1917, 16.

106. [Thomas Ivey], "A Counter 'Watch on the Rhine,'" *NCA,* August 1, 1919, 6–7.

107. Christian Education Movement, "Spies That Cried Calamity," *NCA,* February 4, 1921, 32.

108. *NCA,* February 18, 1921, 32.

109. *NCA,* March 4, 1921, 32.

110. "Banish the Bolshevik," *NCA,* April 1, 1921, 32; "Moral Character or Steel Doors," *NCA,* April 29, 1921, 32.

111. J. B. Game, "State Colleges and the Church," *NCA,* January 18, 1906, 7–9.

112. Rev. O. T. Gilmore, "The Church at Work in State Schools," *NCA,* March 28, 1924, 8–9.

113. [TOS], "Laying the Corner-Stone of Vanderbilt University," *NCA,* May 9, 1874, 5.

Chapter 4. From Temperance to Prohibition: Tennessee Evangelicals and the Legislation of Morality

1. [EEH], "To Our Own People," *NCA,* July 4, 1901, 1.

2. Lacy, "Tennessee Teetotalism," 220.

3. [EEH], "To Our Own People," *NCA,* July 4, 1901, 1.

4. Memphis Conference, Methodist Episcopal Church, South, Journal, 1913, 70, Tennessee Conference, United Methodist Church, Commission on Archives and History, McKendree Methodist Church, Nashville.

5. John Abernathy Smith, *Cross and Flame,* 228–29.

6. Eighmy, *Churches,* 51.

7. Quoted in Wardin, *Tennessee Baptists,* 192.

8. John Abernathy Smith, *Cross and Flame,* 230; Wardin, *Tennessee Baptists,* 192–93.

9. Loveland, *Southern Evangelicals,* 133–35. Brownlow fit Loveland's model, joining forces with the Sons of Temperance and becoming an ardent voice for Prohibition in every forum he entered—his newspaper, the northern Methodist pulpit, or the office of Tennessee governor during Reconstruction (Conklin, "Parson Brownlow Part I," 181–86; John Abernathy Smith, *Cross and Flame,* 230; Wardin, *Tennessee Baptists,* 193).

10. Paul E. Isaac, *Prohibition,* 9; Wardin, *Tennessee Baptists,* 193; John Abernathy Smith, *Cross and Flame,* 230–31.

11. Loveland, *Southern Evangelicals,* 151; Snay, *Gospel,* 41.

12. Loveland, *Southern Evangelicals,* 144–45, 158; John Abernathy Smith, *Cross and Flame,* 230–31. Parsons, "Speculative Philanthropy," suggests the lengths to which southern temperance activists went to evade the charges of being closet abolitionists, even contending that Brownlow was the author of *Speculative Philanthropy,* an anonymous 1859 semifictional temperance "history" that sought to explain the temperance movement's southern roots and distance it from the guilt by association of abolitionism.

13. Paul E. Isaac, *Prohibition,* 7. Johnson's opponent, Whig candidate Meredith P. Gentry, endorsed a local-option provision. In a position they would reverse in the years

after the war, Prohibition leaders in 1855 wanted a stronger, statewide ban and thus were unsatisfied with Gentry's answer to the liquor evil.

14. Paul E. Isaac, *Prohibition*, 8 n.21. However, various military orders prohibited or restricted the sale of alcohol to soldiers or government employees during the war (Leab, "Tennessee Temperance," 52).

15. A short account of Brownlow's place in Tennessee can be found in Forrest Conklin, "Brownlow, William Gannaway 'Parson,' " in West, *Tennessee Encyclopedia*, 98–99; See also Conklin, "Parson Brownlow Part I"; Paul E. Isaac, *Prohibition*, 8–9; Coulter, *William G. Brownlow*.

16. Conklin, "Parson Brownlow Part II," 302–3; Ash, *Middle Tennessee Society*, 206; Conklin, "Brownlow, William Gannaway 'Parson,' " 98; see also Spain, *At Ease*, 176; Gusfield, *Symbolic Crusade*, 54.

17. "Pastoral Letter" quoted in Stowell, *Rebuilding Zion*, 163, 156–61.

18. J. H. Bowman, "Holston Conference," *NCA*, May 18, 1872, 4; John Abernathy Smith, *Cross and Flame*, 231.

19. Conklin suggests three possible explanations for Brownlow's failure to push prohibitory laws through an otherwise compliant Radical legislature: (1) it was too busy with more pressing issues such as the physical rebuilding of the state's infrastructure; (2) his control over the Radicals was political only; or (3) he wisely chose not to push other Radical and moral policies when his racially and politically radical plans were already engendering substantial opposition ("Parson Brownlow Part II," 304–5).

20. Paul E. Isaac, *Prohibition*, 8–9.

21. Leab, "Tennessee Temperance," 55–58; Paul E. Isaac, *Prohibition*, 9.

22. Fairbanks, *History*, 167–69; Paul E. Isaac, *Prohibition*, 10–11; Leab, "Tennessee Temperance," 64–65.

23. Leab, "Tennessee Temperance," 62–63; Paul E. Isaac, *Prohibition*, 32–60. Much of the support for Prohibition came from heavily Republican East Tennessee. A map showing the distribution of votes for and against the proposal appears in Hart, *Redeemers*, 105.

24. Ash, *Middle Tennessee Society*, 245–46. Sparks, *On Jordan's Stormy Banks*, 154, notes that intoxication was the most common charge leveled against white males, though it declined from a high of 45.8 percent of total charges in the decade 1820–30 to only 20.7 percent in 1860–70. Owenby, *Subduing Satan*, 205–7, marks a similar decrease in alcohol-related offenses in the last years of the nineteenth century and first years of the twentieth century.

25. Spain, *At Ease*, 183–86.

26. [TOS], "Saving Souls," *NCA*, August 22, 1874, 8. The 1886 General Conference finally amended the church's General Rules to require strict abstinence.

27. Quoted in Spain, *At Ease*, 185. Eighmy notes that by the 1850s, most Baptist churches included in their doctrinal statements a requirement that members "abstain from the sale and use of intoxicating drinks" (*Churches*, 51).

28. Union Association of Baptists Proceedings, 1890, 10, microfilm publication 836, SBHLA; TBCM, 1893, 40.

29. Owenby, *Subduing Satan*, 207–8.

30. Wilson, *Baptized*, 87–88.

31. Wilson deals more explicitly with religion, although because of his focus on the "civil religion" aspects of the Lost Cause, he makes little effort to separate the efforts of ministers of the Lost Cause from ministers of the Gospel (some but by no means all of whom, of course, were one in the same). Neither Wilson nor Foster has much to say on Prohibition directly, although Wilson provides a couple of paragraphs and Foster's explanation of the malleability of the Lost Cause ideology for present political and social purposes has clearly influenced my thinking in this matter. See Wilson, *Baptized*, 87–88; Foster, *Ghosts*.

32. [OPF], "Sufficiency of the Church," *NCA*, May 3, 1878, 8; [OPF], "The Temporal Functions of the Church," *NCA*, May 14, 1881, 1; [OPF], *NCA*, December 11, 1880, 1; James M. Lawson, *NCA*, January 22, 1881, 8.

33. Owen makes a similar point in his study of Georgia Methodism, *Sacred Flame*, 181. He devotes significant attention to the various factions of modernizers and traditionalists within Georgia Methodism, suggesting further that the death of an older generation of conservative bishops and church leaders in the first decades after the Civil War prepared the ground for a new class of "progressive" and "neoconservative" leaders, most symbolized by Atticus Haygood and Warren Akin Candler, respectively. Haygood would play a prominent role in stirring up southern Methodists' interest in public education; Candler would prove one of the chief critics of Chancellor Kirkland and Vanderbilt University, eventually leading the charge to abandon Vanderbilt in favor of the new Emory University, which was funded by Candler's millionaire brother (Owen, *Sacred Flame*, 151).

34. In his study on Christian lobbyists for federal moral legislation, *Moral Reconstruction*, 128–30, Foster notes the growing willingness of southern Evangelicals to support and even lead campaigns against alcohol, the lottery, and other moral evils.

35. TBCM, 1901, 35.

36. Jones visited Nashville in the early spring of 1885 and returned again that summer. On Fitzgerald's support of Jones, see [OPF], "Rev. Sam Jones," *NCA*, March 28, 1885, 8; [OPF], "Rev. 'Sam' Jones," *NCA*, April 4, 1885, 8. On the Knoxville ministers' endorsement of Jones, see "Rev. Sam P. Jones," *NCA*, April 25, 1885, 4. On Jones's May revivals, see [OPF], "The Nashville Churches," *NCA*, May 16, 1885, 8; "Sam Jones in Nashville," *NCA*, May 16, 1885, 9; " 'Sam' Jones in Nashville," *NCA*, May 23, 1885, 1; " 'Sam' Jones," *NCA*, May 30, 1885, 8. Minnix devotes the first chapter of her biography of Jones, *Laughter in the Amen Corner*, to the 1885 Nashville meeting.

37. In addition to housing Jones's revival services, the Ryman Auditorium became a frequent public gathering place for religious, political, and entertainment groups, housing such disparate events as high-school graduations, gubernatorial inaugurations,

and William Jennings Bryan's 1924 antievolution speech and 1925 memorial service ([OPF], "Sam Jones Declines," *NCA,* June 6, 1885, 17).

38. Kelley, quoted in Farish, *Circuit Rider,* 315 n.1; W. Perkins, "Temperance: Local Option," *NCA,* February 20, 1875, 5; J. S. Thomas, "Temperance," *MB,* November 16, 1878, 601.

39. Quoted in Paul E. Isaac, *Prohibition,* 22.

40. Wright diary, quoted in W. Calvin Dickinson, "Temperance," in West, *Tennessee Encyclopedia,* 913.

41. Like their Methodist counterparts, Tennessee Baptists who recorded their opinions were careful to justify their participation in politics on moral grounds, prefacing their resolution with the statement "since this is a grand moral and religious question, be it therefore be resolved" (Union Association of Baptists Proceedings, 1886, 6).

42. TBCM, 1886, 25.

43. [TOS], "Crime and Vice," *NCA,* September 5, 1874, 8.

44. [OPF], *NCA,* August 14, 1886, 8.

45. [OPF], *NCA,* April 5, 1879, 8.

46. While willing to speak out specifically on alcohol, Fitzgerald was more reticent about less clearly moral questions. Responding to a number of 1879 requests to comment on the controversies surrounding Tennessee's state debt, Fitzgerald demurred, explaining that the church's duty was to teach generally about morality and responsibility but not to comment explicitly because the debt was an expressly political question ([OPF], "State Bonds—Duty of the Religious Press and Pulpit," *NCA,* April 12, 1879, 8–9).

47. [OPF], "The Hand-to-Hand Fight against the Saloon," *NCA,* August 13, 1887, 1.

48. [OPF], "The Editor's Fourth of July Meditation," *NCA,* July 10, 1886, 1.

49. "Temperance Movement," *MB,* January 4, 1879, 698. Graves may have been out of the state when this article was published and may not have been the author. He had, however, already expressed his favor of stricter temperance discipline within the church. Thus, an extension of this nature is not unreasonable but remains problematic given Graves's Landmarkist tendencies, which would militate against a breach of a strict separation of church and state, even for moral legislation such as this.

50. Paul E. Isaac, *Prohibition,* 16.

51. "Duty Concerning Prohibition," *NBR,* September 17, 1887, 6, quoted in Paul E. Isaac, *Prohibition,* 44; [OPF], "The Last Weeks of the Campaign," *NCA,* September 10, 1887, 8; Paul E. Isaac, *Prohibition,* 54.

52. Tennessee Annual Conference, Methodist Episcopal Church, South, Journal, 1887, 22, Tennessee Conference, United Methodist Church, Commission on Archives and History, McKendree Methodist Church, Nashville; "The Tennessee Election," *NCA,* October 8, 1887, 8; TBCM, 1887, 21.

53. The prohibitionist forces disagreed about how best to proceed; see Paul E. Isaac, *Prohibition,* 58–60.

54. Vertrees quoted in Paul E. Isaac, *Prohibition,* 46.

55. H. C. Snodgrass, *Nashville American,* September 24, 1887, quoted in Paul E. Isaac, *Prohibition,* 53.

56. Vertrees quoted in Paul E. Isaac, *Prohibition,* 46.

57. Quoted in ibid., 57–58.

58. Ibid., 23–27. See also Hooper, *Crying,* 199–203. Lipscomb's outspoken stand on the Prohibition matter was not out of character with his larger rejection of politics and civil government. Whereas Tennessee Methodists and Baptists were moving toward a broader embrace of their surrounding society and at least faint traces of postmillennialism, Lipscomb and his members of the Church of Christ clearly maintained a sect mentality in opposition to both the established churches and the larger society. As other Tennessee Evangelicals were making overtures to reforming individuals and society, Lipscomb's apocalyptic worldview gave little room or purpose to social redemption. See Hughes, *Reviving,* 119–34.

59. [OPF], "The Solidarity of Evil Parties," *NCA,* October 8, 1887, 1; Warren A. Candler, "The Duty of a Christian Citizen," *NCA,* September 10, 1887, 2–3.

60. Harvey, " 'Yankee Faith,' " 177; Harvey, *Redeeming,* 22–25.

61. Paul E. Isaac, *Prohibition,* 56, 47.

62. Much of the correspondence on this subject was reprinted in Tennessee Conference, Methodist Episcopal Church, South, Journal, 1890, 25–33; see also John Abernathy Smith, *Cross and Flame,* 235–37.

63. Paul E. Isaac, *Prohibition,* 67. John Abernathy Smith argues that "the bishops' decision to act against Kelley probably derived less from partisan conviction than from fears that holiness preachers would use Kelley's candidacy to justify their habit of deserting assignments for evangelistic work elsewhere" (*Cross and Flame,* 236).

64. TBCM, 1890, 40. As with most convention minutes, those from 1890 do not offer the full text or even the themes of the arguments on the floor, only a listing of some of the discussants. But two of the major figures from the convention, S. E. Jones and G. A. Lofton, continued their argument in the *Baptist and Reflector* throughout November and December 1890, offering some idea of the context of the convention debates. Jones, who had written the original report (which was not adopted), criticized the substitute report as "favoring prohibition, or the third party." Lofton replied that it had been "distinctly averred on the floor of the Convention that our action had nothing to do with the 'third party,' as such, and was so decided by the president, and the resolution was voted for by those who did to believe in a third party." See S. E. Jones, "That Temperance Report Again—Reply to Dr. Lofton," *NBR,* November 13, 1890, 4; G. A. Lofton, "That Temperance Report Again—Reply to Brother S. E. Jones," *NBR,* November 20, 1890, 4.

65. S. E. Jones, "The Report on Temperance," *NBR,* October 30, 1890, 4; George A. Lofton, "The Report on Temperance," *NBR,* November 6, 1890, 1. For the larger context among southern Baptists over distinctions between individual and convention endorsements of civil and moral reform, see Spain, *At Ease,* 42–43.

66. [Edgar Estes Folk], "The Kelley Case," *NBR,* October 16, 1890, 8; G. A. Lofton,

"That Temperance Report Again—Reply to Brother S. E. Jones," *NBR,* November 20, 1890, 4; George A. Lofton, "The Report on Temperance," *NBR,* November 6, 1890, 1. Baptists were not alone in these concerns; Methodists made similar arguments describing temperance as a nonpartisan activity; see J. M. Hawley, "The Church and Moral Issues," *NCA,* December 7, 1893, 3.

67. [OPF], "The Spectator," *NCA,* August 4, 1888, 1; see also [OPF], "The Christian in Politics," *NCA,* June 23, 1888, 1; Tennessee Annual Conference, Methodist Episcopal Church, South, Journal, 1897, 33; [EEH], *NCA,* October 5, 1893, 1.

68. [EEH], "A Shameful Spectacle," *NCA,* May 9, 1895, 1; [EEH], "Local Option League of Tennessee," *NCA,* July 2, 1896, 8; TBCM, 1901, 35.

69. [Edgar Estes Folk], "Political Preachers," *NBR,* February 16, 1905, 8. Folk frequently repeated this justification, for example, in Folk to M. F. Caldwell, July 22, 1904, Edgar Estes Folk Papers, box 1, folder 30, AR 663, SBHLA. Despite his professions to shun partisan politics, Folk's few surviving papers reveal that he was a keen political activist who paid attention to party affairs in his efforts to secure Prohibition. See, for example, a letter from Jonesboro grocer W. S. Hickey advising Folk on the prospects of garnering Republican votes in favor of gubernatorial candidate James Frazier (June 26, 1904, Folk Papers, box 1, folder 84).

70. [George Winton], "Senator Carmack," *NCA,* November 13, 1908, 1; [George Winton], "Prohibition in Tennessee," *NCA,* December 4, 1908, 4. Carmack's martyrdom even included something of a shrine at the place of his death: a rural Tennessee Methodist circuit rider recorded in his diary that while in Nashville, he "visited the spot where Senator Carmack was murdered and put my arm around the post against which he fell. He did not die in vain. His assassins are being tried in the criminal court at this time" (Jeremiah Walker Cullom Diary, ACC 68–384, February 3, 1909, box 2, folder 9, TSLA).

71. [Edgar Estes Folk], "Capt. Ben W. Hooper," *NBR,* August 25, 1910, 4–5; [Thomas Ivey], "Independent Democracy in Tennessee," *NCA,* September 23, 1910, 7.

72. Holt, *Struggle,* 112; Roblyer, "Fight," 28.

73. Fairbanks added the interesting comment that the law had been supported because it did "not affect the cities and incorporated towns," so "the liquor dealers have no direct interest in having it repealed. It is perhaps more in danger from the over-zealous temperance societies and organizations who may, by their efforts to procure more radical legislation, create a reaction." He further boasted that the law "has been a great blessing to this University. . . . An intoxicated person is rarely seen upon the mountain" (Fairbanks, *History,* 168).

74. [OPF], *NCA,* December 4, 1880, 13.

75. D. L. Cougar to B. W. Hooper, November 17, 1912, Governor Ben W. Hooper Papers, 1911–15, box 4, folder 5, TSLA.

76. Leab, "Tennessee Temperance," 59; Tennessee Conference, Methodist Episcopal Church, South, Journal, 1892, p. 37, 1899, p. 35; Big Hatchie Baptist Association Minutes, 1893, 12; *Tennessee Public Acts,* 1895, chapter 180.

77. Brister's inquiry and several responses from city school superintendents are in

Hooper Papers, "Miscellaneous Correspondence 1913," box 7, folder 5; see, for example, the reply of Superintendent Arthur C. Nute of the Union City Public Schools, July 20, 1912.

78. [OPF], *NCA*, November 7, 1885, 8, August 15, 1885, 1; see also Link, *Paradox*, 41.

79. R. N. Price, "A Plea for the Four-Mile Law," *NCA*, January 8, 1903, 10.

80. Quoted in Paul E. Isaac, *Prohibition*, 19.

81. TBCM, 1891, 32.

82. Ibid., 1914, 55; 1910, 48. In his now-classic study of southern Baptist social relations, Eighmy points to the importance of Baptist engagement in temperance reform as the "first major contact between Southern Baptists and social Christianity" that "brought Southern Baptists into the arena of social action, where they soon became aware of issues other than temperance" (*Churches*, 79–80, 56). Similarly, Link focuses on the significance of the temperance and Prohibition campaigns as setting a model for Progressive-era southern social reform. In his explanation, late nineteenth-century moral reform "provided an emotional language and a rhetoric to a variety of reforms that appeared in the subsequent generation." The significance of temperance reform at the end of the century was that the moral reformers changed "the terms of debate from individual to social redemption" (Link, *Paradox*, 57, 51).

83. Benjamin W. Hooper, "Legislative Message of January 31, 1911," in Ash, *Messages*, 9:204. Governor Hooper convened the first Southern Sociological Congress in Nashville in 1912, organizing a number of speakers and presentations and meetings on a wide range of southern social issues. The presenters included many nonsouthern scholars, with addresses on "The Church and Social Service" by Samuel Zane Batten, the general secretary of the Northern Baptist Convention's Social Service Commission, and "The Church and Modern Industry" by Charles S. Macfarland, secretary of the Federal Council of Churches of Christ in America. The papers were printed in McCulloch, *Call*. For a dated account of the organization of the congress, see Charles, "Southern Sociological Congress: Organization"; Charles, "Southern Sociological Congress: Rationale."

84. Eager quoted in Harper, *Quality*, 34.

85. Board of Temperance and Social Service, "Report No. 1," Memphis Conference, Methodist Episcopal Church, South, Journal, 1922, 65.

Chapter 5. Legislating Religion into the Schools: Evangelicals and Public Education, 1900–1925

1. Lester Weaver, "The Church's Choice—Educate or Evacuate," *NCA*, January 28, 1921, 11.

2. Some earlier observers had been suspicious of German intellectuals, including Hoss, who warned in 1891, "We have learned many bad lessons from Germany. If we learn how its religion as a vital force was prostrated, and be wise enough to protect ourselves from the same deplorable results, this lesson will be a salutary one" ([EEH], "A Lesson from Germany," *NCA*, July 11, 1891, 8).

3. [OPF], *NCA,* August 15, 1885, 1.

4. *Knoxville Chronicle,* July 2, 1882, 2.

5. [Edgar Estes Folk], *NBR,* January 15, 1891, 9, April 6, 1899, 12.

6. Tennessee Annual Conference, Methodist Episcopal Church, South, Board of Education, "Annual Report," in Tennessee Annual Conference, Methodist Episcopal Church, South, Journal, 1907, 54; 1910, 46; [Thomas Ivey], "A Campaign against Illiteracy," *NCA,* May 17, 1912, 6.

7. [George Winton], *NCA,* July 14, 1904, 6; [Edgar Estes Folk], *NBR,* September 9, 1915, 9; [Albert Bond], *NBR,* June 21, 1917, 12.

8. W. M. Leftwich, "Religion and Public Education," *NCA,* February 22, 1890, 2; Killebrew, "Second Annual Report," 25; "State Normal Institute," *Knoxville Chronicle,* July 2, 1881, 1.

9. Harry Clark, "Get Your Teachers from Baptist Colleges," *NBR,* March 30, 1922, 8; Harry Clark, "Do You Need Baptist Teachers?" *NBR,* June 15, 1922, 8; "Religious Status in State Schools," *NBR,* March 24, 1921, 3; N. H. Williams, "The Greatest Need of the South," *NCA,* February 15, 1915, 6–7.

10. [Edgar Estes Folk], "Minister and the Public School," *NBR,* April 5, 1917, 8.

11. J. W. Storer, "A Unique Opportunity," *NBR,* May 5, 1921, 5. Storer's letter suggested his recognition that such denominational teaching was far more likely to occur in rural than in urban schools, noting that "it would be impossible to do this in many localities where the Jewish and Catholic elements would be sufficiently strong to object, effectually." The word *effectually* suggests a theme that will be explored later in this chapter—namely, the understanding by some Protestants that others might object to the religion being taught in the public schools and even that such teaching might be unconstitutional, combined with a willingness to overlook or deny any constitutional contradictions in favor of the belief that a majority of citizens were Protestants or sympathized with the goal of religious instruction in the public schools. Storer's use of *effectually* suggests that he did not care whether Catholics or Jews would object, only whether any objections might have some effect. For other examples of similar direct preaching to public school students, see Livingston T. Mays, "A Christian School Superintendent," *NBR,* June 8, 1922, 9.

12. J. R. Wright, "Franklin District Institute," *Nashville Midland Methodist,* February 3, 1915, 4. The *Midland Methodist* was a weekly newspaper jointly operated by the three Methodist Annual Conferences (Tennessee, Memphis, and Holston) that covered Tennessee. The *NCA* increasingly assumed a denomination-wide readership in the twentieth century, although with its editorial offices in Nashville, it remained interested in state and local affairs. Complete files of the *Midland Methodist* do not exist, although some issues can be found on microfilm at the Tennessee Annual Conference of the United Methodist Church, Commission on Archives and History, Nashville.

13. The classic account of the Conference for Education in the South appears in Dabney, *Universal Education,* vol. 2; see also James Riley Montgomery, "Summer School"; Link, *Hard Country,* 98–123. For a more Tennessee-centered approach to rural school reform, see Hoffschwelle, *Rebuilding,* 13–33.

14. Formed in 1901, the Southern Education Board was headed by Robert Curtis Ogden and included philanthropists and southern educational leaders J. L. M. Curry, Charles W. Dabney, Edwin A. Alderman, Charles D. McIver, H. B. Frissell, George Foster Peabody, and Rev. Wallace Buttrick, among others. The board worked to mobilize southern public opinion on behalf of improving the public schools and to encourage and receive gifts from private individuals and groups to aid public education. The latter function was quickly separated and placed under the control of the General Education Board, headquartered in New York. Dabney, *Universal Education*, 2:54–73, details the founding of the board.

15. Holt, *Struggle*, 209–25.

16. Claxton quoted in Holt, *Struggle*, 221; see also Dabney, *Universal Education*, 2:365.

17. Cullom Diary, 1910.

18. Mynders quoted in Holt, *Struggle*, 210.

19. Holt, *Struggle*, 114. Although Leloudis, *Schooling*, gives far more attention and credibility to the opponents of the University of North Carolina, he likewise discounts the ideological differences between religious and secular educators in that state's controversies between Charles Elisha Taylor of Wake Forest and supporters of the state university.

20. Jeffries's letter does not survive in the governor's files, but Brister refers to it in his correspondence with the governor; see J. W. Brister to Ben Hooper, August 25, 1911, Hooper Papers, box 2, folder 4. At least one Methodist minister directly endorsed Hooper's choice of Brister as state superintendent; see Rev. E. C. Atkins to Hooper, April 21, 1911, Hooper Papers, box 2, folder 2.

21. [EEH], "Thanksgiving," *NCA,* November 21, 1891, 1.

22. *NCA,* April 2, 1903, 1.

23. [George Winton], "The Southern Education Board," *NCA,* May 14, 1903, 1; see also [George Winton], "Illiteracy in the South," *NCA,* April 9, 1903, 1; [George Winton], "The Battle against Ignorance," *NBR,* September 27, 1907, 2–3.

24. Rufus Weaver, "Baptists and the Present Public School Situation," *NCA,* March 8, 1917, 16. In later years Weaver continued to stress Baptists' important role in public education, warning in 1926 that "if illiteracy and an impoverished rural life continues, we cannot escape our share of the blame. . . . Until each southern commonwealth assumes the responsibility of providing an adequate elementary education for all of its children wherever they may live, the next generation of Baptists will furnish practically the same number of backward rural churches led by pastors with as limited education as we now have" (Rufus Weaver, "The Contribution of the Christian College to Scholarship and the Teaching Profession" [address], February 1926, box 5, folder 6, Rufus W. Weaver [1870–1947] Collection, AR 99, SBHLA).

25. Rufus Weaver, "Lengthen the Rural Schools," *NBR,* March 15, 1917, 16.

26. For further information on Weaver, see the collection descriptions for the Rufus Washington Weaver Papers, SBHLA. A more extensive collection of Weaver's papers is at Mercer University, Macon, Georgia.

27. Holt, *Struggle,* 94.

28. Rev. S. W. Tyndall, "Evolution of the School Idea," *NBR,* December 31, 1903, 2–3; James W. Sewell, "What the South Will Gain from George Peabody College for Teachers," *NBR,* September 17, 1914, 6.

29. [TOS], "Teachers in Council," *NCA,* May 6, 1876, 9. Vanderbilt quickly discontinued this practice. Kirkland's efforts to affiliate with Peabody, though in the long run a good addition to Vanderbilt University, added unnecessary fuel to already hot fires concerning the direction and control of Vanderbilt within Methodist circles as well as within Nashville. Conkin, *Gone,* 149–84, details the intermingling of Kirkland's "courtship" of Peabody with the separation from the Methodist Episcopal Church, South. After several abortive efforts, Vanderbilt and Peabody finally merged in 1979 (Conkin, *Gone,* 706–14).

30. "Demand Better Public School Teachers," *NBR,* January 26, 1922, 7.

31. G. M. Savage, "Union University," *NBR,* June 24, 1917, 16.

32. Harry Clark, "Get Your Teachers from Baptist Colleges," *NBR,* March 30, 1922, 8.

33. [J. D. Moore], "Our Educational Secretary," *NBR,* January 20, 1921, 5; Harry Clark, "Department of Christian Education," *NBR,* February 10, 1921, 7.

34. N. H. Williams, "The Greatest Need of the South," *NCA,* February 15, 1915, 6–7.

35. S. W. Tyndall, "Evolution of the School Idea," *NBR,* December 31, 1903, 2–3.

36. *Nashville Midland Methodist,* May 27, 1914, 8, March 24, 1915, 9.

37. S. G. Gilbreath, "The Relation of State and Denominational Schools," *NBR,* October 18, 1917, 2–3.

38. *Public Acts of Tennessee,* 1907, chapter 236. In another irony, the bill actually complicated the school bureaucracy. The county board members still ran individual school district advisory boards, but they also had to work with county high school boards. This system, with minor revisions, remained until 1923, when a true county unit system was put in place, creating a school board of seven members elected at large from each county (*Public Acts of Tennessee,* 1923, chapter 79). For the progression of school oversight, see Rhey Boyd Parsons, "Teacher Education," 26–28. Parsons argues that the efforts to block centralization of school authority were purely issues of political patronage, spearheaded in each district by a local politician who "employs and discharges their teachers, and in some cases even demands as the price of appointment either political vassalage or an actual cash bribe. . . . The issue in the struggle today as in the struggle in the past is the issue between administration by petty local politicians and administration by trained educators" (28). Winton supported efforts for better teachers, calling for legislation to remove teacher selection from "the muck of local politics" ("The Southern Education Board," *NCA,* May 14, 1903, 1).

39. Holt, *Struggle,* 243. In 1903, there had been 3,744 school districts in the state, each governed by three school directors. Most of the school districts, except those in towns and cities, encompassed only one school. The 14,232 school directors were not necessarily pleased with the shift in control, and their potential opposition led school reformers to downplay plans to restructure the schools (Holt, *Struggle,* 101).

40. Rhey Boyd Parsons, "Teacher Education," 69–88. County commissioners could and often did grant exceptional licenses to teachers without the state certificate.

41. Rufus W. Weaver, "Lengthen the Rural Schools," *NBR*, March 15, 1917, 16. Weaver continued his criticisms in several other back-page advertisements from the Board of Education of the Tennessee Baptist Convention in the spring of 1917. In his "A Review of Education Legislation by the Present Legislature," Weaver gave some praise to efforts to improve the schools, but continued to criticize appropriations for the university: "Tennessee leads the South in the number of her universities and colleges. Tennessee leads the South, leaving out South Carolina, in providing for her children the shortest term of her elementary schools, and therefore giving them the most limited opportunity for getting an education" (*NBR*, April 12, 1917, 16). See also Rufus Weaver, "The Present Educational System in Tennessee Is Top-Heavy," *NBR*, April 5, 1917, 16.

42. Rhey Boyd Parsons, "Teacher Education," 23.

43. S. G. Gilbreath, "The Relation of State and Denominational Schools," *NBR*, October 18, 1917, 2–3.

44. I thank Ronald Numbers for suggesting this connection. Edward Larson has likewise noted the importance of the growth of high schools. Tennessee high school average attendance increased from ten thousand in 1910 to more than fifty thousand by 1925, the time of the *Scopes* trial (*Summer*, 24).

45. Tennessee *House Journal*, 1885, (HB 119), 156, 505. The original bill is in the legislative archives, TSLA. See also Cartwright, *Triumph*, 112. One possible reason for the failure of Fields's bill was its alarmingly high fines for noncompliance: the law provided that "a willful violation . . . of this act shall be a misdemeanor and punishable by a fine not less than ten nor more than fifty dollars for each offender." A second possible reason for the bill's failure was that it required students to attend school at least 120 days a year at a time when funding was inadequate to provide teachers or schoolhouses for half that number of days for all school-age children in the state. A third reason for the bill's defeat was that it did not seem to have the support of the education lobby. None of the secondary works on education in Tennessee mention this bill. Perhaps this reflects the bias of the majority of educational historians who have written on Tennessee: they have been too closely associated with the Progressive educational reform movement to see beyond its scope. This bill was proposed by a black state legislator, and as far as I have seen, the journals of the State Teachers' Association, which normally proposed all state school legislation, make no mention of this bill.

46. See, for example, Gilbreath, *Biennial Report*, 192, 200; Fitzpatrick, *Annual Report*, 225, 234–35. For public support from the Tennessee Federation of Women's Clubs, see *Nashville American*, February 4, 1898, clipping in Tennessee Federation of Women's Clubs Records, box 3, folder 1, TSLA.

47. In 1905, the first such bill passed, making Tennessee's Claiborne and Union counties the first southern school systems to compel attendance through law. By 1909, when Governor Malcolm Rice Patterson signed the General Education Bill, thirty-five counties had already secured compulsory education through private legislation.

48. *Public Acts of the State of Tennessee,* 1913, chapter 13; Griffith, "Constitutional and Legal Status," 12–50; *Public Acts of the State of Tennessee,* 1919, chapter 143. In the event that a particular county could not operate its schools for eighty days, the law required students to attend the full term for that county.

49. Bardaglio, *Reconstructing,* xii–xiii, 81, 118, 136.

50. Holt, *Struggle,* 20. Bardaglio, *Reconstructing,* 121, points to the irony of the Confederacy's need for troops and supplies leading to a growth in centralized authority that could compel enlistment and forcibly requisition war material; see also Thomas, *Confederacy.*

51. Governor Robert Love Taylor, "Address," in Frank M. Smith, *Proceedings,* 11. On the racial implications of the Blair bill, see Cartwright, *Triumph,* 52.

52. Elliott, *Eagle Wing,* 4, 9, 8, 6. Elliott was not just making this language up; see, for example, the 1865 declaration of the Wisconsin Teachers' Association that "children are the property of the state" (quoted in Kaestle, *Pillars,* 158).

53. Elliott, *Eagle Wing,* 12.

54. *Thirty-eighth Annual Meeting,* 25.

55. [George Winton], *NCA,* November 16, 1905, 6. Chancellor James H. Kirkland of Vanderbilt was also an advocate of compulsory-education laws, arguing that they would help fight the problem of child labor; see Kirkland, "School," 559, where he endorses the "parental power" of the state to supervise the education of children. The *Christian Advocate* included several other endorsements of compulsory education; see, for example, J. D. Hammond, "Compulsory Education," *NCA,* March 22, 1907, 16; [George Winton], "The Battle against Ignorance," *NCA,* September 27, 1907, 3–4.

56. [Edgar Estes Folk], *NBR,* March 8, 1906, 1.

57. [Edgar Estes Folk], "Minister and the Public School," *NBR,* April 5, 1917, 8; see also Harry Clark, "The Opening of the Public Schools," *NBR,* August 21, 1924, 8.

58. Claxton, *Should the General Assembly Enact?* 6.

59. R. W. Snell, "Compulsory Education," *Progressive Teacher and Southwestern School Journal* 9 (May 1903): 41; Griffith, "Constitutional and Legal Status," 8–9.

60. *Cross et al. v. Fisher et al.,* 132 Tenn. 38, 43; Hand, "Need," 301; Milton, "Compulsory Education," 39–41.

61. William S. Johnson, "Our Public School System," *NBR,* May 3, 1894, 2–3.

62. [Alfred Franklin Smith], "The Week-Day School of Religion," *NCA,* April 27, 1923, 6.

63. [OPF], "The Old South and the New," *NCA,* April 19, 1907, 13.

64. [George Winton], "The Southern Education Board," *NCA,* May 14, 1903, 1.

65. *Proceedings of the Seventh and Eighth Annual Sessions,* 25.

66. [EEH], *NCA,* October 18, 1890, 1; see also *NCA,* June 6, 20, 1889, February 22, 1890, April 19, 1894; TBCM, 1889, p. 32, 1890, p. 29, 1895, p. 26.

67. Rhey Boyd Parsons, "Teacher Education," 43–68, details the pay and demographics of Tennessee teachers throughout the period.

68. "A Mortal Wound," *Nashville Banner,* January 15, 1896, 1; "A Bad Example," *Nashville Banner,* January 16, 1896, 4.

69. [George Winton], "Religion and the Public Schools," *NCA*, July 16, 1903, 1.

70. T. S. Ray, "Our Debt to Children," *NBR*, May 10, 1900, 2.

71. [OPF], "Authority," *NCA*, January 28, 1882, 1; [OPF], "The Unity of Family and Church Life," *NCA*, February 14, 1885, 8.

72. [Thomas Ivey], *NCA*, March 16, 1917, 3. Ivey was further incensed that the criticisms of religion in the public schools could come from a member of the clergy: "It is a strange thing to come from a representative of that body which started the movement for universal education, which has fostered all the real educational ideals that are worth anything, and whose stamp will be on education when the proudest colleges and universities of to-day shall have given back their brick and mortar to mother earth." Ivey was probably responding to a recent article in the *Nashville Baptist and Reflector* in which Weaver, while arguing for the necessity of denominational education, explained that the "weakness of American education is to a large degree overcome by the fact that the child while in the public school receives in the home, in the Sunday school, and in the church religious instruction which compensates for the absence of such instruction in the public school" (Rufus Weaver, "A Message on Christian Education," *NBR*, January 3, 1917, 2–4).

73. W. C. Owen, "A Suggested Solution of the Present Situation in Religious Education," *NCA*, October 27, 1922, 11.

74. J. M. Phillips, "A Great Work," *MB*, February 14, 1880, 553.

75. [EEH], *NCA*, November 15, 1894, 1.

76. [EEH], "Religion vs. the Public School," *NCA*, November 11, 1897, 8.

77. Lester Weaver, "The Church's Choice—Educate or Evacuate," *NCA*, January 28, 1921, 11; I. T. Cameron, "Christian Education and the High School," *NCA*, April 8, 1921, 24–25. See also [Alfred Franklin Smith], "The Week-Day School of Religion," *NCA*, April 27, 1923, 6.

78. Rev. W. C. Owen, "A Suggested Solution of the Present Situation in Religious Education," *NCA*, October 27, 1922, 15.

79. W. W. Richeson, "Will the Church Rise to the Needs of the Hour, and Will the Colleges of the Methodist Church, South, Take the Lead?" *NCA*, February 27, 1925, 6–7.

80. David H. Bishop, "The National Educational Association," *NCA*, July 23, 1903, 3.

81. W. P. Lovejoy, "The Place of Religion in Education," *NCA*, August 27, 1903, 8.

82. [George Winton], "Religion and the Public Schools," *NCA*, July 16, 1903, 1.

83. TBCM, 1882, 27; see also Prof. W. S. Woodward, "Why Baptists Should Persist in Education," *NBR*, December 24, 1914, 2–3; J. W. Gillon, "Some Reasons Why I Oppose the Compulsory Use of the Bible in the Public Schools," *NBR*, July 22, 1915, 2.

84. J. B. Gambrell, "Our Public School System," *NBR*, April 19, 1894, 2; see also J. P. Greene, "Our Public School System," *NBR*, April 19, 1894, 2.

85. Charles Elisha Taylor, "Our Public School System," *NBR*, April 19, 1894, 2. Much of Taylor's article concerned his objections to public education beyond the elementary grades and especially to the North Carolina practice of providing reduced tuition at state

colleges and thereby, he believed, unfairly driving religious schools out of existence. Leloudis, *Schooling,* 113–15, focuses almost exclusively on this, perhaps economically motivated, part of Taylor's objections. But Taylor's objections also centered on the question of what kind of education was best for children and young adults, suggesting that a thorough education required training of both the heart and mind and that such an education could only be found within a denominational institution; see "A Citizen of North Carolina" [Charles Elisha Taylor], *How Far;* as well as chapter 3 on arguments about the importance of denominational colleges.

86. William S. Johnson, "Our Public School System," *NBR,* May 3, 1894, 2–3.

87. "Payne, Parkes, and Priest: The New Members of the Board of Education," *Nashville Banner,* January 10, 1896, 4; "City Council in Session," *Nashville Banner,* January 24, 1896, 3; "Sensational Proceedings," *Nashville Banner,* January 28, 1896, 2; "A Lively Discussion," *Nashville Banner,* February 25, 1896, 3; "Bible in the Public Schools," *Nashville Banner,* March 13, 1896, 3.

88. In an argument before the Memphis school board, Alfred Mason noted that the Bible was used in the Nashville schools "with no harm"; see "That Memphis Bible Text Book Question," *Memphis Commercial Appeal,* September 9, 1902, 5.

89. "Proposition Is Withdrawn: So Ends the Controversy over Bibles in Schools," *Memphis Commercial Appeal,* November 11, 1902, 6.

90. "The Bible in School," *Memphis Commercial Appeal,* July 26, 1902, 3. McMillin made his pronouncement at a meeting of the Tennessee State Teachers Association meeting in Monteagle. Presbyterian minister W. H. Neal opposed the Memphis petition, drawing criticism from supporters that was reported in "Dr. Neal Refuses; Daily Reading of Scriptures in the City Schools; Will Not Sign the Petition," *Memphis Commercial Appeal,* October 2, 1902, 7.

91. *NBR,* March 19, 1896, 1, September 18, 1902, 1; *NCA,* September 18, 1902, 3.

92. "Sensational Proceedings," *Nashville Banner,* January 28, 1896, 2.

93. "The Bible in the Schools," *Memphis Commercial Appeal,* July 28, 1902, 4.

94. "Sensational Proceedings," *Nashville Banner,* January 28, 1896, 2. Stokes's arguments closely resembled those presented by Baptist educator R. A. Venable in his 1894 response to Folk's questionnaire about religion and the public schools; see Venable, "Our Public School System," *NBR,* April 19, 1894, 2.

95. [George Winton], "Religion and the Public Schools," *NCA,* July 16, 1903, 1.

96. [Thomas Ivey], "The Church's Quandary," *NCA,* February 13, 1914, 4; [Thomas Ivey], "Correlation of Religious and Secular Instruction," *NCA,* October 9, 1914, 5; [Thomas Ivey], "The Gary Plan for Religious Instruction," *NCA,* February 5, 1915, 19.

97. *Tennessee House Journal,* 1915, 1048. The bill passed the House 64–10 over the objections of Representatives Stanton and Julian G. Straus. The Senate Education Committee's rejection of the bill was changed to a recommendation after an amendment prohibited the reading of the same passage more than twice in a session. The original bill, with amendments, is filed as HB 379 in the Legislative History Department, TSLA.

The final bill, as signed by Governor Thomas Clark Rye, is in *Tennessee Public Acts,* 1915, chapter 102, pp. 23–24.

98. J. W. Gillon, "Some Reasons Why I Oppose the Compulsory Use of the Bible in the Public Schools," *NBR,* July 22, 1915, 2.

99. Gillon's arguments were more in line with the arguments presented in Virginia roughly a decade later in controversies over the required reading of the Bible in the public schools. By that time, the editorial voice of the *Nashville Baptist and Reflector* strongly favored daily Bible reading in the public school, even to the point of entering into an editorial attack and response with Rev. Dr. R. H. Pitt, editor of the *Richmond Religious Herald.* See [J. D. Moore], "Bible in Public Schools," *NBR,* April 24, 1924, 2; [J. D. Moore], "Bible in Public Schools Approved," *NBR,* May 8, 1924, 1; [J. D. Moore], "Dr. Pitt Puzzled," *NBR,* May 29, 1924, 2. The Baptist state secretary of education, Harry Clark, went so far as to reprint the Tennessee law requiring daily Bible reading in the spring of 1925; see Harry Clark, "Remember This Law," *NBR,* April 9, 1925, 8.

100. [Thomas Ivey], "The Coming Reunion," *NCA,* March 19, 1915, 4. A few weeks later Ivey, in an article criticizing efforts to exclude the Bible from the public schools in some states, pointedly stated that such actions were directly "responsible for the world's being now at war" ([Thomas Ivey], "Can We Afford It?" *NCA,* April 16, 1915, 4).

101. The original article was published on February 28, 1918; Bond's editorial comments appeared in "The Fundamental Factor," *NBR,* March 28, 1918, 9.

102. W. A. Candler, "Our Educational Work Is Now Missionary Work Also," *NCA,* August 13, 1915, 12. Candler was the first president of the new Methodist Episcopal Church, South, university in Atlanta, Emory University, and was very interested in setting up a teacher training department at the school. Rev. William F. Quillian, another Emory supporter, made similar arguments after the war about the necessity of training teachers in "safe" institutions: "our quickest and surest way to bring permanent peace to the disordered nations is by the training of our young men and maidens in schools which recognize and honor the Peacemaker imperial of all ages. To do this we must have teachers who can rightly lead in this glorious crusade" (Quillian, "Building for Peace," *NCA,* February 14, 1919, 23).

103. Stonewall Anderson, "Christian Culture and German Kultur," *NCA,* August 2, 1918, 10–11.

104. [Thomas Ivey], "Education in War Times," *NCA,* July 27, 1917, 4.

105. [Thomas Ivey], "One Hundred Per Cent American," *NCA,* March 28, 1919, 7; see also Lester Weaver, "The Church's Choice—Educate or Evacuate," *NCA,* January 28, 1921, 11, which is quoted at the beginning of this chapter.

106. W. C. Owen, "A Suggested Solution of the Present Situation in Religious Education," *NCA,* October 27, 1922, 11, 15.

107. [Thomas Ivey], "The Bible in a Democracy," *NCA,* June 2, 1916, 1; [Thomas Ivey], "A Citizen's Right," *NCA,* June 16, 1916, 5.

108. Mrs. Evelyn Baker [Mary Louise] Dodd, "The Bible in the Public Schools," *NCA,* April 7, 1904, 3. Dodd contributed other articles to the *Advocate,* including another

explanation of the Christian Constitution in 1909: Mary Louise Dodd, "The Christian Spirit of the Constitution," *NCA,* August 6, 1909, 9.

109. [Alfred Franklin Smith], "The Bible in the Schools," *NCA,* November 2, 1923, 3; Harry Clark, "Bible in the Public Schools," *NBR,* October 6, 1921, 8; C. H. Briggs, "Clarence Darrow and American Institutions," *NCA,* July 31, 1925, 1082–83; *Nashville Midland Methodist,* January 6, 1915, 1.

110. [Thomas Ivey], *NCA,* March 23, 1917, 3.

111. [EEH], "A Fatal Blunder," *NBR,* January 11, 1900, 9.

112. [J. D. Moore], "Bible in Public Schools," *NCA,* April 24, 1924, 2. Tennessee Attorney General Tom Stewart, debating the constitutionality of Tennessee's antievolution law with John Scopes's attorney, Dudley Field Malone, explained to the court that "the Saint James version of the Bible is the recognized one in this section of the country. The laws of the land recognize the Bible; the laws of the land recognize the law of God and Christianity as a part of the common-law" (Stewart quoted in Moran, *Scopes Trial,* 85).

113. [EEH], "A Fatal Blunder," *NCA,* January 11, 1900, 9.

114. [George Winton], "Religion and the Public Schools," *NCA,* July 16, 1903, 1.

115. [J. D. Moore], "Dr. Pitt Puzzled," *NBR,* May 29, 1924, 2.

116. W. T. Callaway, "Shall the Bible Be Read in Our Public Schools?" *NBR,* April 29, 1926, 6. Several other postwar writers similarly noted their increased perceptions of moral decay in Tennessee homes and society; see, for example, E. K. Cox, "The Why of the Crime Wave," *NBR,* September 22, 1921, 2–3; [Thomas Ivey], "The Bible in School and Home," *NCA,* October 31, 1919, 13; [Thomas Ivey], "Message of our Bishops," *NCA,* November 21, 1919, 8–10.

117. W. T. Callaway, "Shall the Bible Be Read in Our Public Schools?" *NBR,* April 29, 1926, 6.

Chapter 6. Evolution and Education: Science and Religion in Church and Public Schools

1. M. M. Black, "Christianity and Evolution," *NCA,* July 31, 1925, 7–9.

2. John Darby to Holland N. McTyeire, September 11, 1873, Garland Papers (personal), box 1, file 3.

3. John Darby, "The Cosmogony of Moses," *NCA,* January 25, 1873, 3, February 1, 1873, 3; see also Thomas O. Summers Jr., "The Conflict between Religion and Science," *NCA,* January 16, 1875, 1.

4. [OPF], *NCA,* December 14, 1878, 1.

5. Lula Bowen, "The Two Revelations," *MB,* July 13, 1878, 497.

6. M. M. Black, "Christianity and Evolution," *NCA,* July 31, 1925, 7.

7. The quotation comes from the title of a series of lectures published under the auspices of Vanderbilt University's Cole Lecture Foundation in 1926. Delivered by Dean O. E. Brown of the Vanderbilt School of Religion, Chancellor James H. Kirkland,

and Professor Edwin Mims of the Vanderbilt English department, the three lectures attempted to position the Vanderbilt of 1925—much as university founders had asserted a half century earlier—as a safe place for the investigation of both science and religion (Brown, Kirkland, and Mims, *God*). In his 1925 address on the school's fiftieth anniversary, Kirkland pointedly referred to the recent *Scopes* trial, suggesting, "The answer to the episode at Dayton is the building of new laboratories on the Vanderbilt campus for the teaching of science. The remedy for a narrow sectarianism and a belligerent fundamentalism is the establishment on this campus a School of Religion, illustrating in its methods and its organization the strength of a common faith and the glory of a universal worship" (quoted in Conkin, *Gone*, 255).

8. Cash, *Mind*, 137–41; Eaton, *Mind*, 156. For more generous assessments of the quantity if not quality of southern scientific interests, see Davenport, "Scientific Interests"; Midgette, "In Search," 597; Numbers and Numbers, "Science"; Numbers with Stephens, "Darwinism"; Stephens, *Science*. A particularly sensitive and intelligent portrayal of one southerner's struggles to reconcile science, religion, and denominational higher education in the New South is Hall, *William Louis Poteat*.

9. [TOS], "The Church and Its Enemies," *NCA*, September 27, 1877, 3; [OPF], "Religion and Science at the Vanderbilt University," *NCA*, August 17, 1878, 1; J. T. Christian, "Evolution," *MB*, November 27, 1880, 393.

10. Judge John Lea quoted in Summerville, "Science," 319–20.

11. Marsh quoted in Summerville, "Science," 322.

12. TOS, "Geology and the Bible," *NCA*, April 26, 1879, 6–7; TOS, "Skepticism—Speculation," *NCA*, September 27, 1879, 7.

13. By far the best analysis of American theologians' encounter with theories of evolution is Roberts, *Darwinism*. A more regional approach to Darwinism in the American South, suggestive in theme but limited by the brevity of its essay format, is Numbers with Stephens, "Darwinism."

14. [TOS], "The American Association for the Advancement of Science," *NCA*, September 15, 1877, 8. Using scientific disagreements over the specifics of evolutionary or geological theories has been a common trope not just of Summers but of several generations of antievolutionists and creationists who have followed him. One of his successors at the *Christian Advocate*, Winton, asserted his freedom to believe as he chose "when doctors differ" ([George Winton], "When Doctors Differ," *NCA*, July 6, 1905, 5).

15. Roberts, *Darwinism*, 95. Numbers provides a prosographical approach to the question, surveying the stance of naturalists in the National Academy of Sciences on evolution in "Darwinism and the Dogma of Separate Creations: The Responses of American Naturalists to Evolution," in Numbers, *Darwinism*, 24–48. An even more ambitious attempt to catalog naturalists' responses to evolution appears in Sulloway, *Born*.

16. *Vanderbilt University Register*, 1875, 9, VUSC; Winchell quoted in Roberts, *Darwinism*, 139. Summers praised Winchell's orthodoxy in this article and a similar article from a year earlier ("New Publications," *NCA*, July 22, 1876, 2, June 23, 1877, 8).

17. Roberts explains that the acceptance of evolution did not equate to an acceptance of Darwin's mechanism of natural selection until well into the twentieth century with the rediscovery of Mendelian genetics and the neo-Darwinian synthesis (*Darwinism,* 87). Bowler summarizes the "eclipse of Darwinism" in *Evolution,* 246–81, and more extensively in *Non-Darwinian Revolution.*

18. Winchell went to great pains to argue that his notion of Preadamites would establish Anglo-Saxon racial superiority and refute polygenesis, but misconceptions or misunderstandings of this part of his theory apparently intensified some of the criticisms lodged against him ([OPF], "Vanderbilt University and the Critics," *NCA,* July 13, 1878, 2).

19. Accounts of Winchell's dismissal are legion in the intellectual history of the South, most of which take it as an example of the region's intellectual intolerance at the time; see Roberts, *Darwinism,* 227–29; Davenport, "Scientific Interests," 514–18; Conkin, *Gone,* 60–63; Cash, *Mind,* 137–41; Farish, *Circuit Rider,* 139, 294–98; Mims, *History,* 100–105. While conceding that both Winchell's case and the closely following dismissal of James Woodrow from South Carolina's Presbyterian seminary point to the extreme regional intolerance of evolutionary teaching, Numbers and Stephens argue that southern evolutionists far more frequently kept their jobs in both state and denominational colleges despite accepting evolution ("Darwinism," 67–71).

20. Roy Talbert, "A Brief Sketch of the Career of Alexander Winchell, with Some Comment on His Difficulties at Vanderbilt," November 26, 1969, typescript report in RG-100, Centennial History Collection, Administration, Evolution, Winchell folder, VUSC. For a sensitive investigation of Winchell's internal religious and scientific dialogue before his termination from Vanderbilt, see Harrold, "Alexander Winchell's 'Science with a Soul.'"

21. Quoted in Davenport, "Scientific Interests," 518.

22. [TOS], "Vanderbilt University and the Critics," *NCA,* July 13, 1878, 5; TOS, "Skepticism—Speculation," *NCA,* September 27, 1879, 7; [OPF], "Religion and Science at the Vanderbilt University," *NCA,* August 17, 1878, 1.

23. [James R. Graves], *MB,* February 5, 1881, 536; [George Winton], "When Doctors Differ," *NCA,* July 6, 1905, 5. Tennessee Methodists writing in the *Nashville Christian Advocate* appeared to have more balance on evolution than Tennessee Baptists: most antievolution arguments in the Methodist paper were quickly answered by professions of the possibility of theistic evolution; see G.W.R., "The New Learning," *NCA,* November 14, 1901, 5; J. G. Halls, "'The New Learning,'" *NCA,* March 6, 1902, 9.

24. Ivey made clear the application of his warning by continuing, "our choice is whether education shall be Christian or heathen, and in that choice we determine the civilization of the future" ([Thomas Ivey], "Is It Worth the Effort?" *NCA,* January 7, 1921, 6).

25. Lofton, quoted in [Edgar Estes Folk], "Tennessee Baptist Convention Minutes," *NBR,* October 20, 1910, 4. Andrew S. Moore, in his study of several East Tennessee Baptist associations during this period, notes the importance of the postwar timing of

Baptist concern for the schools and particularly the teaching of evolution: "In their minds it became their duty to recreate the pre-war Christian civilization to counteract the rest of the nation's turning away from God" (" 'To Advance the Redeemer's Kingdom,' " 87).

26. Roberts, *Darwinism,* 236–37, 327 n.5. Roberts does not really emphasize regional variations in his assessment of the clerical response to Darwinism but does suggest that "a slightly disproportionate number [of antievolutionists] resided in the southern and border states. This was doubtless due in large measure to the strength of Princeton Seminary's influence in those regions, but it may have also been at least partly the result of the fact that the commitment of clergy and theologians to the epistemological priorities of modern culture was most attenuated in regions further from the levers of cultural power within American society" (*Darwinism,* 222). Roberts's arguments are persuasive for the intellectual activities of these thinkers, and his is perhaps the best account of the mental and ideological responses to Darwinism, but I believe that the southern and particularly the Tennessee response to the antievolution campaigns of the early twentieth century had more to do with other cultural concerns—notably the efforts to sanctify southern schools, the lingering sectionalism, and the related necessity of maintaining a belief in southern religious distinctiveness—than the particular legacies of Princeton theology in the region.

27. Warren A. Candler, "Liberalism Proposing to Liberate the South," *NCA,* September 18, 1925, 5. James J. Thompson Jr. emphasizes the importance of the postwar atmosphere for controversies among southern Baptists in *Tried,* 3–11.

28. M. M. Black, "Christianity and Evolution," *NCA,* July 31, 1925, 7.

29. For the best account of the fundamentalist resurgence as a national movement, see Marsden, *Fundamentalism.* But as I will argue in this chapter, it is important to see Tennessee's antievolution battles as more than just an extension of a national movement; they were grounded in the state's history of public education and religion. Glass, *Strangers,* looks more closely at southern fundamentalism than does Marsden and suggests how national fundamentalism eventually took root in the South and why it took so long to do so.

30. Kenneth K. Bailey, "Enactment." Good historiographical essays on antievolution and the *Scopes* trial can be found in Larson, *Summer,* 225–46; Numbers, "The Scopes Trial: History and Legend," in *Darwinism,* 76–91.

31. L. H. Brown, "Evolution and the Bible," *NCA,* August 22, 1901, 4. As had been the model in nineteenth-century Tennessee Methodism, Brown's article was answered by another Methodist who saw no danger in evolution, in fact asserting that after close study he believed in evolution as a theory because he could see in it the "footprints of design," or the evidence of God's handiwork; see Professor E. H. Randle, " 'Evolution and the Bible,' " *NCA,* March 6, 1902, 10.

32. [George Winton], "Church Schools and Science," *NCA,* July 10, 1908, 4–5.

33. Union University Faculty Minutes, October 10, 1921, quoted in Ward, *History,* 68. The faculty minutes for this period are no longer available at Union University, having

been lost apparently after Ward wrote his history. The student and faculty resolutions in support of Davis's "integrity, Christian character, and orthodoxy" and commendations of "him heartily and fully as being in every way safe and trustworthy as a teacher in Science for youth in a Christian College" were printed in the school newspaper (*Cardinal and Cream*, February 24, 1922, 4, University Archives, Emma Watters Summar Library, Union University, Jackson). These resolutions as well as a report of a special investigating committee were reported to the executive committee of the Tennessee Baptist Convention and through the *Nashville Baptist and Reflector* to the larger constituency of Tennessee Baptists (W. L. Pickard, Edward Stubblefield, and G. T. Mayo, "To the Executive Board," *NBR*, April 6, 1922, 7; [Jesse D. Moore], "Union University Matter Settled," *NBR*, April 6, 1922, 2; "Statement by Prof. Davis," *NBR*, June 29, 1922, 2).

34. W. L. Pickard, Edward Stubblefield, and G. T. Mayo, "To the Executive Board," *NBR*, April 6, 1922, 7. Davis provided a longer explanation of his beliefs and the origin of the controversy to the assembled students and faculty of Union University in a chapel service; see "Dr. Davis Explains His Position on Evolution," *Cardinal and Cream*, December 16, 1921, 1, 4.

35. Selsus E. Tull, "The Evolution Issue at Union University," *NBR*, October 27, 1921, 3. Tull continued his attacks on evolution at the school, but the student newspaper reported that he was satisfied with the outcome of the investigation ("Evolution Issue at Union University Settled," *Cardinal and Cream*, March 31, 1922, 1). The *Cardinal and Cream*'s judgment was a bit premature, however, for Tull voted against Davis's reappointment at the May 1922 meeting of the Union University Board of Trust and, when outvoted, opted to resign from the board. Following his resignation, Tull presented the board with a typed list of his reasons for objecting to Davis to be put into the minutes, among them Tull's argument that "Prof. Davis is a confessed Evolutionist of a type which I cannot accept or endorse in a teacher in a Baptist School" (Union Board Minutes, May 29, 1922, 2:397).

36. Moore's reason for urging caution was evident from his reminder that the purpose of the paper was in part to supervise denominational institutions but was also to "build up our institution of learning along lines which are consistent with our established faith" ([Jesse D. Moore], "The Evolution Discussion," *NBR*, November 3, 1921, 1). Moore continued this theme of caution throughout his short career at the paper, warning his fellow Baptists in 1924 about the dangers of always looking for heresy. A diligent investigator could find heresy wherever he wanted to, but the cost to the denomination and its institutions would be great. Though he did not mention William Louis Poteat by name, Moore's editorial was likely written in response to the growing agitation in North Carolina and the SBC as a whole over Poteat's scientific and theological teachings ([Jesse D. Moore], "Heresy Hunters," *NBR*, June 5, 1924, 1). For more on the Poteat controversy, see especially Hall, *William Louis Poteat*, 133–55; James J. Thompson Jr., *Tried*, 101–36; Gatewood, *Preachers*, 59–76.

37. T. A. J. Beasley, "Progression or Degeneration, Which?" *NBR*, May 12, 1921, 7; George W. Read, "What about Our Church Schools?" *NCA*, March 31, 1922, 410–11.

38. Marsden, *Understanding,* 174–75.

39. [EEH], "Mr. Bryan," *NCA,* March 18, 1897, 8; see also [George Winton], "Mr. Bryan in Nashville," *NCA,* February 11, 1904, 4, as well as the praise for his peace efforts during World War I in "The Principle of Peace," *Nashville Midland Methodist,* June 16, 1915, 1. After Bryan's death, one of the few outspoken critics of his antievolution crusade, Rembert G. Smith, nonetheless pointed to Bryan's leadership in the antidrink campaign, praising him as "a sincere and courageous prohibitionist" who "rightly regarded the laws of the nation" ("A Great Christian," *NCA,* August 28, 1925, 10).

40. Leuba quoted in Larson, *Summer,* 41; Bryan quoted in Larson, *Summer,* 41–43.

41. [Jesse D. Moore], "Evolution in Kentucky," *NBR,* March 23, 1922, 1. The *Nashville Christian Advocate* responded to the Kentucky evolution matter with contradictory articles and editorials, the first being a lukewarm endorsement of an article by Lyman Abbott suggesting that there were several ways to interpret evolution, not all of which would contradict the Bible. The second was a reprint from evangelist Bob Schuler staunchly supporting the antievolution movement; see "Evolution—'God's Way of Doing Things,' " *NCA,* March 3, 1922, 4; R. A. Schuler, " 'Bob' Schuler on Evolution," *NCA,* March 24, 1922, 4. Bill L. Weaver, "Kentucky Baptists' Reaction," gives an account of the Baptist situation in Kentucky but does not report on the 1921 resolution by the state mission board.

42. O. L. Hailey, "Church or State, Who Shall Define the Education of Our Children? Shall the State Teach Evolution?" *NBR,* August 10, 1922, 4–5.

43. Northern and Hailey's correspondence grew increasingly ungracious, much of it hinging on Northern's condescension for Hailey's unscientific understanding and nonspecific allegations: "Some of us are already fighting materialism wherever we find it, but have not been able to locate it as definitely as you seem to have done. If we knew better where to locate this octopus our efforts would be more efficient. Some of us have heard broad statements and, undertaking to act on them have found ourselves shelling the woods where no enemy existed. Some of us have been shelled by those fighting for the same cause that we were supporting" (E. E. Northern, "An Open Letter to Dr. O. L. Hailey," *NBR,* September 7, 1922, 4–5).

44. O. L. Hailey, "In Response to Professor Northern," *NBR,* October 26, 1922, 4; T. A. J. Beasley, "Progression or Degeneration, Which?" *NBR,* May 12, 1921, 7; [Thomas Ivey], "A Citizen's Right," *NCA,* June 16, 1916, 5. Larson, *Trial and Error,* 7–27, surveys the science textbooks widely used from the late nineteenth century through the height of the antievolution controversy in the 1920s and 1930s.

45. Larson, *Summer,* 44. There is room for interpretation about whether the parents or the legislature is ultimately writing the check. Bryan elaborated in other speeches, stating that since the people elected the legislators and educational boards, "all authority goes back at last to the people; they are the final source of authority" (Bryan quoted in Moran, *Scopes Trial,* 190).

46. A. M. Mann, "Partial Review of 'King Knut Redivivus,' " *NCA,* July 24, 1925, 30; see also J. L. Campbell, "Dr. Campbell Defends Tennessee," *NBR,* July 2, 1925,

6–7. Campbell was a professor at the Baptists' Carson-Newman University, not far from Dayton.

47. [Alfred Franklin Smith], "American Education Week," *NCA,* October 24, 1924, 4; [Jesse D. Moore], "Bible in Public Schools," *NBR,* April 24, 1924, 2.

48. Bryan quoted in Larson, *Summer,* 50.

49. O. L. Hailey, "In Response to Professor Northern," *NBR,* October 26, 1922, 4.

50. The article was reprinted in the Tennessee Baptist paper; see "The Law against Teaching Evolution," *NBR,* August 20, 1925, 6. As far as I can tell, there was no law in Tennessee to prohibit the use of the Bible in the public schools; in fact, the 1915 Bible-reading law required its use. In part, this contradiction might arise because of vague understandings of "teaching" the Bible in the public schools. Even in arguments for daily Bible reading, most Tennessee Baptists and Methodists remained squeamish about the notion of "teaching" the Bible in the public school. Any effort at explaining the Bible would invariably involve sectarian or doctrinally debatable issues, so both Baptists and Methodists objected to "teaching" the Bible except perhaps in weekday "release-time" Bible classes. On the argument that if religion could not be taught, neither could evolution, see also O. L. Hailey, "Professor Northern Again," *NBR,* November 9, 1922, 6; [Jesse D. Moore], "Evolution Legislation," *NBR,* February 19, 1925, 2; [Jesse D. Moore], "Evolution Legislation," *NBR,* March 29, 1923; 2; J. H. Thomas, "Tennessee's Evolution Law," *NBR,* June 25, 1925, 9; J. L. Campbell, "Dr. Campbell Defends Tennessee," *NBR,* July 2, 1925, 6–7.

51. The bills were defeated outright in Alabama, Georgia, Tennessee, and West Virginia, while Oklahoma "added a rider to its public-school textbook law providing 'that no copyright shall be purchased, nor textbook adopted that teaches the "Materialistic Conception of History" (i.e.) the Darwin Theory of Creation versus the Bible Account of Creation.' The Florida legislature chimed in with a nonbinding resolution declaring 'that it is improper and subversive to the best interest of the people' for public school teachers 'to teach as true Darwinism or any other hypothesis that links man in blood relationship to any form of lower life' " (Larson, *Summer,* 47).

52. Whitfield labeled the bill "by request," but it is not clear who made the request. A House bill met a similar fate. The original Senate Bill 681 is filed in the legislative archives, TSLA. The legislative history of the two bills can be found in Tennessee *House Journal,* 1923, 666, 719, 720; Tennessee *Senate Journal,* 1923, 599, 617, 668.

53. Kenneth K. Bailey, "Antievolution Crusade," 78–79.

54. [Jesse D. Moore], "Evolution Legislation," *NBR,* March 29, 1923, 2.

55. Interestingly, Moore utilized some of the same arguments used in the antievolution campaign in his writings in favor of Sunday-observance laws: "Legislation regarding Sunday may not be so easy. But Tennessee is a Christian commonwealth, and it has a right to enforce such regulations governing Sunday which may be thought needful to the peace and success of the State" ([Jesse D. Moore], "Important Legislation," *NBR,* January 11, 1923, 2).

56. Tennessee General Assembly, 1923, Senate Bill 681, TSLA.

57. *Nashville Banner,* April 1, 1923, quoted in Kenneth K. Bailey, "Antievolution Crusade," 81.

58. Larson, *Summer,* 48; [Alfred Smith], "Mr. Bryan on the Bible," *NCA,* February 1, 1924, 3.

59. Keith, *Country People,* 183–210, provides by far the freshest and most sympathetic view of Butler and his antievolution stand in her rural-studies book on Butler's native Upper Cumberland region (north of the Cumberland River in Middle Tennessee, bordering Kentucky, and including Macon, Clay, Pickett, Smith, Jackson, Overton, Fentress, Putnam, Dekalb, White, and Cumberland counties). Much as I do in this chapter, she argues that efforts to require Bible reading and ban the teaching of evolution were reactions against the formalization of education and local communities' perceived lack of control over schools and curriculum. Further, she notes how people such as Butler reacted to modern centralizing legislation by co-opting state power to enforce their local values, such as a belief in the literal truth of the Bible. We differ in opinion, however, on the value of Butler's bill. Keith sees it as a victory for local control, whereby local values reasserted themselves through the machinery of the state school system so that "in the end the traditionalists won—and won in such a way that their influence, reflected in the Butler Act, was extended nationwide." I would, however, suggest that the Butler bill, if it was a protest against the loss of local control, ended up imposing the rural or local values of some people on the whole state. The Butler bill, like the Bible-reading statutes, succeeded by obscuring the constitutional protection of minority religious, scientific, or social views behind the demagogic smokescreen of majority rule.

60. The most succinct account of the bill's legislative career can be found in Kenneth K. Bailey, "Enactment"; see also Larson, *Summer,* 49–59.

61. [Jesse D. Moore], "Evolution Legislation," *NBR,* February 19, 1925, 2; A. M. Mann, "Partial Review of 'King Knut Redivivus,'" *NCA,* July 24, 1925, 30.

62. Kenneth K. Bailey, "Antievolution Crusade," 92–94; Mims to Morgan, February 8, 1925, reprinted in James Riley Montgomery and Gaither, "Evolution," 149; Morgan to Peay, February 9, 1925, reprinted in James Riley Montgomery and Gaither, "Evolution," 151. Morgan's ducking of the issue is difficult to swallow, especially in light of the courageous stand taken by Frank McVey, his counterpart at the University of Kentucky, only a couple of years earlier. Morgan was a botanist who taught evolution in his classes, but in 1925 he was confronted with a very difficult choice: speak out for a long-term concept and risk the financial and administrative ruin of the university or quietly allow a symbolic bill to pass unnoticed and, hopefully, unenforced. In an era when the university had to depend almost exclusively on the state legislature for support, Morgan was perhaps wise not to oppose so powerful a figure as Hill. But the negative public opinion piled on Tennessee during and after 1925, when the bill was enforced and the nation took notice of Tennessee's supposed intellectual backwardness, unfortunately stamped a seemingly indelible image on the state and its university for decades to come.

63. M. M. Black, "Christianity and Evolution," *NCA,* July 31, 1925, 9; Kenneth K. Bailey, "Antievolution Crusade," 93, 477. After the bill passed the legislature, Owenby

appealed more directly to Governor Peay; see Owenby to Peay, March 17, 1925, Governor Austin Peay Papers, GP-40, box 43, folder 1, TSLA.

64. Rembert G. Smith, "King Knut Redivivus," *NCA,* July 3, 1925, 7–8.

65. A. M. Mann, "Partial Review of 'King Knut Redivivus,' " *NCA,* July 24, 1925, 30; Kenneth K. Bailey, "Antievolution Crusade," 96.

66. Norton, *Religion,* 102; John Abernathy Smith, *Cross and Flame,* 273. The votes on the bill do not break down into any easy-to-categorize pattern, but legislators from urban districts and especially Memphis/Shelby County were more likely to oppose the bill.

67. [O. E. Bryan], "Evangelicalism Fundamental," *NBR,* April 2, 1925, 2; [Alfred Smith], "The Case of Evolution," *NCA,* July 31, 1925, 4; [Alfred Smith], "The Single Aim," *NCA,* July 24, 1925, 3.

68. For a summary of Peay's gubernatorial career, see Stephen V. Ash, "Austin Peay, 1923–1927," in Ash, *Messages,* 10:61–96. Most of Peay's official papers have been preserved in the TSLA, and some of his campaign speeches have been published in Peay, *Austin Peay,* but unfortunately most of his private correspondence and family materials have been lost, precluding an extensive biography or any better insight into his decision to sign the Butler bill in 1925. More on Peay and the political climate of reform and reaction during 1920s Tennessee can be found in Lee, *Tennessee,* 19–75.

69. Macpherson, "Democratic Progressivism," 361; Peay, "Inaugural Address of January 19, 1925," in Ash, *Messages,* 10:159; Wood to Peay, March 14, 1925, White to Peay, April 15, 1925, Peay Papers, box 43, folder 1. Writers from Mississippi and Texas, in addition to commending his support of the bill, asked him for copies of the measure to be introduced in those states; see L. Walter Evans, Edinburgh, Miss., to Peay, October 1, 1925, W. H. Fortney, Port Neches, Tex., to Peay, March 24, 1925, Peay Papers, box 43, folder 1.

70. A. C. Hardy, Aspen Hill, Tenn., to Peay, March 5, 1925, Jeanette Moore King, Rutherford County, to Peay, March 23, 1925, Peay Papers, box 43, folder 1. A variety of other opponents wrote to Peay, including Bishop Coadjutor James M. Maxon, Protestant Episcopal Church; T. W. Talley, professor of chemistry, Fisk University; N. W. Dougherty, professor of civil engineering, University of Tennessee–Knoxville; and James L. Graham, dean, Fisk University.

71. Expatriate Tennessean Krutch excoriated Peay in 1925 in "Tennessee," 88–89. Ash suggests that Peay, "though favorably inclined toward the old-time religion, disliked the obscurantist spirit of the bill and agonized for days before signing it" ("Austin Peay," 79). Macpherson, who has written the only full-length biography of Peay (at least of his legislative career), concluded that Peay was more in sympathy with the Butler bill than many of his latter-day supporters have been willing to concede ("Democratic Progressivism," 387). Conkin suggests that Peay was "reluctant" but signed the bill "to gain legislative support for his reform package" (*When All the Gods Trembled,* 81–83). Larson depicts Peay as "trapped between fundamentalism and progressivism," mildly criticizing him for convincing himself that "majoritarianism [w]as an excuse for the

law. Caught in the same bind, Bryan saw it as the law's ultimate justification" (Larson, *Summer*, 58).

72. Austin Peay, "Special Message of March 23, 1925 to the Honorable House of Representatives," in Ash, *Messages*, 10:171–74. As governor, Peay was a member of the state textbook commission, which was charged with choosing authorized books for state schools (with the goal of lowering costs to districts with bulk purchases and to prevent fraud by local districts). The commission had approved George W. Hunter's *Civic Biology*, the book from which John T. Scopes admitted to having taught evolution. John Randolph Neal, a former University of Tennessee law professor and part of Scopes's defense team, wrote Peay a letter of warning in the months before the trial. Neal sarcastically cautioned Peay that were the Butler bill to be upheld and were the textbook commission to select any book "containing any reference to the theory of Evolution, it would be in our opinion a violation of the law on the part of the Commission, and criminal prosecution will be immediately initiated against every member participating in said act" (Neal to Peay, June 1, 1925, Peay Papers, box 43, folder 1). On the presence of evolutionary concepts in most textbooks, particularly in Hunter's *Civic Biology* (the book adopted by Tennessee and used in Dayton), see Larson, *Trial and Error*, 21.

73. The State Constitution of Tennessee explicitly recognized a belief in God in Article 9, Section 3: "No person who denies the being of God or a future state of rewards and punishment, shall hold any office in the Civil Department of this State."

74. Ash, *Messages*, 10:173. Attorney General Tom Stewart argued this point in Dayton, persuading Judge John T. Raulston to uphold Scopes's indictment. As the judge explained, "the relations between the teacher and employer are completely contractual." Scopes could believe whatever he wanted and preach about it as much as he wanted on the street corner, but as a state employee, he could teach only as directed by the legislature or its designees; see *World's Most Famous Court Trial*, 65, 102.

75. Ash, *Messages*, 10:173–74; John D. Freeman, "Putting the Day at Dayton," *NBR*, July 16, 1925, 3.

76. House Bill 185 (1925). In this argument, I build on Fields's suggestion of how "white supremacy" acted as a slogan in her seminal essay, "Ideology and Race in American History."

77. A Chattanooga rabbi wrote to Peay about the proposed law, complaining that it would deny an "American citizen the right granted to him in the first amendment to the Constitution of the United States which clearly prohibits the passing of laws respecting the establishment of religion and laws that prohibit the free exercise thereof" (Samuel R. Shillman to Peay, February 4, 1925, Peay Papers, box 96, folder 1). Peay responded to a similar letter; see Peay to Sarah Rudoff, YWHA, Chattanooga, Peay Papers, reel 2.

78. House Bill 252, Tennessee *House Journal*, 1925, 225, 233, 318, 423–24, 439. The original bill and amendments are filed in the legislative archives, TSLA. Kenneth K. Bailey, "Antievolution Crusade," 102–3, refers to this bill but suggests that its importance was that a majority of the House was not willing to regulate what teachers thought but only what they taught as state employees. Several county boards of education attempted

to pass similar requirements on local levels. In June 1925, the Carroll County School Board announced that "the board will inquire into the religious beliefs of candidates to teach in the schools before electing the teachers in July" ("School Board Will Apply Religious Test to Teacher Applicants," *NBR*, June 11, 1925, 7). To some degree, such resolutions might have merely formalized procedures or expectations that members of the school boards had previously used in making hiring decisions.

79. Ash, *Messages*, 10:174.

80. The origins, conduct, and historical representation of the trial have been more than adequately represented in Larson, *Summer*. Larson gives an excellent depiction of many of the religious, political, scientific, and social issues surrounding the trial, but even he falls into the trap of seeing the trial as spectacle, to be examined as an incident. In fairness to Larson, he gives the trial an admirable level of context in *Summer,* and in his previous contribution, *Trial and Error,* situates the trial within the preceding and following debates on the legal and legislative efforts to deal with evolution. I argue that the trial, however important, is less important than the Butler bill. Both make more sense when seen in the context of the fifty years of contention and debate over control of the schools.

81. S. K. Hicks to William Jennings Bryan, [May 21, 1925], reprinted in Eigelsbach and Linder, " 'If Not the People Who?' " 117–18.

82. William Jennings Bryan to S. K. Hicks, May 28, 1925, reprinted in Eigelsbach and Linder, " 'If Not the People Who?' " 118. Larson has discussed the origins and legacies of Bryan's majoritarian arguments in "*Scopes* Trial." Bryan thought his strongest legal arguments were on this majoritarian ground, but he did nonetheless desire that the trial vindicate his campaign on religious and scientific grounds by "surprising" the defense with overwhelming evidence not just of the Tennessee law's constitutionality but also of the falsity of the theory of evolution, taking advantage of the national stage and accompanying media attention.

83. [O. E. Bryan], "Tennessee's Evolution Trial," *NBR*, May 28, 1925, 2–3. This was a common theme in the Baptist paper, as can be seen in the similar arguments from S. M. Ellis, "State Authority in Public Education," *NBR*, July 9, 1925, 4; [John D. Freeman], "Evolution Issue Warm," *NBR*, July 9, 1925, 2–3.

84. Larson, *Summer*, 191–92. The scientists' statements are recorded in *World's Most Famous Court Trial*, 231–80.

85. M. M. Black, "Christianity and Evolution," *NCA*, July 31, 1925, 8–9.

86. Responding to Scopes's question, "Did I win or did lose?" Darrow responds that Scopes won, explaining, "What jury? Twelve men? Millions of people will say you won. They'll read in their papers tonight that you smashed a bad law. You made it a joke!" (Jerome Lawrence and Robert E. Lee, *Inherit the Wind* [stage play, 1955], quoted in Larson, "*Scopes* Trial," 521–22 n.121). Numbers places most of the blame for the "broken Bryan" and defeat of fundamentalism interpretation on Frederick Lewis Allen's *Only Yesterday* (1931), on which *Inherit the Wind* picked up ("Scopes Trial," 85).

87. In an even more explicit expression, Mencken supposedly exclaimed, "We killed the son-of-a-bitch!" (quoted in Larson, *Summer*, 200).

88. Ginger describes Bryan's posttrial days as "feverish," signifying "desperation, a frore [*sic*] presentiment that the current of fundamentalist adulation was about to dump him on some exposed and arid mud flat" (*Six Days*, 192–93).

89. McMinn County Baptist Association, "McMinn County Resolutions," *NBR*, October 15, 1925, 7. Smith praised Bryan, noting, "He was always the champion of the right as God gave him to see the right, and in the broad conceptions of the right he made no compromises" ([Alfred Smith], "William Jennings Bryan," *NCA*, August 7, 1925, 3). Similar support for the antievolution statute came from Shelby County Baptists: "Shelby County Uncompromising," *NBR*, July 30, 1925, 5–6.

90. T. H. Farmer, "A Plea for Clarence Darrow," *NBR*, February 4, 1926, 6, compared Bryan to a previous martyr to Tennessee evangelical causes, Edward Ward Carmack, the martyred champion of Prohibition whose death mobilized support to secure passage of the statewide prohibition law. Ginger also recognizes the "galvanic" importance of Bryan's death: "In these bitter circumstances Bryan did the most effective thing possible to regain his fundamentalist support—he died" (*Six Days*, 193).

91. Numbers, "Scopes Trial," 88. Larson reports further that regional opinion in favor of the Butler bill and similar measures had so solidified that in 1926, after Mississippi passed its antievolution law, the American Civil Liberties Union could not find a Mississippi teacher willing to stand for a test case (*Summer*, 212). The Arkansas law was passed by popular initiative, providing more detailed voting records, which Gray has analyzed in "Anti-Evolution Sentiment."

92. Quoted in Larson, *Summer*, 217.

93. *Scopes v. State*, 154 Tenn. 105 (1927). Some efforts to repeal the law through the Tennessee legislature occurred, but the measure remained in effect, although not formally enforced, until the General Assembly repealed the law in 1967, just one year before the U.S. Supreme Court struck down Arkansas's antievolution law in *Epperson v. Arkansas*, 393 U.S. 97 (1968) (Larson, *Summer*, 237; George E. Webb, *Evolution Controversy*, 145–49). For the legacy of the *Scopes* trial and its influence on the opinion of Justice Abe Fortas, who had been a Jewish schoolchild in Memphis, Tennessee, at the time of the *Scopes* trial, see Larson, "*Scopes* Trial," 524–27.

94. [TOS], "New Publications," *NCA*, November 2, 1872, 9; [Alfred Smith], "Education in the South," *NCA*, June 26, 1925, 5. Smith was introducing a special issue of the paper on southern education.

Chapter 7. Before and after Scopes: Social Christianity, Formal Education, and the Scopes Legacy

1. Dr. W. J. Young, "The Church School and the Salvation of the World," *NCA*, March 11, 1921, 9.

2. TBCM, 1883, 11.

3. Tennessee Association of Baptists Minutes, 1904, quoted in Andrew S. Moore, " 'To Advance the Redeemer's Kingdom,' " 62.

4. James D. Anderson, in his excellent cultural and institutional history of black

education in the New South, takes a similar approach to the concept of education, and I have found it instructive and helpful. Anderson uses debates about black education—from white, black, northern, southern, religious, industrial, and other varied perspectives—as "a better lens through which to comprehend the separate and distinct social visions of a New South. For it was through differing forms of training the young that each class and race tried to shape its own future and translate its particular experiences, ideas, values, and norms into a legitimate projection of broader social relations" (*Education*, 279). I have sought to similarly use the educational sphere to investigate the role of religion in the New South period, to reveal both white southern Evangelicals' understanding of the place of themselves and their religion in the culture and governance of the region and the effects of injecting explicitly religious goals into education and governance.

5. Stonewall Anderson, "Relation of Religious Education to General Education," *NCA*, April 2, 1926, 9–10.

6. See especially Tyack, "Tribe." Link, *Hard Country*, 3–70, likewise details the community orientation of late-nineteenth-century Virginia rural public schools.

7. John M. Fleming, *Tennessee School Report, 1874*, quoted in Robert Hiram White, *Development*, 123–24.

8. W. W. Richeson, "Will the Church Rise to the Needs of the Hour, and Will the Colleges of the Methodist Church, South, Take the Lead?" *NCA*, February 27, 1925, 6–7; W. T. Callaway, "Shall the Bible Be Read in Our Public Schools?" *NBR*, April 29, 1926, 6.

9. [OPF], *NCA*, July 17, 1880, 8; Elizabeth Denty Abernethy, "The Future of the South," *NCA*, September 29, 1916, 22–23.

10. Rufus Weaver, "The Obligation of Southern Baptists to Improve the Rural Elementary School and the Method Which Ought to Be Employed to Secure This Result," *NBR*, January 31, 1918, 1, 4.

11. Best, "Education," 10–12; Link, *Hard Country*, 65–68.

12. "Memorial to General Assembly," in *Twenty-ninth Annual Meeting*, 16–17; *Thirty-seventh Annual Meeting*, 19; see also Fred A. Bailey, "Textbooks."

13. Lippmann, *American Inquisitors*, 29–30.

14. [Thomas Ivey], "A Citizen's Right," *NCA*, June 16, 1916, 5.

15. H. E. Watters, "Why I Retained Dr. Davis," *NBR*, October 29, 1926, 1. I have been unable to find Davis's textbook, if he did indeed write one. See also Skoog, "Topic"; Larson, *Trial and Error*, 7–27.

16. Porter Claxton to Philander Priestly Claxton, March 24, 1925, quoted in James Riley Montgomery and Gaither, "Evolution," 153. Porter Claxton relates that the plan was suggested to him by W. R. "Sawney" Webb, a Methodist layman and teacher at a private Middle Tennessee boys school.

17. "Sex Hygiene in the Public Schools," *Nashville Midland Methodist*, April 29, 1914, 1.

18. Numbers, *Creationists;* Larson, *Trial and Error;* Witham, *Where Darwin Meets the Bible*.

19. "March Madness Please, Not Another Monkey Trial," *Little Rock Arkansas Democrat-Gazette*, March 23, 2001.

20. Michael Rowett, "Evolution Proposal Shot Down in House," *Little Rock Arkansas Democrat-Gazette*, March 24, 2001.

21. *Epperson v. Arkansas*, 393 U.S. 97 (1968). Arkansas subsequently passed an equal-time law in 1981 after Tennessee did so in 1973; federal courts found both states' laws unconstitutional. The issues in the Arkansas case (*McLean v. Arkansas Board of Education*, 529 F. Supp. 1255 [1982]) were finally reviewed in a similar case from Louisiana, *Edwards v. Aguillard* (482 U.S. 578 [1987]), in which the U.S. Supreme Court found that mandatory equal time for creation science was unconstitutional.

22. Larson, *Summer*, 262–64. In the 1967 debates about amending or repealing the Butler law, Tennessee legislators worried about a pending legal challenge and repealed the law to spare the state "the ordeal of another trial in which a proud state is required to make a monkey of itself in a court of law" (Larson, *Summer*, 252–53).

23. [OPF], "Education," *NCA*, February 4, 1882, 1.

24. Larson and Witham, "Inherit," 26. In the wake of the Kansas controversy, the editors of the *Journal of Law and Policy* prepared a summary of the current state of laws on the teaching of evolution; see "Appendix: Other States' Treatment of the Evolution Issue," *Journal of Law and Policy* 9 (2001): 691–708. In the third edition of *Trial and Error* (New York: Oxford University Press, 2003), Larson provides a brief summary of the creation-evolution debates in the 1990s. For a longer exploration of the status of the conflict at the end of the decade, see Reule, "New Face."

25. Darrow and Malone quoted in *World's Most Famous Court Trial*, 87, 187. Federal courts have to this point shown themselves to be unsympathetic to this argument for academic freedom or fostering "critical thinking" when presented by creationist teachers; see, for example, *Peloza v. Capistrano Unified School District*, 37 F.3d 517 (1994); *Freiler v. Tangipahoa Parish Board of Education*, 185 F.3d 337 (1999).

Bibliography

Archival Material

Memphis Room, Memphis-Shelby County Library, Memphis. Memphis Board of Education Annual Report. Shelby County School Superintendent Annual Report.

Southern Baptist Historical Library and Archives, Nashville. Beulah Baptist Association Proceedings. Big Hatchie Baptist Association Proceedings. Campbell Country Baptist Association Proceedings. Thomas T. Eaton Papers. Edgar Estes Folk Papers. General Association of Baptists of East Tennessee Proceedings. Holston Baptist Association Minutes. Mountain Mission Schools Files. Tennessee Association of Baptists Proceedings. Tennessee Baptist Convention Proceedings. Union Association of Baptists Proceedings. Rufus Washington Weaver Papers.

Tennessee Conference, United Methodist Church, Commission on Archives and History, McKendree Methodist Church, Nashville. Holston Conference, Methodist Episcopal Church, South, Journal. Memphis Conference, Methodist Episcopal Church, South, Journal. Tennessee Conference, Methodist Episcopal Church, South, Board of Education Minutes. Tennessee Conference, Methodist Episcopal Church, South, Journal.

Tennessee Room, Jackson-Madison County Library, Jackson. Annual Report of the Superintendent of Schools of the City of Jackson. Jackson City Schools History, 1879–1972. Madison County Schools History.

Tennessee State Library and Archives, Nashville. Bethel Association of Regular Baptist Churches Records, 1846–1965. Beulah Methodist Episcopal Church, South, Rutherford County, Tennessee, Records 1889–1927. Alexander Cotton Cartwright Family Papers. Jeremiah Walker Cullom Diary. Collins D. Elliott Papers, 1810–99. Albert Theodore Goodloe Journal, 1893–1902. Governor Ben W. Hooper Papers, 1911–15. Legislative Archives. Plautus Iberus Lipsey Diary. William D. Mooney Papers. William West Mooney Diary, 1866–73. J. Emerick Nagy Collection and Addition. Nashville College for Young Ladies Papers, 1888–1949. Governor Austin Peay Papers, 1923–27. R. B. Polk Daybook, 1892–1928. Salem Baptist Church, Dayton, Rhea County, Records, 1807–1937. State Superintendent of Public Instruction Annual Reports, 1870–1926. Tennessee Federation of Women's Clubs Records. Tennessee State Teachers Association Proceedings. William Trousdale Papers, 1828–1940.

University Archives, Emma Watters Summar Library, Union University, Jackson. *Cardinal and Cream*. Central Baptist Association Minutes. Southwestern Baptist University Board of Trustees Minutes. Union University Board of Trustees Minutes. Union University Bulletin. Union University Catalog.

Bibliography

University Archives and Special Collections, Jean and Alexander Heard Library, Vanderbilt University, Nashville. Centennial History Collection. Chancellor's Office Papers. Landon C. Garland Papers. *The Hustler.* James Hampton Kirkland Papers. John Thomas McGill Papers. McTyeire-Baskerville Papers. John James Tigert IV Papers. Wilbur Fiske Tillett Papers. Vanderbilt University Board of Trust Minutes. *Vanderbilt University Bulletin.* Vanderbilt University General Files. *Vanderbilt University Quarterly. Vanderbilt University Register.*

Serials

Bulletin of the Tennessee State Teachers Association, 1922–27
Memphis Baptist, 1875–89
Memphis Commercial Appeal, 1902
Nashville American, 1896–98
Nashville Banner, 1896–98
Nashville Baptist and Reflector, 1889–1926
Nashville Christian Advocate, 1870–1926
Nashville Midland Methodist, 1898–1912
The Progressive Teacher and Southwestern School Journal, 1895–1922
Tennessee *House Journal,* 1865–1929
Tennessee *Senate Journal,* 1865–1929

Published Sources

Abbott, Lyman. *The Evolution of Christianity.* 1892; reprint, New York: Johnson, 1969.
Alberstadt, Leonard. "Alexander Winchell's Preadamites—A Case for Dismissal from Vanderbilt University." *Earth Sciences History* 13 (1994): 97–112.
Alexander, J. E. *A Brief History of the Synod of Tennessee from 1817–1887.* Knoxville: Ross and Goodheart, 1890.
Allen, Frederick Lewis. *Only Yesterday: An Informal History of the 1920s.* New York: Harper and Row, 1931.
Allison, Clinton B. "Training Dixie's Teachers: The University of Tennessee's Summer Normal Institutes." *Journal of Thought* 28 (1983): 27–36.
Anderson, James D. *The Education of Blacks in the South, 1860–1935.* Chapel Hill: University of North Carolina Press, 1988.
Ash, Stephen V. *Messages of the Governors of Tennessee.* Vol. 9, *1907–1921.* Nashville: Tennessee Historical Commission, 1990.
―――. *Messages of the Governors of Tennessee.* Vol. 10, *1921–1933.* Nashville: Tennessee Historical Commission, 1990.
―――. *Middle Tennessee Society Transformed, 1860–1870: War and Peace in the Upper South.* Baton Rouge: Louisiana State University Press, 1988.
Ayers, Edward L. *The Promise of the New South: Life after Reconstruction.* New York: Oxford University Press, 1992.

Bailey, Fred A. "Caste and the Classroom in Antebellum Tennessee." *Maryland Historian* 13 (1982): 39–54.

—. "The Textbooks of the 'Lost Cause': Censorship and the Creation of Southern State Histories." *Georgia Historical Quarterly* 65 (1981): 119–37.

Bailey, Hugh C. *Liberalism in the New South.* Coral Gables, Fla.: University of Miami Press, 1969.

Bailey, Kenneth K. "The Antievolution Crusade of the Nineteen-Twenties." Ph.D. diss., Vanderbilt University, 1953.

—. "The Enactment of Tennessee's Antievolution Law." *Journal of Southern History* 16 (1950): 472–90.

—. *Southern White Protestantism in the Twentieth Century.* New York: Harper and Row, 1964.

Bailyn, Bernard. *Education in the Forming of American Society: Needs and Opportunities for Study.* Chapel Hill: University of North Carolina Press for the Institute of Early American History and Culture, 1960.

Bardaglio, Peter W. *Reconstructing the Household: Families, Sex, and the Law in the Nineteenth-Century South.* Chapel Hill: University of North Carolina Press, 1995.

Bauman, Mark K. "Confronting the New South Creed: The Genteel Conservative as Higher Educator." In *Education and the Rise of the New South,* edited by Ronald K. Goodenow and Arthur O. White, 92–113. Boston: Hall, 1981.

Belissary, Constantine G. "The Rise of Industry and the Industrial Spirit in Tennessee, 1865–1885." *Journal of Southern History* 19 (1953): 193–215.

Bell, Marty G. "James Robinson Graves and the Rhetoric of Demagogy: Primitivism and Democracy in Old Landmarkism." Ph.D. diss., Vanderbilt University, 1991.

Berger, Peter L. *The Sacred Canopy: Elements of a Sociological Theory of Religion.* New York: Anchor, 1967.

Bergeron, Paul H., Stephen V. Ash, and Jeanette Keith. *Tennesseans and Their History.* Knoxville: University of Tennessee Press, 1999.

Beringer, Richard E., Herman Hattaway, Archer Jones, and William N. Still Jr. *Why the South Lost the Civil War.* Athens: University of Georgia Press, 1986.

Berkeley, Kathleen C. *"Like a Plague of Locusts": From an Antebellum Town to a New South City, Memphis, Tennessee, 1850–1880.* New York: Garland, 1991.

Bernabo, Lawrence Mark. "The Scopes Myth: The Scopes Trial in Rhetorical Perspective." Ph.D. diss., University of Iowa, 1990.

Best, John Hardin. "Education in the Forming of the American South." In *Essays in Twentieth-Century Southern Education: Exceptionalism and Its Limits,* edited by Wayne J. Urban, 3–18. New York: Garland, 1999.

Bledstein, Burton J. *The Culture of Professionalism: The Middle Class and the Development of Higher Education in America.* New York: Norton, 1976.

Bode, Frederick. *Protestantism and the New South: North Carolina Baptists and Methodists in Political Crisis, 1894–1903.* Charlottesville: University Press of Virginia, 1975.

Boles, John B. "The Discovery of Southern Religious History." In *Interpreting Southern*

History: Historiographical Essays in Honor of Sanford W. Higginbotham, edited by John B. Boles and Evelyn Thomas Nolen, 510–48. Baton Rouge: Louisiana State University Press, 1987.

———. "Evangelical Protestantism in the Old South: From Religious Dissent to Cultural Dominance." In *Religion in the South,* edited by Charles Reagan Wilson, 13–34. Jackson: University Press of Mississippi, 1985.

———. *The Great Revival: Beginnings of the Bible Belt.* Lexington: University Press of Kentucky, 1996.

———. *The Great Revival: Origins of the Southern Evangelical Mind.* Lexington: University Press of Kentucky, 1972.

———. *The Irony of Southern Religious History.* New York: Lang, 1994.

———. *Religion in Antebellum Kentucky.* Lexington: University Press of Kentucky, 1976.

———. "The Southern Way of Religion." *Virginia Quarterly Review* 75 (1999): 226–47.

Bone, Winstead P. *A History of Cumberland University.* Nashville: Parthenon, 1935.

Borum, Joseph H. *Biographical Sketches of Tennessee Baptist Ministers.* Memphis: Rogers, 1880.

Bowler, Peter J. *Evolution: The History of an Idea.* Rev. ed., Berkeley: University of California Press, 1989.

———. *The Non-Darwinian Revolution: Reinterpreting a Historical Myth.* Baltimore: Johns Hopkins University Press, 1988.

Boyce, Everett Robert, ed. *The Unwanted Boy: The Autobiography of Governor Ben W. Hooper.* Knoxville: University of Tennessee Press, 1963.

Bozeman, Theodore Dwight. "Joseph LeConte: Organic Science as 'Sociology' for the South." *Journal of Southern History* 39 (1973): 565–82.

———. *Protestants in an Age of Science: The Baconian Ideal and Antebellum American Religious Thought.* Chapel Hill: University of North Carolina Press, 1977.

Brooks, J. C. *First Annual Report of the Superintendent of Schools of the City of Jackson for the Scholastic Year 1879–80.* Jackson, Tenn.: Balch, 1880.

Brooks, Richard Donoho. *One Hundred and Sixty-two Years of Middle Tennessee Baptists.* Nashville: Cullom and Ghertner, 1958.

Brown, Oswald Eugene, James Hampton Kirkland, and Edwin Mims. *God and the New Knowledge.* Nashville: Cole Lecture Foundation, 1926.

Brumfield, Thomas Mason. "Religion as Being Interpreted in Nashville among Negroes." Ph.D. diss., University of Chicago, 1928.

Bullock, Henry Morton. *A History of Emory University.* Nashville: Parthenon, 1936.

Burtchaell, James Tunstead. "The Alienation of Christian Higher Education in America: Diagnosis and Prognosis." In *Schooling Christians: "Holy Experiments" in American Education,* edited by Stanley Hauerwas and John H. Westerhoff, 129–83. Grand Rapids, Mich.: Eerdmans, 1992.

———. *The Dying of the Light: The Disengagement of Colleges and Universities from Their Christian Churches.* Grand Rapids, Mich.: Eerdmans, 1998.

Carr, Isaac Newton. *History of Carson-Newman College.* Jefferson City, Tenn.: Carson-Newman College, 1959.

Carter, Cullen T. *History of Methodist Churches and Institutions in Middle Tennessee, 1787–1956.* Nashville: Parthenon, 1956.

———. *History of the Tennessee Conference and a Brief Summary of the General Conferences of the Methodist Church from the Frontier in Middle Tennessee to the Present Time.* Nashville: Parthenon, 1948.

———. *Methodist Leaders in the Old Jerusalem Conference, 1812–1962.* Nashville: Parthenon, 1961.

Cartwright, Joseph H. *The Triumph of Jim Crow: Tennessee Race Relations in the 1880s.* Knoxville: University of Tennessee Press, 1976.

Carty, James W. *Nashville as a World Religious Center.* Nashville: Cullom and Ghertner, 1958.

Cash, W. J. *The Mind of the South.* New York: Knopf, 1941.

Caudill, Edward. "The Roots of Bias: An Empiricist Press and Coverage of the Scopes Trial." *Journalism Monographs* 114 (1989): 1–37.

Chaffin, Nora C. *Trinity College, 1839–92: The Beginnings of Duke University.* Durham, N.C.: Duke University Press, 1950.

Charles, Chatfield E. "The Southern Sociological Congress: Organization of Uplift." *Tennessee Historical Quarterly* 19 (1960): 328–47.

———. "The Southern Sociological Congress: Rationale of Uplift." *Tennessee Historical Quarterly* 20 (1961): 51–64.

Cherry, Conrad. *Hurrying toward Zion: Universities, Divinity Schools, and American Protestantism.* Bloomington: Indiana University Press, 1995.

Chitty, Arthur B., Jr. *Reconstruction at Sewanee: The Founding of the University of the South . . . , 1857–72.* Sewanee, Tenn.: University of the South, 1954.

Clark, Constance Areson. "Evolution for John Doe: Pictures, the Public, and the Scopes Trial Debate." *Journal of American History* 87 (2001): 1275–1301.

Clark, Norman H. *Deliver Us from Evil: An Interpretation of American Prohibition.* New York: Norton, 1976.

Claxton, Philander Priestly. *Should the General Assembly of Tennessee Enact a Compulsory School Attendance Law?* N.p., 1907.

Clayton, Bruce. *The Savage Ideal: Intolerance and Intellectual Leadership in the South, 1890–1914.* Baltimore: Johns Hopkins University Press, 1972.

Clough, Dick B. "A History of Teachers' Institutes in Tennessee, 1875–1915." Ph.D. diss., Memphis State University, 1975.

Conkin, Paul K. *Gone with the Ivy: A Biography of Vanderbilt University.* Knoxville: University of Tennessee Press, 1985.

———. *Peabody College: From a Frontier Academy to the Frontiers of Teaching and Learning.* Nashville: Vanderbilt University Press, 2002.

———. *When All the Gods Trembled: Darwinism, Scopes, and American Intellectuals.* Lanham, Md.: Rowman and Littlefield, 1998.

Conklin, Forrest. "Parson Brownlow Joins the Sons of Temperance, Part I." *Tennessee Historical Quarterly* 39 (1980): 178–94.

———. "Parson Brownlow—Temperance Advocate, Part II." *Tennessee Historical Quarterly* 39 (1980): 292–309.

Corkran, W. D. *The Sumner County Educator: Edited and Published in the Interest of the Free Schools.* Gallatin, Tenn.: N.p., 1879.

Corlew, Robert E. *Tennessee: A Short History.* Knoxville: University of Tennessee Press, 1981.

Coulter, E. Merton. *College Life in the Old South.* Athens: University of Georgia Press, 1928.

———. *William G. Brownlow: Fighting Parson of the Southern Highlands.* Chapel Hill: University of North Carolina Press, 1937.

Cremin, Lawrence Arthur. *American Education: The Metropolitan Experience, 1876–1980.* New York: Harper and Row, 1988.

———. *American Education: The National Experience, 1783–1876.* New York: Harper and Row, 1980.

Crowther, Edward R. " 'Religion Has Something . . . to Do with Politics': Southern Evangelicals and the North, 1845–1860." In *Religion and the Antebellum Debate over Slavery,* edited by John R. McKivigan and Mitchell Snay, 317–42. Athens: University of Georgia Press, 1998.

Cullom, Jeremiah W. *Warm Hearts and Saddlebags: Journal of the Reverend Jeremiah W. Cullom (1828–1915).* Edited by James R. Cox. Nashville: Tennessee Conference Historical Society, n.d.

Curran, Francis X., S.J. *The Churches and the Schools: American Protestantism and Popular Elementary Education.* Chicago: Loyola University Press, 1954.

Dabney, Charles William. *Universal Education in the South.* 2 vols. Chapel Hill: University of North Carolina Press, 1936.

Daly, John Patrick. *When Slavery Was Called Freedom: Evangelicalism, Proslavery, and the Causes of the Civil War.* Lexington: University Press of Kentucky, 2002.

Dannelly, Clarence. "The Development of Collegiate Education in the Methodist Episcopal Church, South, 1846–1902." Ph.D. diss., Yale University, 1933.

Davenport, F. Garvin. "Scientific Interests in Kentucky and Tennessee, 1870–1890." *Journal of Southern History* 14 (1948): 500–521.

Davis, Derek H. "Kansas Schools Challenge Darwinism: The History and Future of the Creationism-Evolution Controversy in American Public Education." *Journal of Church and State* 41 (1999): 661–76.

Davis, Edward B. "Debating Darwin: The 'Intelligent Design' Movement." *Christian Century* 115 (July 15, 1998): 678–81.

Davis, John H. *St. Mary's Cathedral, Memphis.* Jackson, Tenn.: McCowat-Mercer, 1958.

DeCamp, L. Sprague. *The Great Monkey Trial.* Garden City, N.Y.: Doubleday, 1968.

Dellinger, David Worth. " 'My Way or the Highway': The Hawkins County Textbook Controversy." Ed.D. diss., University of Tennessee, 1991.

DeLozier, Mary Jean. *The Tennessee Supreme Court on Religious Liberty, 1900–1960.* Master's thesis, Tennessee Technological University, 1966.

Dennis, Pamela R. "Music in Jackson, Tennessee: 1875–1917." Ph.D. diss., University of Memphis, 2000.

Doherty, Herbert J., Jr. "Alexander J. McKelway: Preacher to Progressive." *Journal of Southern History* 24 (1958): 177–90.

———. "Voices of Protest from the New South, 1875–1910." *Mississippi Valley Historical Review* 42 (1955–56): 45–66.

Doyle, Don H. *Nashville in the New South, 1880–1930.* Knoxville: University of Tennessee Press, 1985.

Dyer, Thomas G. "Higher Education in the South since the Civil War: Historiographical Issues and Trends." In *The Web of Southern Social Relations: Women, Family, and Education,* edited by Walter J. Fraser Jr., R. Frank Saunders Jr., and Jon L. Wakelyn, 127–45. Athens: University of Georgia Press, 1985.

Eaton, Clement. *The Mind of the Old South.* Baton Rouge: Louisiana State University Press, 1964.

Eigelsbach, William B., and Jamie Sue Linder, comps. "'If Not the People Who?': Prosecution Correspondence Preparatory to the Scopes Trial." *Journal of East Tennessee History* 70 (1998): 109–45.

Eighmy, John Lee. *Churches in Cultural Captivity: A History of the Social Attitudes of Southern Baptists.* 1972; reprint, Knoxville: University of Tennessee Press, 1987.

Elliott, C. D. *The Eagle Wing vs. the Mayflower; or, Familyism in Education vs. Stateism; or, Tennessee vs. Massachusetts in Schools.* Columbia, Tenn.: Scotch-Irish Congress, 1886.

———. *Family-Craft; or, The Scotch-Irish in Education: Nashville, Davidson County, Tennessee, from 1780 to 1880.* Nashville: Staddan, 1880.

Ellis, John H. "Memphis' Sanitary Revolution, 1880–1890." *Tennessee Historical Quarterly* 23 (1964): 59–72.

Ellis, William E. "Evolution, Fundamentalism, and the Historians: A Historiographical Review." *Historian* 44 (1981): 15–35.

Evans, Edith Snyder. "The Progressive Party in Tennessee in 1912." Master's thesis, University of Tennessee, 1933.

Ezell, J. S. "A Southern Education for Southrons." *Journal of Southern History* 17 (1951): 303–27.

Fair, Harold L. "Southern Methodists on Education and Race, 1900–1920." Ph.D. diss., Vanderbilt University, 1972.

Fairbanks, George R. *History of the University of the South at Sewanee, Tennessee.* Jacksonville, Fla.: Drew, 1905.

Farish, Hunter Dickinson. *The Circuit Rider Dismounts: A Social History of Southern Methodism, 1865–1900.* Richmond, Va.: Dietz, 1938.

Faust, Drew Gilpin. "Christian Soldiers: The Meaning of Revivalism in the Confederate Army." *Journal of Southern History* 53 (1987): 63–90.

—. *The Creation of Confederate Nationalism: Ideology and Identity in the Civil War South.* Baton Rouge: Louisiana State University Press, 1988.

Few, William Preston. "Some Educational Needs of the South." *South Atlantic Quarterly* 3 (1904): 201–11.

Fields, Barbara Jeanne. "Ideology and Race in American History." In *Region, Race, and Reconstruction: Essays in Honor of C. Vann Woodward,* edited by J. Morgan Kousser and James M. McPherson, 143–77. New York: Oxford University Press, 1982.

Fisher, John E. "Life on the Common Level: Inheritance, Conflict, and Instruction." *Tennessee Historical Quarterly* 26 (1967): 304–22.

Fitzgerald, Oscar P. *Dr. Summers: A Life-Study.* Nashville: Methodist Publishing House, 1884.

—. *John B. McFerrin: A Biography.* Nashville: Methodist Publishing House, 1888.

Fitzpatrick, Morgan C. *Annual Report of the State Superintendent of Public Instruction for Tennessee for the Scholastic Year ending June 30, 1900.* Nashville: Gospel Advocate, 1900.

Flanigen, George J., ed. *Catholicity in Tennessee: A Sketch of Catholic Activities in the State, 1541–1937.* Nashville: Ambrose, 1937.

Fleming, Cynthia Griggs. "The Development of Black Education in Tennessee, 1865–1920." Ph.D. diss., Duke University, 1977.

—. "Knoxville College: A History and Some Recollections of the First Fifty Years, 1875–1925." *East Tennessee Historical Society's Publications* 58–59 (1986–87): 89–111.

—. "A Survey of the Beginnings of Tennessee's Black Colleges and Universities, 1865–1920." *Tennessee Historical Quarterly* 39 (1980): 195–207.

Flynt, J. Wayne. "Southern Protestantism and Reform, 1890–1920." In *Varieties of Southern Religious Experience,* edited by Samuel S. Hill, 135–57. Baton Rouge: Louisiana State University Press, 1988.

Folmsbee, Stanley J., Robert E. Corlew, and Enoch L. Mitchell. *History of Tennessee.* New York: Lewis Historical Publishing, 1960.

Folsom, Burton W. "The Scopes Trial Reconsidered." *Continuity: A Journal of History* 12 (1988): 103–27.

Fortieth Annual Meeting of the Tennessee State Teachers' Association. Clarksville, Tenn.: Titus, 1906.

Forty-first Annual Meeting of the Tennessee State Teachers' Association. Clarksville, Tenn.: Titus, 1907.

Fosdick, Harry Emerson. "Shall the Fundamentalists Win?" *Christian Work* 102 (June 10, 1922): 716–22.

Foster, Gaines M. *Ghosts of the Confederacy: Defeat, the Lost Cause, and the Emergence of the New South.* New York: Oxford University Press, 1987.

—. "Guilt over Slavery: A Historiographical Analysis." *Journal of Southern History* 56 (1990): 665–94.

—. *Moral Reconstruction: Christian Lobbyists and the Federal Legislation of Morality, 1865–1920.* Chapel Hill: University of North Carolina Press, 2002.

Fox, Sister Mary Loyola. *A Return of Love: The Story of the Sisters of Mercy in Tennessee, 1866–1966.* Nashville: Bruce, 1967.

Francis, Joyce F. "Creationism v. Evolution: The Legal History and Tennessee's Role in that History." *Tennessee Law Review* 63 (1996): 753–74.

Fraser, James W. *Between Church and State: Religion and Public Education in a Multicultural America.* New York: St. Martin's, 1999.

Freund, Paul A., and Robert Ulich. *Religion and the Public Schools.* Burton Lecture and Inglis Lecture. Cambridge: Harvard University Press, 1965.

Friedman, Jean E. *The Enclosed Garden: Women and Community in the Evangelical South, 1830–1900.* Chapel Hill: University of North Carolina Press, 1985.

Frost, Dan R. *Thinking Confederates: Academia and the Idea of Progress in the New South.* Knoxville: University of Tennessee Press, 2000.

Fuller, T. O. *History of the Negro Baptists of Tennessee.* Memphis: Haskins, 1936.

Gatewood, Willard B., Jr., ed. *Controversy in the Twenties: Fundamentalism, Modernism, and Evolution.* Nashville: Vanderbilt University Press, 1969.

————. *Preachers, Pedagogues, and Politicians: The Evolution Controversy in North Carolina, 1920–1927.* Chapel Hill: University of North Carolina Press, 1966.

Geertz, Clifford. "Religion as a Cultural System." In *The Interpretation of Cultures,* edited by Clifford Geertz, 87–125. New York: Basic Books, 1973.

Genovese, Eugene D. *A Consuming Fire: The Fall of the Confederacy in the Mind of the White Christian South.* Athens: University of Georgia Press, 1998.

Gershenberg, Irving. "Southern Values and Public Education: A Revision." *History of Education Quarterly* 10 (1970): 413–22.

Gilbreath, S. G. *Biennial Report of the State Superintendent of Public Instruction for Tennessee for the Scholastic Year ending June 30, 1896.* Nashville: n.p., 1896.

Ginger, Ray. *Six Days or Forever? Tennessee v. John Thomas Scopes.* New York: Oxford University Press, 1958.

Glass, William R. *Strangers in Zion: Fundamentalists in the South.* Macon, Ga.: Mercer University Press, 2001.

Gobbel, Luther L. *Church-State Relationships in Education in North Carolina since 1776.* Durham, N.C.: Duke University Press, 1938.

Godbold, Albea. "Bishop William McKendree and His Contribution to Methodism." *Methodist History* 8 (1969–70): 3–12.

————. *The Church College of the Old South.* Durham, N.C.: Duke University Press, 1944.

Goodenow, Ronald K., and Arthur O. White, eds. *Education and the Rise of the New South.* Boston: Hall, 1981.

Grammich, Clifford Anthony, Jr. "The Bible and Political Change: A Study of White Bible-Based Protestant Southerners." Ph.D. diss., University of Chicago, 1996.

Grantham, Dewey W. *Southern Progressivism: The Reconciliation of Progress and Tradition.* Knoxville: University of Tennessee Press, 1983.

Gray, Virginia. "Anti-Evolution Sentiment and Behavior." *Journal of American History* 57 (1970): 352–66.

Green, John W. *Lives of the Judges of the Supreme Court of Tennessee, 1796–1947.* Knoxville: University of Tennessee Press, 1947.

Greene, Lee Seifert, and Robert Sterling Avery. *Government in Tennessee.* Knoxville: University of Tennessee Press, 1962.

Griffin, Paul R. "Black Founders of Reconstruction Era Methodist Colleges: Daniel A. Payne, Joseph C. Price, and Isaac Lane, 1863–1890." Ph.D. diss., Emory University, 1983.

Griffith, Chester Clinton. "Constitutional and Legal Status of Compulsory Education in Tennessee." Ph.D. diss., George Peabody College, 1935.

Grime, John H. *History of Middle Tennessee Baptists with Special References to Salem, New Salem, Enon, and Wiseman Associations, Containing Sketches of Associations, Churches, Deceased Ministers, and Deacons, with Ministerial Directory: Also Chapters on Separate Baptists, Christian Baptists, Feet Washing.* Nashville: Baptist and Reflector, 1902.

Gross, John O. "The Bishops versus Vanderbilt University." *Tennessee Historical Quarterly* 22 (1963): 53–65.

Gusfield, Joseph R. *Symbolic Crusade: Status Politics and the American Temperance Movement.* Urbana: University of Illinois Press, 1966.

Hall, Randal L. *William Louis Poteat: A Leader of the Progressive-Era South.* Lexington: University Press of Kentucky, 2000.

Halliburton, R., Jr. "The Adoption of Arkansas' Anti-Evolution Law." *Arkansas Historical Quarterly* 23 (1964): 271–83.

———. "Mississippi's Contribution to the Anti-Evolution Movement." *Journal of Mississippi History* 35 (1973): 175–82.

———. "The Nation's First Anti-Darwin Law." *Southwestern Social Science Quarterly* 41 (1960): 123–34.

Hand, William H. "The Need of Compulsory Education in the South." In *Proceedings of the Fifteenth Conference for Education in the South,* 55–70. Washington, D.C.: Executive Committee of the Conference, 1912.

Handy, Robert T. *A Christian America: Protestant Hopes and Historical Realities.* 2d ed. New York: Oxford University Press, 1984.

Hardacre, Paul H. "History and Historians at Vanderbilt, 1875–1918." *Tennessee Historical Quarterly* 25 (1966): 22–31.

Harkness, Georgia. *The Methodist Church in Social Thought and Action—A Summary.* New York and Nashville: Abingdon, 1964.

Harlan, Louis R. *Separate and Unequal: Public School Campaigns and Racism in the Southern Seaboard States, 1901–1915.* Chapel Hill: University of North Carolina Press, 1958.

Harper, Keith. *The Quality of Mercy: Southern Baptists and Social Christianity, 1890–1920.* Tuscaloosa: University of Alabama Press, 1996.

Harrell, David Edwin, Jr. "Disciples of Christ Pacifism in Nineteenth Century Tennessee." *Tennessee Historical Quarterly* 21 (1962): 263–74.

———. *Quest for a Christian America: The Disciples of Christ and American Society.* Nashville: Disciples of Christ Historical Society, 1966.

———, ed. *Varieties of Southern Evangelicalism.* Macon, Ga.: Mercer University Press, 1981.

Harris, William A. "Is Education the Prerogative of the Church or State?" *Methodist Quarterly Review* 12 (1858): 78–92.

Harrison, Joseph W. "The Bible, The Constitution, and Public Education." *Tennessee Law Review* 29 (1962): 1–56.

Harrold, Philip E. "Alexander Winchell's 'Science with a Soul': Piety, Profession, and the Perils of Nineteenth Century Popular Science." *Methodist History* 36 (1998): 97–112.

Hart, Roger L. *Redeemers, Bourbons, and Populists: Tennessee, 1870–1896.* Baton Rouge: Louisiana State University Press, 1975.

Harvey, Paul. *Redeeming the South: Religious Cultures and Racial Identities among Southern Baptists, 1865–1925.* Chapel Hill: University of North Carolina Press, 1997.

———. "'Yankee Faith' and Southern Redemption: White Southern Baptist Ministers, 1850–1890." In *Religion and the American Civil War,* edited by Randall M. Miller, Harry S. Stout, and Charles Reagan Wilson, 167–86. New York: Oxford University Press, 1998.

Haunton, Richard H. "Education and Democracy: The Views of Philip Lindsley." *Tennessee Historical Quarterly* 21 (1962): 131–39.

Hawkins, Hugh. "Charles W. Eliot, University Reform, and Religious Faith in America, 1869–1909." *Journal of American History* 51 (1964): 191–213.

Haygood, Atticus G. *The Church and the Education of the People: An Address Delivered before the Alumni Association of Emory College.* Nashville: Publishing House of the Methodist Episcopal Church, South, 1874.

———. *Pleas for Progress.* Nashville: Publishing House of the Methodist Episcopal Church, South, 1889.

Henderson, Jerry. "Nashville's Ryman Auditorium." *Tennessee Historical Quarterly* 27 (1968): 305–28.

Herron, W. W. "A History of Lambuth College." *West Tennessee Historical Society Papers* 10 (1956): 20–37.

Heyrman, Christine Leigh. *Southern Cross: The Beginnings of the Bible Belt.* New York: Knopf, 1997.

Higginbotham, Evelyn Brooks. *Righteous Discontent: The Women's Movement in the Black Baptist Church, 1880–1920.* Cambridge: Harvard University Press, 1993.

Hill, Samuel S., ed. *Encyclopedia of Religion in the South.* Macon, Ga.: Mercer University Press, 1984.

———. *One Name but Several Faces: Variety in Popular Christian Denominations in Southern History.* Athens: University of Georgia Press, 1996.

———, ed. *Religion and the Solid South.* Nashville: Abingdon, 1972.

———. "The Shape and Shapes of Popular Southern Piety." In *Varieties of Southern*

Evangelicalism, edited by David Edwin Harrell Jr., 89–114. Macon, Ga.: Mercer University Press, 1981.

———. *The South and the North in American Religion.* Athens: University of Georgia Press, 1980.

———. *Southern Churches in Crisis.* Chicago: Holt, Rinehart, and Winston, 1966.

———, ed. *Varieties of Southern Religious Experience.* Baton Rouge: Louisiana State University Press, 1988.

Hoffschwelle, Mary S. *Rebuilding the Rural Southern Community: Reformers, Schools, and Homes in Tennessee, 1900–1930.* Knoxville: University of Tennessee Press, 1998.

Hofstadter, Richard, and Walter P. Metzger. *Academic Freedom in the Age of the College.* New York: Columbia University Press, 1955.

Holifield, E. Brooks. *The Gentlemen Theologians: American Theology in Southern Culture, 1795–1860.* Durham, N.C.: Duke University Press, 1978.

Hollow, Elizabeth Patton. "Development of the Brownsville Baptist Female College: An Example of Female Education in the South, 1850–1910." *West Tennessee Historical Society Papers* 32 (1978): 48–59.

Holt, Andrew David. *The Struggle for a State System of Public Schools in Tennessee, 1903–1936.* New York: Bureau of Publications, Teachers College, Columbia University, 1938.

Hood, John O. *History of the Chilhowee Baptist Association.* Nashville: Curley, 1970.

Hooper, Robert E. *Crying in the Wilderness: A Biography of David Lipscomb.* Nashville: David Lipscomb College, 1979.

Hopkins, Charles Henry. *The Rise of the Social Gospel Movement in American Protestantism, 1865–1914.* New Haven: Yale University Press, 1940.

Hovenkamp, Herbert. *Science and Religion in America, 1800–1860.* Philadelphia: University of Pennsylvania Press, 1978.

Howell, Sarah McCanless. "The Editorials of Arthur S. Colyar, Nashville Prophet of the New South." *Tennessee Historical Quarterly* 27 (1968): 74–106.

Hughes, Richard T. *Reviving the Ancient Faith: The Story of Churches of Christ in America.* Grand Rapids, Mich.: Eerdmans, 1996.

Hunt, Thomas C., and James C. Carper. *Religion and Schooling in Contemporary America: Confronting Our Cultural Pluralism.* New York: Garland, 1997.

Hunter, George W. *A Civic Biology: Presented in Problems.* New York: American Book, 1914.

Iannone, Carol. "The Truth about *Inherit the Wind.*" *Trinity Journal* 70 (1997): 28–33.

Isaac, Paul E. "The Problems of a Republican Governor in a Southern State: Ben Hooper of Tennessee, 1910–1914." *Tennessee Historical Quarterly* 27 (1968): 229–48.

———. *Prohibition and Politics: Turbulent Decades in Tennessee, 1885–1920.* Knoxville: University of Tennessee Press, 1965.

Isaac, Rhys. *The Transformation of Virginia.* Chapel Hill: University of North Carolina Press for the Institute of Early American History and Culture, 1982.

Israel, Charles A. "From Biracial to Segregated Churches: Black and White Protestants in Houston, Texas, 1840–1870." *Southwestern Historical Quarterly* 101 (1998): 428–58.

Johnston, Charles D. *Higher Education of Southern Baptists: An Institutional History, 1826–1954*. Waco, Tex.: Baylor University Press, 1955.

Joiner, James. "A History of Sunday Laws in Tennessee." Ph.D. diss., University of Tennessee, Knoxville, 1954.

Jones, Robert B. *Tennessee at the Crossroads: The State Debt Controversy, 1870–1883*. Knoxville: University of Tennessee Press, 1977.

Jorgenson, Lloyd P. *The State and the Non-Public School, 1825–1925*. Columbia: University of Missouri Press, 1987.

Kaestle, Carl F. *Pillars of the Republic: Common Schools and American Society, 1780–1860*. New York: Hill and Wang, 1983.

Keith, Jeanette. *Country People in the New South: Tennessee's Upper Cumberland*. Chapel Hill: University of North Carolina Press, 1995.

Kiger, Joseph C. "Social Thought as Voiced in Rural Middle Tennessee Newspapers, 1878–1898." *Tennessee Historical Quarterly* 9 (1950): 131–54.

Kincheloe, Joe Lyons. "The Antebellum Southern Evangelical and State-Supported Colleges: A Comparative Study." Ed.D. diss., University of Tennessee, 1980.

————. "The Battle for the Antebellum Southern Colleges: The Evangelicals vs. the Calvinists in Tennessee." *Journal of Thought* 18 (1983): 119–33.

Kirby, James E. "The McKendree Chapel Affair." *Tennessee Historical Quarterly* 25 (1966): 360–70.

Kirkland, James H. "The School as a Force Arrayed against Child Labor." *Annals of the American Academy of Political and Social Science* 25 (1905): 558–62.

————. "Twenty-Five Years of University Work." *Vanderbilt University Quarterly* 1 (1901): 86–99.

Knight, Edgar W. *Public Education in the South*. Boston: Ginn, 1922.

Knox, John Ballenger. *The People of Tennessee: A Study of Population Trends*. Knoxville: University of Tennessee Press, 1949.

Kousser, J. Morgan. "Post-Reconstruction Suffrage Restrictions in Tennessee: A New Look at the V. O. Key Thesis." *Political Science Quarterly* 88 (1973): 655–83.

————. "Progressivism—For Middle-Class Whites Only: North Carolina Education, 1880–1910." *Journal of Southern History* 46 (1980): 169–94.

Krutch, Joseph Wood. "Tennessee: Where Cowards Rule." *Nation* 121 (1925): 88–89.

Kyriakoudes, Louis M. *The Social Origins of the Urban South: Race, Gender, and Migration in Nashville and Middle Tennessee, 1890–1930*. Chapel Hill: University of North Carolina Press, 2003.

Lacy, Eric Russell. "Tennessee Teetotalism: Social Forces and the Politics of Progressivism." *Tennessee Historical Quarterly* 24 (1965): 219–40.

Lamon, Lester C. *Black Tennesseans, 1900–1930*. Knoxville: University of Tennessee Press, 1977.

————. "The Tennessee Agricultural and Industrial Normal School: Public Education for Black Tennesseans." *Tennessee Historical Quarterly* 32 (1973): 42–58.

Larson, Edward J. "The *Scopes* Trial and the Evolving Concept of Freedom." *Virginia Law Review* 85 (1999): 503–29.

————. *Summer for the Gods: The Scopes Trial and America's Continuing Debate over Science and Religion.* New York: Basic Books, 1997.

————. *Trial and Error: The American Controversy over Creation and Evolution.* 2d ed. New York: Oxford University Press, 1989.

Larson, Edward J., and Larry Witham. "Debating Evolution: The God Who Would Intervene." *Christian Century* 116 (October 27, 1999): 1026–27.

————. "Inherit an Ill Wind." *The Nation,* October 4, 1999, 25–29.

————. "Scientists and Religion in America." *Scientific American,* September 1999, 88–93.

Leab, Grace. "Tennessee Temperance Activities, 1870–1899." *East Tennessee Historical Society's Publications* 21 (1949): 52–68.

Lee, David D. *Tennessee in Turmoil: Politics in the Volunteer State, 1920–1932.* Memphis: Memphis State University Press, 1979.

Leloudis, James L. *Schooling the New South: Pedagogy, Self, and Society in North Carolina, 1880–1920.* Chapel Hill: University of North Carolina Press, 1996.

Leslie, W. Bruce. *Gentlemen and Scholars: College and Community in the "Age of the University," 1865–1917.* University Park: Pennsylvania State University Press, 1992.

Levine, Lawrence W. *Defender of the Faith: William Jennings Bryan, the Last Decade, 1915–1925.* New York: Oxford University Press, 1965.

Levy, Leonard W. *The Establishment Clause: Religion and the First Amendment.* 2d ed. Chapel Hill: University of North Carolina Press, 1994.

Lewis, Charles Lee. *Philander Priestly Claxton: Crusader for Public Education.* Knoxville: University of Tennessee Press, 1948.

Lewis, J. Eugene. "The Tennessee Gubernatorial Campaign and Election of 1894 [Part I]." *Tennessee Historical Quarterly* 13 (1954): 99–126.

————. "The Tennessee Gubernatorial Campaign and Election of 1894 [Part II]." *Tennessee Historical Quarterly* 13 (1954): 224–43.

————. "The Tennessee Gubernatorial Campaign and Election of 1894 [Part III]." *Tennessee Historical Quarterly* 13 (December 1954): 301–28.

Limbo, Ernest Maurice. "Economic Transformation and the Old, Old Story: Evangelicals Respond to a Changing World in Southern Middle Tennessee." Ph.D. diss., University of Mississippi, 1998.

Linder, Robert D. "The Resurgence of Evangelical Social Concern [1925–1975]." In *The Evangelicals,* edited by David F. Wells and John D. Woodbridge, 189–210. Nashville: Abingdon, 1975.

Linder, Suzanne C. "William Louis Poteat and the Evolution Controversy." *North Carolina Historical Review* 40 (1963): 135–57.

Link, William A. *A Hard Country and a Lonely Place: Schooling, Society, and Reform in Rural Virginia, 1870–1920.* Chapel Hill: University of North Carolina Press, 1986.

————. "Making the Inarticulate Speak: A Reassessment of Public Education in the Rural South, 1870–1920." *Journal of Thought* 18 (1983): 63–75.

————. *The Paradox of Southern Progressivism, 1880–1930.* Chapel Hill: University of North Carolina Press, 1992.

————. "The School That Built a Town: Public Education and the Southern Social Landscape, 1880–1930." In *Essays in Twentieth-Century Southern Education: Exceptionalism and Its Limits,* edited by Wayne J. Urban, 19–42. New York: Garland, 1999.

Lippmann, Walter. *American Inquisitors: A Commentary on Dayton and Chicago.* Barbour-Page Lectures at the University of Virginia. New York: Macmillan, 1928.

Livingstone, David N. *Darwin's Forgotten Defenders: The Encounter between Evangelical Theology and Evolutionary Thought.* Grand Rapids, Mich.: Eerdmans, 1987.

Loewenberg, Bert James. "The Reaction of American Scientists to Darwinism." *American Historical Review* 38 (1933): 686–701.

Loveland, Anne C. *Southern Evangelicals and the Social Order, 1800–1860.* Baton Rouge: Louisiana State University Press, 1980.

Luker, Ralph E. *A Southern Tradition in Theology and Social Criticism, 1830–1930: The Religious Liberalism and Social Conservatism of James Warley Miles, William Porcher Dubose, and Edgar Gardner Murphy.* Studies in American Religion, vol. 11. New York: Mellen, 1984.

Macpherson, Joseph Tant. "Democratic Progressivism in Tennessee: The Administrations of Governor Austin Peay, 1923–1927." Ph.D. diss., Vanderbilt University, 1969.

Madison, James H. "Reformers and the Rural Church, 1900–1950." *Journal of American History* 73 (1986): 645–68.

Mann, Harold. *Atticus Greene Haygood: Bishop, Editor, and Educator.* Athens: University of Georgia Press, 1965.

Marion, Forrest L. "East Tennessee and the Sabbath Question, 1828–1838." *Journal of East Tennessee History* 66 (1994): 9–31.

Marsden, George M. *Fundamentalism and American Culture: The Shaping of Twentieth-Century Evangelicalism, 1870–1925.* New York: Oxford University Press, 1980.

————. *The Soul of the American University: From Protestant Establishment to Established Nonbelief.* New York: Oxford University Press, 1994.

————. *Understanding Fundamentalism and Evangelicalism.* Grand Rapids, Mich.: Eerdmans, 1991.

Marsden, George M., and Bradley J. Longfield, eds. *The Secularization of the Academy.* New York: Oxford University Press, 1992.

Martin, Isaac Patton. *Elijah Embree Hoss, Ecumenical Methodist.* Nashville: Parthenon, 1942.

————. *Methodism in Holston.* Knoxville: Methodist Historical Society of Holston Conference, 1945.

———. *A Minister in the Tennessee Valley: Sixty-seven Years.* Nashville: Methodist Historical Society of Holston Conference, 1954.

Massengale, Robert. "Collegiate Education in the Methodist Episcopal Church, South, 1902–1939." Ph.D. diss., Yale University, 1950.

Mathews, Donald G. *Religion in the Old South.* Chicago: University of Chicago Press, 1977.

———. " 'We Have Left Undone Those Things Which We Ought to Have Done': Southern Religious History in Retrospect and Prospect." *Church History* 67 (1998): 305–25.

Maurer, Beryl B. "The Rural Church and Organized Community: A Study of Church-Community Relations in Two East Tennessee Communities." Master's thesis, University of Tennessee, 1953.

May, Lynn E., Jr. *The First Baptist Church of Nashville, Tennessee, 1820–1970.* Nashville: First Baptist Church, 1970.

McAfee, Ward M. *Religion, Race, and Reconstruction: The Public School in the Politics of the 1870s.* Albany: State University of New York Press, 1998.

McBride, Robert M., and Dan M. Robison. *Biographical Directory of the Tennessee General Assembly.* Vol. 2, *1861–1901.* Nashville: Tennessee State Library and Archives and Tennessee Historical Commission, 1979.

McClellan, B. Edward. *Moral Education in America: Schools and the Shaping of Character from Colonial Times to the Present.* New York: Teachers College, Columbia University Press, 1999.

McCulloch, James E., ed. *The Call of the New South: Addresses Delivered at the Southern Sociological Congress, Nashville, Tennessee.* Nashville: Southern Sociological Congress, 1912.

McDowell, John Patrick. *The Social Gospel in the South: The Woman's Home Mission Movement in the Methodist Episcopal Church, South, 1886–1939.* Baton Rouge: Louisiana State University Press, 1982.

McMillen, Sally G. *To Raise Up the South: Sunday Schools in Black and White Churches, 1865–1915.* Baton Rouge: Louisiana State University Press, 2001.

McMillin, Laurence. *The Schoolmaker: Sawney Webb and the Bell Buckle Story.* Chapel Hill: University of North Carolina Press, 1971.

Mencken, H. L. "Sahara of the Bozart." In *Prejudices: Second Series,* 136–54. New York: Knopf, 1924.

Merriam, Lucius Salisbury. *Higher Education in Tennessee.* Bureau of Education Circular 5. Washington, D.C.: U.S. Government Printing Office, 1893.

Methodist Publishing House. *Since 1789: The Story of the Methodist Publishing House.* Nashville: Abingdon, 1964.

Meyer, Alfred M. "A History of the Southern Association of Colleges and Secondary Schools." Ph.D. diss., George Peabody College of Teachers, 1933.

Midgette, Nancy Smith. "In Search of Professional Identity: Southern Scientists, 1883–1940." *Journal of Southern History* 54 (1988): 597–622.

Miller, Nicholas P. "Life, the Universe, and Everything Constitutional: Origins in the Public Schools." *Journal of Church and State* 43 (2001): 483–510.

Miller, William D. *Memphis during the Progressive Era, 1900–1917.* Memphis: Memphis State University Press, 1957.

———. "The Progressive Movement in Memphis." *Tennessee Historical Quarterly* 15 (1956): 3–16.

Milton, George Fort. "Can Minds Be Closed by Statute?" *World's Work* 50 (1925): 323–28.

———. "Compulsory Education and the Southern States." *Sewanee Review* 16 (1908): 25–42.

Mims, Edwin. *The Advancing South.* Garden City, N.Y.: Doubleday, 1968.

———. *Chancellor Kirkland of Vanderbilt.* Nashville: Vanderbilt University Press, 1940.

———. *History of Vanderbilt University.* Nashville: Vanderbilt University Press, 1946.

Minnix, Kathleen. *Laughter in the Amen Corner: The Life of Evangelist Sam Jones.* Athens: University of Georgia Press, 1993.

Modey, Yao Foli. "The Struggle over Prohibition in Memphis, 1880–1930." Ph.D. diss., Memphis State University, 1983.

Montgomery, James Riley. "The Summer School of the South." *Tennessee Historical Quarterly* 22 (1963): 361–81.

———. "Threshold of a New Day: The University of Tennessee, 1919–1946." *University of Tennessee Record* 74 (1971): 1–432.

Montgomery, James Riley, Stanley J. Folmsbee, and Lee Seifert Greene. *To Foster Knowledge: A History of the University of Tennessee, 1794–1970.* Knoxville: University of Tennessee Press, 1984.

Montgomery, James Riley, and Gerald Gaither. "Evolution and Education in Tennessee: Decisions and Dilemmas." *Tennessee Historical Quarterly* 28 (1969): 141–55.

Montgomery, William E. *Under Their Own Vine and Fig Tree: The African-American Church in the South, 1865–1900.* Baton Rouge: Louisiana State University Press, 1993.

Moore, Andrew S. " 'To Advance the Redeemer's Kingdom': East Tennessee Southern Baptists amid Social and Cultural Transition, 1890–1929." Master's thesis, University of Tennessee, 1994.

Moore, James R. *The Post-Darwinian Controversies: A Study of the Protestant Struggle to Come to Terms with Darwin in Great Britain and America, 1870–1900.* Cambridge: Cambridge University Press, 1979.

Moore, R. Laurence. "Bible Reading and Nonsectarian Schooling: The Failure of Religious Instruction in Nineteenth-Century Public Education." *Journal of American History* 86 (2000): 1581–99.

Moran, Jeffrey P. "Reading Race into the Scopes Trial: African American Elites, Science, and Fundamentalism." *Journal of American History* 90 (2003): 891–911.

————. *The Scopes Trial: A Brief History with Documents.* Boston: Bedford/St. Martin's, 2002.

————. "The Scopes Trial and Southern Fundamentalism in Black and White: Race, Region, and Religion." *Journal of Southern History* 70 (2004): 95–120.

Muelder, Walter G. *Methodism and Society in the Twentieth Century.* 4 vols. New York: Abingdon, 1961–62.

Murphy, Edgar Gardner. *Problems of the Present South: A Discussion of Certain of the Educational, Industrial, and Political Issues in the Southern States.* New York: Macmillan, 1904.

Newton, John C. Calhoun. *The New South and the Methodist Episcopal Church, South.* Baltimore: King, 1887.

Nord, Warren A. *Religion and American Education: Rethinking a National Dilemma.* Chapel Hill: University of North Carolina Press, 1995.

Norton, Herman A. *Religion in Tennessee, 1777–1945.* Knoxville: University of Tennessee Press and Tennessee Historical Commission, 1981.

————. *Tennessee Christians: A History of the Christian Church in Tennessee.* Nashville: Reed, 1971.

Numbers, Ronald L. *The Creationists: The Evolution of Scientific Creationism.* Berkeley: University of California Press, 1998.

————. *Darwinism Comes to America.* Cambridge: Harvard University Press, 1998.

Numbers, Ronald L., and Janet L. Numbers. "Science in the Old South: A Reappraisal." *Journal of Southern History* 48 (1982): 163–84.

Numbers, Ronald L., and John Stenhouse, eds. *Disseminating Darwinism: The Role of Place, Race, Religion, and Gender.* New York: Cambridge University Press, 1999.

Numbers, Ronald L., with Lester D. Stephens. "Darwinism in the American South: From the Early 1860s to the Late 1920s." In *Darwinism Comes to America,* by Ronald L. Numbers, 58–75. Cambridge: Harvard University Press, 1998.

Olasky, Marvin N. "The Real Story of the Trial That 'Disgraced Fundamentalism.'" *Fundamentalist Journal* 6 (1987): 23–26.

Owen, Christopher H. *The Sacred Flame of Love: Methodism and Society in Nineteenth-Century Georgia.* Athens: University of Georgia Press, 1998.

————. "'To Keep the Way Open for Methodism': Georgia Wesleyan Neutrality toward Slavery, 1844–1861." In *Religion and the Antebellum Debate over Slavery,* edited by John R. McKivigan and Mitchell Snay, 109–33. Athens: University of Georgia Press, 1998.

Owenby, Ted. *Subduing Satan: Religion, Recreation, and Manhood in the Rural South, 1865–1920.* Chapel Hill: University of North Carolina Press, 1990.

Pace, C. Robert. *Education and Evangelism: A Profile of Protestant Colleges.* New York: McGraw-Hill, 1972.

Paine, Donald F. "State of Tennessee v. John Scopes Revisited." *Tennessee Bar Journal* 32 (1996): 32–34.

Parker, Franklin. "George Peabody's Influence on Southern Educational Philanthropy." *Tennessee Historical Quarterly* 20 (1961): 65–74.

Parsons, Elaine Frantz. "Speculative Philanthropy: The Dilemmas of Temperance Reform in Late Antebellum Tennessee." Paper presented at the annual meeting of the Southern Historical Association, Baltimore, November 2002.

Parsons, Rhey Boyd. "Teacher Education in Tennessee." Ph.D. diss., University of Chicago, 1935.

Pattie, Frank A. ed. "The Last Speech of William Jennings Bryan." *Tennessee Historical Quarterly* 6 (1947): 265–83.

Peay, Mrs. Austin. *Austin Peay, Governor of Tennessee, 1923–25, 1925–27, 1927–29: A Collection of State Papers and Public Addresses with a Biography by T. H. Alexander.* Kingsport, Tenn.: Southern, 1929.

Perko, F. Michael. "Religious Schooling in America: An Historiographic Reflection." *History of Education Quarterly* 40 (2000): 320–38.

Phillips, Margaret I. *The Governors of Tennessee.* Gretna, La.: Pelican, 1978.

Piper, David H. "The Administration of Governor Ben W. Hooper of Tennessee." Master's thesis, George Peabody College for Teachers, 1929.

Plank, David N., and Rick Ginsberg, eds. *Southern Cities, Southern Schools: Public Education in the Urban South.* New York: Greenwood, 1990.

Poole, C. H. "Thomas O. Summers: A Biographical Study." Ph.D. diss., Vanderbilt University, 1957.

Porter, Curt. "Chautauqua and Tennessee: Monteagle and the Independent Assemblies." *Tennessee Historical Quarterly* 22 (1963): 347–60.

Posey, Walter Brownlow. "The Earthquake of 1811 and Its Influence on Evangelistic Methods in the Churches of the Old South." *Tennessee Historical Magazine,* 2d ser., 1 (1931): 107–14.

Potts, David B. "American Colleges in the Nineteenth Century: From Localism to Denominationalism." *History of Education Quarterly* 11 (1971): 363–80.

Price, Richard N. *Holston Methodism: From Its Origin to the Present Time.* 5 vols. Nashville: Methodist Publishing, 1903–13.

———. "Methodism in East Tennessee: Before, during, and since the War." *Methodist Quarterly Review* 57 (1908): 293–303.

Proceedings of the Seventh and Eighth Annual Sessions of the Tennessee State Teachers' Association. Nashville: Wheeler, Marshall, and Bruce, 1873.

Proceedings of the Tennessee State Teachers' Association. Nashville: University Press, 1897.

Provenzo, Eugene F., Jr. *Religious Fundamentalism and American Education.* Albany: State University of New York Press, 1990.

Rabinowitz, Howard N. *The First New South: 1865–1920.* Arlington Heights, Ill.: Harlan Davidson, 1992.

Reed, Ralph Eugene, Jr. "Fortresses of Faith: Design and Experience at Southern Evangelical Colleges, 1830–1900." Ph.D. diss., Emory University, 1991.

"Religion and Science at Vanderbilt." *Popular Science Monthly* 13 (1878): 492–95.

Reule, Deborah A. "The New Face of Creationism: The Establishment Clause and the Latest Efforts to Suppress Evolution in Public Schools." *Vanderbilt Law Review* 54 (November 2001): 2555–2610.

Roberts, Jon H. *Darwinism and the Divine in America: Protestant Intellectuals and Organic Evolution, 1859–1900.* Madison: University of Wisconsin Press, 1988.

Robinson, Dan M. "Governor Robert Love Taylor and the Blair Educational Bill in Tennessee." *Tennessee Historical Magazine,* 2d ser., 2 (1931): 28–49.

Roblyer, Leslie F. "The Fight for Local Prohibition in Knoxville, Tennessee, 1907." *East Tennessee Historical Society's Publications* 26 (1954): 27–37.

Rutledge, Rosa Dyer. "Union University through the Century (1834–1950)." *West Tennessee Historical Society Papers* 4 (1950): 83–96.

Schweiger, Beth Barton. *The Gospel Working Up: Progress and the Pulpit in Nineteenth-Century Virginia.* New York: Oxford University Press, 2000.

Settle, Mary Lee. *The Scopes Trial: The State of Tennessee v. John Thomas Scopes.* New York: Watts, 1972.

Shahan, Joe Michael. "Reform and Politics in Tennessee: 1906–1914." Ph.D. diss., Vanderbilt University, 1981.

Shapiro, Karin A. *A New South Rebellion: The Battle against Convict Labor in the Tennessee Coalfields, 1871–1896.* Chapel Hill: University of North Carolina Press, 1998.

Sharber, Patricia Farrell. "The Social Attitudes of the Episcopal Church in Tennessee, 1865–1898." Ph.D. diss., Vanderbilt University, 1970.

Shattuck, Gardiner H., Jr. " 'Appomattox as a Day of Blessing': Religious Interpretations of Confederate Defeat in the New South Era." *Journal of Confederate History* 7 (1991): 1–18.

Singal, Daniel Joseph. *The War Within: From Victorian to Modernist Thought in the South, 1919–1945.* Chapel Hill: University of North Carolina Press, 1982.

Sizer, Theodore R. *The Age of the Academies.* New York: Columbia University Teachers College Bureau of Publications, 1964.

Skoog, Gerald. "The Topic of Evolution in Secondary School Biology Textbooks: 1900–1977." *Science Education* 63 (1979): 620–36.

Sledge, Robert Watson. *Hands on the Ark: The Struggle for Change in the Methodist Episcopal Church, South, 1914–1939.* Lake Junaluska, N.C.: United Methodist Church Commission on Archives and History, 1975.

Smith, Charles Foster. "Southern Colleges and Schools." *Atlantic Monthly* 56 (1885): 738–50.

Smith, Frank M. *Proceedings of the Convention of County Superintendents, Held in the City of Nashville, December 6th and 7th, 1887.* Nashville: Marshall and Bruce, 1887.

Smith, John Abernathy. *Cross and Flame: Two Centuries of United Methodism in Middle Tennessee.* Nashville: Parthenon Press for the Commission on Archives and History of the Tennessee Conference, United Methodist Church, 1984.

Smith, Timothy L. *Revivalism and Social Reform in Mid–Nineteenth Century America.* Nashville: Abingdon, 1957.

Snay, Mitchell. *Gospel of Disunion: Religion and Separatism in the Antebellum South.* Cambridge: Cambridge University Press, 1993.

Snyder, Henry N. "The Denominational College in Southern Education." *South Atlantic Quarterly* 5 (1906): 8–20.

Spain, Rufus B. *At Ease in Zion: A Social History of Southern Baptists, 1865–1900.* Nashville: Vanderbilt University Press, 1961.

Sparks, Randy J. *On Jordan's Stormy Banks: Evangelicalism in Mississippi, 1773–1876.* Athens: University of Georgia Press, 1994.

————. "Religion in the Pre–Civil War South." In *A Companion to the American South,* edited by John B. Boles, 156–75. Oxford: Blackwell, 2002.

————. " 'To Rend the Body of Christ': Proslavery Ideology and Religious Schism from a Mississippi Perspective." In *Religion and the Antebellum Debate over Slavery,* edited by John R. McKivigan and Mitchell Snay, 273–95. Athens: University of Georgia Press, 1998.

Stephens, Lester D. *Joseph LeConte: Gentle Prophet of Evolution.* Baton Rouge: Louisiana State University Press, 1982.

————. *Science, Race, and Religion in the American South: John Bachman and the Charleston Circle of Naturalists, 1815–1895.* Chapel Hill: University of North Carolina Press, 2000.

Stetar, Joseph M. "In Search of a Direction: Southern Higher Education after the Civil War." *History of Education Quarterly* 25 (1985): 341–67.

Stowell, Daniel W. *Rebuilding Zion: The Religious Reconstruction of the South, 1863–1877.* New York: Oxford University Press, 1998.

Sulloway, Frank J. *Born to Rebel: Birth Order, Family Dynamics, and Creative Lives.* New York: Pantheon, 1996.

Summerville, James. "Science in the New South: The Meeting of the AAAS at Nashville, 1877." *Tennessee Historical Quarterly* 45 (1986): 316–28.

Szasz, Ferenc M. *The Divided Mind of Protestant America, 1880–1930.* University: University of Alabama Press, 1982.

————. "The Scopes Trial in Perspective." *Tennessee Historical Quarterly* 30 (1971): 288–98.

Tatum, Noreen Dunn. *A Crown of Service: A Story of Women's Work in the Methodist Episcopal Church, South, from 1878–1940.* Nashville: Abingdon, 1960.

Taylor, Alrutheus A. "Fisk University and the Nashville Community." *Journal of Negro History* 39 (1954): 111–26.

[Taylor, Charles Elisha.] *How Far Should a State Undertake to Educate? or, A Plea for the Voluntary System in the Higher Education.* Raleigh, N.C.: Edwards and Broughton, 1894.

Tennessee Department of Agriculture. *Makers of Millions: Not for Themselves—But for You.* Nashville: State of Tennessee, 1951.

Tennessee State Planning Commission. *Guide to Church Vital Statistics in Tennessee.* Nashville: State of Tennessee, 1942.

Tewksbury, Donald G. *The Founding of American Colleges and Universities before the Civil War.* 1932; reprint, Hamden, Conn.: Archon, 1965.

Thirty-eighth Annual Meeting of the Tennessee State Teachers' Association. Clarksville, Tenn.: Titus, 1903.

Thirty-ninth Annual Meeting of the Tennessee State Teachers' Association. Clarksville, Tenn.: Titus, 1905.

Thirty-seventh Annual Meeting of the Tennessee State Teachers' Association. Clarksville, Tenn.: Titus, 1902.

Thomas, Emory M. *The Confederacy as a Revolutionary Experience.* 1971; Columbia: University of South Carolina Press, 1991.

Thompson, Ernest Trice. *Presbyterians in the South.* 3 vols. Richmond: Knox, 1963–73.

Thompson, James J., Jr. *Tried as by Fire: Southern Baptists and the Religious Controversies of the 1920s.* Macon, Ga.: Mercer University Press, 1982.

Tigert, John J. *Bishop Holland Nimmons McTyeire.* Nashville: Abingdon, 1955.

Tillett, Wilbur Fisk. *Methodism and Higher Education in the Tennessee Conference: An Address Delivered at the Centennial Session of the Tennessee Annual Conference of the Methodist Episcopal Church, South, Held in Nashville, Tenn., October 9–14, 1912.* Nashville: Publishing House of the Methodist Episcopal Church, South, 1913.

Tindall, George B. "Business Progressivism: Southern Politics in the Twenties." *South Atlantic Quarterly* 62 (1963): 92–106.

Tompkins, Jerry R., ed. *D-Days at Dayton: Reflections on the Scopes Trial.* Baton Rouge: Louisiana State University Press, 1965.

Trousdale, Leon. "A Plea for Universal Education by the State, as the Correlative of Citizenship." Nashville: Tavel, Eastman, and Howell, 1875.

Turner, Elizabeth Hayes. *Women, Culture, and Community: Religion and Reform in Galveston, 1880–1920.* New York: Oxford University Press, 1997.

Turner, Frank. *Without God, without Creed: The Origins of Unbelief in America.* Baltimore: Johns Hopkins University Press, 1986.

Twenty-ninth Annual Meeting of the Tennessee State Teachers' Association. N.p.: 1894.

Twenty-seventh Annual Meeting of the Tennessee State Teachers' Association. N.p.: 1891.

Tyack, David B. "The Tribe and the Common School: Community Control in Rural Education." *American Quarterly* 24 (1972): 3–19.

Urban, Wayne J. "History of Education: A Southern Exposure." *History of Education Quarterly* 21 (1981): 131–45.

———. "Stasis or Change: Recent Histories of Twentieth-Century Southern Education." In *Essays in Twentieth-Century Southern Education: Exceptionalism and Its Limits,* edited by Wayne J. Urban, 227–56. New York: Garland, 1999.

U.S. Bureau of the Census. *Religious Bodies: 1906.* Vol. 1. Washington, D.C.: U.S. Government Printing Office, 1910.

———. *Religious Bodies: 1916.* Vol. 1. Washington, D.C.: U.S. Government Printing Office, 1919.

Utley, Buford C. "The Early Academies of West Tennessee." *West Tennessee Historical Society Papers* 8 (1954): 5–38.

Valentine, Foy Don. "A Historical Study of Southern Baptists and Race Relations, 1917–1947." Th.D. thesis, Southwestern Baptist Theological Seminary, 1949.

Van Fleet, Alanson A. "Teachers as Cultural Brokers: Historical and Anthropological Evidence." *Journal of Thought* 18 (1983): 56–62.

"Vanderbilt University Again." *Popular Science Monthly* 14 (1878): 237–39.

Vanderwood, Paul. *Night Riders of Reelfoot Lake.* Memphis: Memphis State University Press, 1969.

Waggoner, Jennings L. "Higher Education and Transition in Southern Culture: An Exploratory Apologia." *Journal of Thought* 18 (1983): 104–18.

Waggoner, Paul M. "The Historiography of the Scopes Trial: A Critical Reevaluation." *Trinity Journal,* new ser., 5 (1984): 155–74.

Waller, William, ed. *Nashville, 1900–1910.* Nashville: Vanderbilt University Press, 1972.

Ward, Richard Hiram. "The Development of Baptist Higher Education in Tennessee." Ed.D. diss., George Peabody College for Teachers, 1953.

———. *A History of Union University.* Jackson, Tenn.: Union University Press, 1975.

———. "Union University and Its Predecessors: Historical Highlights." *West Tennessee Historical Society Papers* 29 (1975): 55–63.

Wardin, Albert W., Jr. *Tennessee Baptists: A Comprehensive History, 1779–1999.* Brentwood, Tenn.: Executive Board of the Tennessee Baptist Convention, 1999.

Weaver, Bill L. "Kentucky Baptists' Reaction to the National Evolution Controversy, 1922–1926." *Filson Club Historical Quarterly* 49 (1975): 266–75.

Webb, George E. *The Evolution Controversy in America.* Lexington: University Press of Kentucky, 1994.

Webb, William R., Jr. "Sawney Webb, My Father and His Ideals of Education." *Sewanee Review* 50 (1942): 227–40.

Wedell, Marsha. *Elite Women and the Reform Impulse in Memphis, 1875–1915.* Knoxville: University of Tennessee Press, 1991.

Welsh, John R. "George F. Mellen: A Versatile Tennessean." *Tennessee Historical Quarterly* 8 (1949): 220–47.

West, Carroll Van, ed. *Tennessee Encyclopedia of History and Culture.* Nashville: Tennessee Historical Society and Rutledge Hill Press, 1998.

Wheeler, Majorie S., ed. *Votes for Women: The Woman Suffrage Movement in Tennessee, the South, and the Nation.* Knoxville: University of Tennessee Press, 1995.

Whitaker, Arthur P. "The Public School System of Tennessee, 1834–1860." *Tennessee Historical Magazine* 2 (1916): 1–30.

White, Edward A. *Science and Religion in American Thought: The Impact of Naturalism.* Stanford, Calif.: Stanford University Press, 1952.

White, Robert Hiram. *Development of the Tennessee State Educational Organization.* Kingsport, Tenn.: Southern, 1929.

Wiebe, Robert H. *The Search for Order, 1877–1920.* New York: Hill and Wang, 1967.

Williams, David Craig. "Progressive Education in Microccosm [*sic*]: Knoxville, Tennessee, A Case Study." Ed.D. diss., University of Tennessee, 1993.

Williams, Frank B., Jr. "The East Tennessee Education Association, 1903–1954." *East Tennessee Historical Society's Publications* 27 (1955): 49–76.

Wilson, Charles Reagan. *Baptized in Blood: The Religion of the Lost Cause, 1865–1920.* Athens: University of Georgia Press, 1980.

————. *Judgment and Grace in Dixie: Southern Faiths from Faulkner to Elvis.* Athens: University of Georgia Press, 1995.

Windrow, J. E. "Collins D. Elliott and the Nashville Female Academy." *Tennessee Historical Magazine,* 2d ser., 3 (1935): 74–106.

Winn, Thomas H. "Liquor, Race, and Politics: Clarksville during the Progressive Period." *Tennessee Historical Quarterly* 49 (1990): 207–17.

Witham, Larry A. *Where Darwin Meets the Bible: Creationists and Evolutionists in America.* New York: Oxford, 2002.

Witherington, Henry Carl. "A History of State Higher Education in Tennessee." Ph.D. diss., University of Chicago, 1931.

Wolfe, Margaret Ripley. "Bootleggers, Drummers, and National Defense: Sideshow to Reform in Tennessee, 1915–1920." *East Tennessee Historical Society's Publications* 49 (1977): 77–91.

————. *Lucius Polk Brown and Progressive Food and Drug Control: Tennessee and New York City, 1908–1920.* Lawrence: Regents Press of Kansas, 1978.

Woodrow, James. "Evolution." *Southern Presbyterian Review* 35 (July 1884): 341–68.

Woodward, C. Vann. *Origins of the New South, 1877–1913.* Baton Rouge: Louisiana State University Press, 1951.

Wooley, Davis C., and Norman W. Cox, eds. *Encyclopedia of Southern Baptists.* 3 vols. Nashville: Broadman, 1958–71.

Woolverton, John F. "Philip Lindsley and the Cause of Education in the Old Southwest." *Tennessee Historical Quarterly* 19 (1960): 3–22.

The World's Most Famous Court Trial: Tennessee Evolution Case: A Word-for-Word Report of the Famous Court Test of the Tennessee Anti-Evolution Act, at Dayton, July 10 to 21, 1925, Including Speeches and Arguments of Attorneys, Testimony of Noted Scientists, and Bryan's Last Speech. 1925; reprint, Dayton, Tenn.: Bryan College, 1990.

Wrenn, Lynette Boney. *Crisis and Commission Government in Memphis: Elite Rule in a Gilded Age City.* Knoxville: University of Tennessee Press, 1998.

Wright, Absalom B. *Autobiography of Rev. A. B. Wright, of the Holston Conference, Methodist Episcopal Church South.* Edited by J. C. Wright. Cincinnati: Cranston and Curtis, 1896.

Wyatt-Brown, Bertram. *Yankee Saints and Southern Sinners.* Baton Rouge: Louisiana State University Press, 1985.

Zimmerman, Jonathan. *Whose America? Culture Wars in the Public Schools.* Cambridge: Harvard University Press, 2002.

Index

Cowan, 153

Creationists, 163. *See also* Antievolution

Creation science, 163. *See also* Antievolution

Cullom, Jeremiah, 103

Cumberland River, 70

Cunnyngham, W. G. F., 25, 35, 41

Dabney, Robert Louis, 15, 28, 38

Darby, John, 130

Darrow, Clarence, 3, 128, 151, 153, 165

Darwin, Charles, 35, 131, 136, 139

Darwinism. *See* Evolution

Davis, C. W., 139–40, 161

Dayton, 128, 150, 151, 154, 164

Democratic Party: and Bryan, 140; and prohibition, 75, 85–86, 87–88, 90–91

Dilton, 114

Disciples of Christ, 147

Doak, Samuel, 19

Eager, George Broadman, 94

East Tennessee Normal School, 106

East Tennessee University, 50. *See also* University of Tennessee

Eaton, Clement, 131

Eaton, John, 22, 24

Eaton, Joseph, 45

Edgefield Baptist Church (Nashville), 148

Education: antebellum, 7, 12, 19–21, 158, 160; and Bible reading, 124, 126; and Blair bill, 24, 110, 174 (n. 46); and control of future, 116–17, 136, 141, 154–55, 156–57, 159, 162; and denominational colleges, 17, 27, 29, 32–33, 34–35, 38, 42, 43–67, 156–57; and Germany, 66, 97–98, 123–24, 125, 136, 138, 152–53, 195 (n. 2); and health, 91–93, 162–63; historiography on, 172–73 (n. 28); informal sources of, 6–7, 11, 18–19, 24–26, 37, 41–42, 98, 158–59, 160; of ministers, 46–48;

as morality promoter, 25–27, 96; Progressive-Era campaigns for, 101–8, 110–11, 159; and prohibition, 91–93, 116–17, 162; and race, 12, 23–24, 30, 175 (n. 52), 215–16 (n. 4); and religion, 7–8, 26, 112, 113–27, 143–44, 154–55, 157–59, 162; as religion's social mission, 40; and religious control of teaching, 97–100, 105–6; and religious opposition to evolution, 128–29, 138, 141; and sectionalism, 160–61; and state universities, 50–51, 57–58, 103, 107, 114, 146, 148–49; and textbooks, 142, 160–62. *See also* Public schools; Universities, church-affiliated; *and specific schools*

Edwards v. Aguillard (1987), 164

Elliott, Collins D., 12, 20, 26, 27, 29–30, 38, 110, 112

Elliott, Stephen, 14, 15, 16

Emory University (Ga.), 63, 66, 105

Episcopalians, 44

Epperson v. Arkansas (1968), 164, 215 (n. 93)

Evangelicals: and alcohol, 68–96; antebellum, 13, 19–20, 70; and black Christians, 4–5, 16; Christian nation argument of, 94, 98, 124–25, 143; and church discipline, 78–79; and evolution, 128–55; and female education, 19–20, 37, 66, 157; and geology, 132–33; and Germany, 66, 136, 140, 152; majority rule argument by, 93–94, 125–26, 142–43, 153, 154, 165; and non-Protestants, 28, 31, 36–37, 46, 120, 125–27, 143, 196 (n. 11); and prohibition, 9, 70–75, 77–95, 111; as public school officials, 34, 35, 99–100, 105, 185 (n. 60); publishing enterprises of, 17; and sectionalism, 75, 80, 81, 87, 136–37; and slavery, 14, 57–58; support of, for public schools, 2–3, 4,